Fighting Eviction
Tribal Land Rights and Research-in-Action

———

Daniel Buckles and Rajeev Khedkar
with
Bansi Ghevde and Dnyaneshwar Patil

FOUNDATION®
B ⦿ ⦿ K S

Delhi • Bengaluru • Mumbai • Kolkata • Chennai • Hyderabad
Pune • Thiruvananthapuram

Published by
Cambridge University Press India Pvt. Ltd.
under the imprint of Foundation Books
Cambridge House, 4381/4 Ansari Road, Daryaganj, **New Delhi** 110 002

Cambridge University Press India Pvt. Ltd.
C-22, C-Block, Brigade M.M., K.R. Road, Jayanagar, **Bengaluru** 560 070
Plot No. 80, Service Industries, Shirvane, Sector-1, Nerul, **Navi Mumbai** 400 706
10 Raja Subodh Mullick Square, 2nd Floor, **Kolkata** 700 013
21/1 (New No. 49), 1st Floor, Model School Road, Thousand Lights, **Chennai** 600 006
House No. 3-5-874/6/4, (Near Apollo Hospital), Hyderguda, **Hyderabad** 500 029
Agarwal Pride, 'A' Wing, 1308 Kasba Peth, Near Surya Hospital, **Pune** 411 011
T.C. 25/2731 Lukes Lane, Ambujavilasam Road, **Thiruvananthapuram** 695 001

© Cambridge University Press India Pvt. Ltd.

First Published 2013

ISBN 978-93-8226-493-4

Published by Manas Saikia for Cambridge University Press India Pvt. Ltd.

Dedicated to
Dwarkanath Lakhma Ghogharkar,
a Katkari leader and musician with great vision and heart

Contents

List of Tables

List of Figures

List of Images

Foreword

The Katkari of India cope with great hardship on a daily basis, from gruelling physical labour to inadequate food or shelter, exploitation and forced indebtedness to employers. Most families, children included, live at brick kilns for five to six months a year, producing on average 1,500 bricks per day, six days a week. They literally form with their own hands the raw material going into the edifices of one of the most populous regions of the world – Mumbai, Panvel, New Mumbai, Thane and Kalyan. On top of this heavy load comes the weight of stereotypes, discrimination and open contempt directed against the Katkari as a former 'criminal tribe'. Ignored by the general public and an indifferent government, the Katkari seem to be the epitome of subalterns – poverty-stricken people without voice in social life or agency in the public sphere.

The work of Buckles and Khedkar is a major contribution to lifting the silence and shame that surrounds the story of the Katkari today. It also contributes to a critical rethinking of social anthropology. This is a discipline that is sometimes reproached for having served colonial and post-colonial interests, directly or indirectly. Most anthropologists, however, are now firm in their commitment to understanding cultural difference and otherness as manifestations of our common humanity. Still, as they pursue this noble mission, students of other cultures and ways of life must consciously choose between paths. One option is to follow in the footsteps of mainstream positive science, by pursuing knowledge for its own sake, with detachment from the struggles of history. If this perspective is applied to the Katkari, the tribe would constitute a distinct object of study, a culture to be studied as a discrete social entity more or less preserved from outside influence. For those who choose this path, the advancement of knowledge hinges on the disengagement of science from the entanglements of broader systems of power, injustice and sheer misery.

Many social scientists have learned to become distrustful of this legacy of 'hard science' and its hidden agenda, and rightly so. Objections to the illusion of scientific objectivity in anthropology are widely known. A more critical attitude towards the lessons of history and the social sciences typically follows one of two guide-posts. The first is wedded to the spirit of advocacy – using anthropological inquiry to 'speak on behalf' of those otherwise without a voice. Researchers act as spokespersons for groups of people that are vulnerable and oppressed, using the expert knowledge they have to support and provide legitimacy to worthy causes, such as protecting the land of the Katkari. The second critical stance consists in 'giving voice' to others, 'empowering' them to convey their own voices, stories and hopes to key audiences, decision makers and the powers that be. Instead of representing the issues and movements of marginalized peoples, anthropologists provide assistance to 'others' in their own struggle to think and speak for themselves.

Buckles and Khedkar choose none of the above. Their work is a remarkable contribution to another kind of anthropology – a story of authentic conversations between the research team and the Katkari, where all parties contribute to flexible yet rigorous action research grounded in history. The role of social scientists becomes one of articulating the links between sources of knowledge and competing ways of making sense of and acting on reality. In this approach, researchers do not act as ventriloquists speaking for others. Nor do they hide behind the voiceless to help them 'speak for themselves'. Instead, the research team and the Katkari engage with each other so they can learn from each other, plan together, and change the world – starting with their own.

Inquiry that is both methodical and dialogical is key on this road to an engaged social science. Walking the talk is by no means easy. Buckles and Khedkar are on this difficult road, fully conscious of the many challenges of tribal life in India, the imponderables of action research in difficult circumstances, and the necessity of careful reasoning and actions that make sense and make things happen. Given these many challenges, the authors take care to create moments of rich dialogue between themselves and the Katkari and among the Katkari themselves. To facilitate in-depth group thinking on a wide range of pressing issues, they apply ground-breaking methods that pay more than lip service to local knowledge and problem-solving systems. The results speak volumes about what engaged research can contribute to meaningful learning and social change. The authors demonstrate how anthropologists can achieve collaborative inquiry and social engagement with unparalleled rigour –

the kind that is called for in complex situations. Gems of people-based and evidence-based thinking and action documented in the book include a joint investigation into the root causes and effects of not having legal title to a village site and the means to secure it. The conversation informed and consolidated Katkari resolve to stand firm and helped articulate a vision of the future. The collective analysis of stakeholder positions on a proposed land claim facilitated by the research team is equally impressive. So is the reported Katkari account of forces that drive or counteract the threat of eviction in Sarang Katkarwadi and disagreements among men, women and youth regarding livelihoods of priority interest to the Katkari (living in Talaiwadi). The book even shows how to adapt input–output and principal component analysis, advanced analytical tools, to support discussions between literate and non-literate stakeholders exploring livelihood systems and the root causes of fear in Narsurwadi. Action research is taken to a bold new level where participation is synonymous with advanced reasoning rather than quick-and-easy consultation.

This is anthropology at its best. It is richly detailed, flexibly methodical, grounded in complex community life, with a firm commitment to difference and otherness in all senses of the words – including building the foundations and laying the bricks of another, altogether different world. The story told is all the more inspiring as the initiative has led to real change. Tangible results of action research include security of tenure for households in 52 hamlets (out of 212 vulnerable to eviction). Many other hamlets have formally registered petitions for a village site. Raising awareness among landholders and officials about possible prosecution under the Prevention of Atrocities Act has succeeded in curbing forced enclosures and full-scale evictions. As a result of the joint actions they have taken with the research team, the Katkari are now better informed of their rights as a tribal people in India and less fearful of those with the power to ignore them. The spell of isolation in silence and hopelessness is starting to break as the Katkari develop self-confidence, stronger leadership and better organizational skills (creating labour unions, developing small businesses and acquiring caste certificates).

These accomplishments must be celebrated. The gains are nevertheless reversible. Authentic conversations across boundaries must continue, with the support of engaged anthropology, if justice is to prevail.

Jacques M. Chevalier
Chancellor's Professor, Carleton University
Ottawa, Canada

Acknowledgements

The list of people who have been part of the study, and who have helped us in our work, is very long indeed. First and foremost, we would like to place on record our thanks to the Katkari families in Mohmalwadi and Ambewadi in Karjat taluka, Nadodewadi, Asrawadi, Mil Katkarwadi and Sarangwadi in Khalapur taluka and Narsurwadi, Siddheshwarwadi, Wavloliwadi, Wakanwadi and Dhoklewadi in Sudhagad taluka. Katkari in other communities where we worked also deserve our sincere thanks.

We would also like to thank people who have believed in and supported our work with the Katkari community. In alphabetical order, these are Anja Mertineit (Misereor, Germany), David Watters (Onaway Trust, UK), Emmanuel Yap (Belgium), Manjusha Khedkhar (ADS), Merle Faminow (IDRC, Canada), the late Jeeja Bansi Ghevde, John Seed (Rainforest Information Centre, Australia), Julie Smit (ASTM, Luxembourg), Meenakshi Sundram (Onaway Trust, India), Neera Burra (UNDP, New Delhi), Sudhirendar Sharma (Delhi), Vijay Sathe (Murbad).

Several people also took time out to read our work at various stages in its development and provided valuable feedback. We would like to express our deep appreciation to Jacques M. Chevalier (Carleton University, Canada), who constantly inspired and guided us with his creative and grounded approach to participatory action research. We are also very grateful for the admirably efficient and thoughtful editorial work of Debra Huron (Ottawa, Canada). If the text is easy to read, it owes much to her keen eye for clear and engaging language. Several readers provided very useful and encouraging feedback, especially Neema Pathak Broome (Kalpavriksh, Pune), Rudolf C. Heredia (Mumbai) and anonymous reviewers. The editorial team at Cambridge University Press India Pvt Ltd was very kind and professional in its support to the publication process. Thanks go also to Dan Patterson and his students at

Carleton University (Canada) for producing maps of Katkari hamlets, and to Janelle Anderson (Canada) for her help with analysis of survey data. Any errors that remain are ours alone.

All photographs except three are by Daniel Buckles. Image 5.2 was taken by Bansi Ghevde and Image 6.1 by Rajeev Khedkar. The cover photograph of a Katkari woman carrying bricks was taken by Clement Cousin.

The research was possible thanks in part to grants from the International Development Research Centre (Canada), Onaway Trust (United Kingdom), the Rainforest Information Centre (Australia), ASTM (Luxembourgh) and Misereor (Germany).

Daniel Buckles, Rajeev Khedkar,
Bansi Ghevde and Dnyaneshwar Patil

Introduction

The persistent gap between the lived experience of the Adivasis as a class of citizens and the equality provisions in the Constitution of India continues to trouble people and organizations concerned about justice for marginalized communities in India. Large disparities in living standards, displacement from traditional lands and territorial resources, exploitation in the workplace and humiliation in day-to-day transactions mark the Adivasis as a population apart. As such, they are far from realizing the country's constitutional ideals of equality, justice and freedom.

While there is a well recognized need to address these urgent problems, solutions tend to focus on the constitutional and administrative mechanisms alone. Special laws and policies have been put in place to 'uplift' the Adivasis through a combination of political will and an effective bureaucracy (Béteille, 1992). Caste-based voting patterns have lent support to the formation of a political elite among some Adivasi communities and the emergence of new forms of tribal politics (Devalle 1992; Ghosh 2006; Oommen 2010; Radhakrishnan 2003; Shah 2010; Sinha 2010). Affirmative action (reservation policies) with respect to access to education and government jobs has also led to concrete improvements for some individuals, although they are mainly the upwardly mobile and dominant sections of particular groups. The vast majority of Adivasi communities have not benefited directly from these policies (Kijima 2006), despite the expenditure of considerable financial and human resources over the years. Development initiatives by state and federal tribal ministries and departments in different parts of the country have also attempted to address the problems, but implementation has been very weak (Chalam 2007; Chaudhury and Patnaik 2008; Das 2003; Dash Sharma 2006; Karade 2008; Kumar 2006; Swagata and Nirupama 2008; Uma and Bharihoke 2006).

However important these constitutional and administrative endeavours may be, they can be seen purely as the hardware of a liberal democracy. The software part, which involves the exercise of public reason in problem solving and attention to people's own efforts (a key element in Gandhi's concept of *swaraj*), is largely absent in the modern 'tribal project' of the Indian Constitution. Originally conceived as a temporary measure, constitutional protections have become entrenched and mired in an administrative apparatus not yet endowed with eyes to see or ears to hear. Policy and advocacy failures continue unabated, not because the subaltern cannot speak (Spivak 1988), but rather because they cannot be heard. The fundamental processes of knowledge making, public deliberation and democratic decision making do little to actively engage the Adivasi in co-constructing a mutually meaningful understanding of problems or courses of action. The reasoning of academics and institutions (state, private and non-profit) is simply imposed in ways unrelated to the practical concerns and analytical traditions of the grassroots.

In our view, the root of the problem is the tenacious attachment of the powers that be to their own values and views of the world and to their own individual and class interests. Corporations, governments and academics alike resist sincere dialogue, collaborative inquiry into problems and solutions and mutual learning across social boundaries. Even in successful Adivasi social and political movements, concern with creating the impression of unity often overrides efforts to foster internal democracy, independent thought and informed debate (Baviskar 2008; Whitehead 2007).

Significant improvements in Adivasi life can no longer rely on notions of charity and solutions designed by well-meaning experts and leaders. This archaic and sterile dynamic continues to drive the worlds of India apart. Nor can Adivasi issues be divorced from the myriad struggles of oppressed people everywhere (Kamat 2001). To move beyond the many divides, people must combine constitutional measures, political lobbies and scientific investigations with concerted efforts to engage the Adivasi in the making and sharing of knowledge. Struggles for justice, equality and freedom need to be grounded in a process of collaborative inquiry and the co-construction of knowledge that leads to collective social action.

This book recounts an attempt to find vital ways to converse and inquire with the Adivasi and thereby to contribute to an engaged social science serving a larger purpose. It focuses on a concrete problem: the enclosure and eviction of the Katkari, a former 'criminal tribe' and 'particularly vulnerable tribal group' (PTG),[1] from their hamlets on private lands outside of caste (Hindu) villages on the coastal plains of Maharashtra. Rising land prices due to the economic boom in the Mumbai Metropolitan Region are prompting legal landholders to sell their lands. This has in turn led to attempts to evict the Katkari forcibly from land they have lived on for generations. Landholders who once valued easy access to cheap agricultural labour – the reason they allowed the Katkari to settle on marginal lands near their fields in the first place – have come to understand the current value of these plots. This has broken the patron–client relationship that once provided some security to the Katkari. Entire communities have been surrounded by barbed-wire fences as landholders attempt to intimidate residents into moving to other locations. In some cases, houses have been levelled and families forced to move. For the Katkari, a people already living on the edge of survival, the situation is replete with pain and expense. It is also a significant cause of conflict and hardening of relationships with the caste communities they interact with.

The Katkari struggle to remain in their hamlets provides an important contrast to the land tenure problems facing urban slum dwellers (Council for Social Development 2010; Municipal Corporation of Greater Mumbai 2009; Nijman 2008) or Adivasis in remote areas displaced by large-scale development projects (Baviskar 1995; Ghosh 2006). Unlike Adivasis impacted by mega-projects, unpredictable forces at the micro level are driving the Katkari from their homes – haphazardly and one hamlet at a time. And unlike the situation in many urban slums, the Katkari did not squat in public and private spaces illegally, but rather settled where they had been invited to do so by landholders and other employers in need of labourers who could be easily bonded. A set of mutual responsibilities was created, which the Katkari honoured by providing cheap labour to the landholders and others in the caste community. Despite these arrangements, the Katkari were not given the housing rights normally associated with permanent settlement and membership in a village. Tenure over the land where they built their homes remained in private

---

[1] Until recently, the Katkari and 74 other tribal groups in India were classified as 'primitive tribal groups'. The pejorative term 'primitive' was recently expunged from the official lexicon and replaced with the phrase 'particularly vulnerable tribal groups'. The acronym PTG is still in use.

hands rather than being incorporated into a legal village site called a
gaothan.[2]

The vulnerability of the Katkari extends to their livelihoods. Most are
landless workers with only periodic and tenuous connections to their
original nomadic, forest-based livelihoods. In recent decades, many have
become bonded labourers working on the brick kilns and charcoal units
that feed urban growth in contemporary India. They are brutally exploited
by their employers, forced into long-term debt and even robbed of their
personal identity papers in attempts to keep them bound to a place of
work. Sexual exploitation of and assaults on Katkari women are common
at brick kilns, and Katkari men are regularly beaten. Any sort of complaint
from the Katkari is usually met with indifference from the police, thanks
in part to the stigma and institutionalized culture of discrimination against
the Katkari dating back to the 1871 Criminal Tribes Act enacted under
British rule.

Today, Katkari in hamlets without a secure gaothan live under the yoke
of the landholders. Almost without exception, landholders do not permit
residents to do anything on the land: no cultivation of a backyard garden,
no extension to the house, no raising of small livestock. Nor do they allow
or support the development of civic amenities in Katkari hamlets. Katkari
without a gaothan cannot avail themselves of government programmes
to improve their hamlet, such as construction of schools and health posts,
installation of wells, streets and approach roads, or electrification. As a
result, living conditions in Katkari hamlets are primitive, filthy and
crowded, in stark contrast to the neighbouring non-tribal villages.

To make matters worse, the Katkari community is firmly excluded
from membership in village society. Particular expressions of
untouchability, including physical exclusion, the assumption of criminality
and a visceral reaction to Katkari food habits have created an extreme
distance of the Katkari from the caste-based agrarian order. They are

---

[2] In Maharashtra, a village site is known by the Marathi word *gaothan*. A gaothan
is called *abadi* in Hindi. It is a site designated for villages and associated hamlets,
including individual housing sites (*ghartan*) and the space needed for basic
infrastructure such as streets, public buildings, water services and waste
management. From ancient times to the present, the village site has remained a
fundamental feature of human settlement in India. It establishes the tangible
boundaries of the village and helps to define membership in the social and political
institutions of village life. For a contemporary rethinking of villages and the
anthropological study of the village, see Mines and Yazgi (2010).

marginalized even by other tribal communities. These acts of social exclusion have left the Katkari in an amorphous world where they are unrecognized and unprotected, neither fully tribal nor fully integrated into the caste hierarchy. The Katkari's resulting vulnerability allows landholders, government officials, the police and the general public to sweep aside legal and ethical responsibilities, and to assert dominant class and caste interests with virtual impunity. That this should occur while much of the state of Maharashtra booms with economic growth and prosperity is deeply unjust.

This Inquiry's Genesis and Approach

This book tells the story of an extended and action-oriented inquiry into the lack of legal title to village sites among the Katkari and efforts to secure a gaothan. The inquiry began in 2005 and continues into the present, building on many previous years of engagement with the Katkari by three members of the research team: Rajeev Khedkar and Bansi Ghevde of the Academy of Development Science (ADS) and Dnyaneshwar Patil of SOBTI.[3] These individuals and their organizations have advocated for the land and livelihood rights of the Katkari for more than 15 years, facing many obstacles and achieving some successes along the way. Their longstanding relationship with Katkari communities made it possible to plan and develop an intensely collaborative process of inquiry and action. Daniel Buckles, an anthropologist based in Ottawa, Canada, led the inquiry process, provided training, participated directly in many of the research activities over the years, and drafted this book in collaboration with Rajeev Khedkar. Together, we worked as a team to support, document and validate a collaborative inquiry into Katkari land rights and efforts to fight eviction.

Engagement between the research team and the Katkari involved hundreds of meetings and dozens of detailed assessments of the situation by the Katkari themselves. These meetings made use of, but were not limited to, various tools from participatory rural appraisal (PRA). PRA, and its successor, participatory learning and action (PLA), are the most widely known of participatory methods in the international development field and in South Asia. The main contribution of PRA and PLA to

---

[3] SOBTI is not an acronym but rather a name created by members of the community-based organization.

development practice has been the creative, pluralistic and dynamic use of visual and tangible forms of expression and group analysis. Maps, models, diagrams, pile sorting, ranking and rating, storytelling, ice breakers and role play are signature tools of the practice, giving rise to numerous and large collections adapted to various contexts with support from development agencies around the world (cf. Pretty et al. 1995). Underlying the tools is a commitment to eliminate or reduce ruinous sources of bias in community-oriented initiatives: the spatial bias of urban perspectives over remote rural realities, the bias of the educated and the powerful over people with low literacy and low social standing, and the bias of professionals over non-experts or simply 'people who are not professionals' (Satheesh 2009). The visual and tangible tools help tap into the bodily expression of ideas and emotions, although they rely also on subtle and personal behaviours, attitudes and mindsets subject to many influences. Turning researchers into facilitators and participants into leaders and active learners ('role reversals') is a critical, and very difficult, requirement of the practice (Chambers 1993).

The strengths of PRA and PLA, including flexibility and the licence to 'use your own best judgment at all times' (Chambers 2008), also present significant risks. The practice of PRA and PLA can easily override existing legitimate decision-making processes, fall prey to powerful voices within a group, and displace local and traditional ways of thinking and learning (Cooke and Kothari 2001). The consensual focus can obscure diverging interests and the actual exercise of power during the PRA process itself (Cornwall 2004; Reason and Bradbury 2008). Cooptation of PRA and PLA by development bureaucracies and scant attention to the power structures that advocate for and promote its use have led to highly manipulated outcomes (Brown 2004). A common lament is that the practice of PRA may simply legitimize agency-driven agendas, making too much of participation and too little of who decides and what actions are ultimately taken. A lack of rigour in PRA's tools can also lead to superficial assessments and complaints from other researchers that results are anecdotal and of questionable validity. These persistent gaps, and insufficient attention within the tradition to theorizing participatory strategies for social change (Bebbington 2004; Hickey and Mohan 2006), probably explain, at least in part, why the practice has made few inroads into academic research and training.

Our inquiry into the gaothan problem used familiar PRA tools such as the problem tree, timeline and resource mapping to engage with the Katkari. However, the work we did was *not* an exercise in PRA.

Critical and fundamental new directions from the work of Chevalier and Buckles (2012) were from the start built into the rules of engagement, the research process and the methods (See Annex I). The inquiry involved a formal action research process carried out on various scales in the context of a broader social undertaking and with a view to promoting the practice and spirit of group analysis, joint interpretation and stakeholder decision making. This was more in keeping with the much older and larger tradition of participatory action research (PAR) going back to Kurt Lewin's experiments in 'action research' (1948) and the work of the Tavistock Institute in the United Kingdom. Other roots include the study clubs of the Canadian Antigonish movement (Coady 1939), community development initiatives in North America during the 1960s, the adult education methods that Freire (1970) developed in Brazil and pioneering work in South Asia by De Silva et al. (1979) and Rahman (1993), as well as in Latin America by Fals Borda (1979). These practitioners and theorists showed that regular small meetings among poor people with low levels of education could generate meaningful and sophisticated understandings of the situations they faced and agreement on actions needed to address them. Our practice drew inspiration from these traditions by focusing on engaging the Katkari in self-directed problem solving and emancipatory action. It also tried to go beyond PAR by fashioning new tools, techniques and ways of knowing in support of structured conversations with the Katkari on matters of importance to them. We were not concerned with extracting information or simply moving directly to action. As in Gandhian and Buddhist philosophy, the inquiry employed 'skilful means', that is, motivations and practices that embed the ends in the means. (For a detailed discussion of the history of PAR and new contributions to the practice of participatory action research, see Chevalier and Buckles 2012).

Over a period of several years, the Katkari explored and interpreted, from their own perspective, various aspects of the gaothan problem, weighing the pros and cons of proposed actions. They reflected on what they and others had done in the past to address the problem and why those responses failed. They also identified new actions and developed agreements among themselves about what they needed to do and how best to proceed. The research team facilitated the inquiry process and responded to requests from the Katkari to address particular problems by providing information and supporting their analysis and decision making. What started as a targeted study of insecure village sites was broadened by the Katkari over time to include actions aimed at addressing persistent constraints they faced, namely, systemic and systematic government neglect, bondage to migratory livelihoods and the absence of a collective political voice. The engagement process moved progressively from fewer to more hamlets and from a specific problem to broader concerns and actions defined by stakeholders along the way.

Creating Dialogue across Boundaries

The book documents the results from a process of making sense of the world through efforts to transform it, as opposed to simply observing Katkari views about their situation in the hope that change would happen somewhere down the road. It also presents and analyzes detailed information from other sources, much of which was discussed directly with the Katkari.

The research team examined the origins, scope and impacts of insecure gaothan among the Katkari and the policies governments have established to protect the rights of citizens but failed to implement for one of their most vulnerable populations. Collaborative analysis of possible actions drew on information collected from government records and the few existing published documents on the Katkari. Team members also mapped the location of Katkari hamlets without secure village sites in three talukas[4] – Karjat, Khalapur and Sudhagad – using a global positioning system, and conducted many interviews with government officials, landholders, village leaders and other stakeholders. An original village-level survey of 313 Katkari communities provided additional context, as did a detailed key informant survey of household livelihood activities conducted in a sample of villages. The research team shared the facts emerging from these various sources with the Katkari and other stakeholders in various ways over the course of the study. This helped guide new inquiries and actions.

From the beginning of the inquiry, two processes – reflexive action by and with the Katkari, and action research by the research team into specific issues and policies – moved in tandem in response to the persistent complexity and uncertainty surrounding the gaothan problem. The Katkari contributed content and context from within their own bodies of knowledge and experience. The research team also developed and shared analyses and interpretations of its own, thereby contributing to a collaborative

---

[4] A taluka is an administrative division below the district level in India and Pakistan. A taluka usually comprises a city or large town which serves as its headquarters and a number of other towns and villages.

understanding of the situation and an ongoing dialogue about what to do next. We tried to make these discussions both people-based (by being respectful and caring of our relationship with people) and evidence-based (by paying careful attention to the data and information available).

When brought together in a single story, the account illustrates key challenges faced by practitioners of PAR and contributes to a significant rethinking of what it means to do research 'with' people rather than 'on' people. The first challenge consists in reconciling the split between science and democracy, or, described differently, between evidence-based reasoning and people-centred thinking. While deeply committed to applying the principles of participatory democracy in the sphere of knowledge, at no time did the research team opt to 'dumb down' the data collection, analysis and interpretation process under the pretext that the Katkari are by and large non-literate and extremely poor. What challenged us in our attempts to support sound action research with the Katkari was not their limited knowledge about the broader issues or their untrained thinking skills, but rather constraints on our own ability to think creatively when designing each step in the inquiry process. The challenge was to ground inquiry in local concepts and ways of knowing, and to facilitate respectful and reciprocal dialogue. We needed to continuously select and adapt methods for the right fit between the 'means' and the 'ends' of both science and democracy (Chevalier and Buckles 2012). Among other things, this meant designing processes that were not too simple for the question at hand or so cumbersome as to postpone conclusions and actions to a distant future. It meant that we had to scale or calibrate each step of the action inquiry to the level of detail and the kind of evidence appropriate in each situation. For the Katkari, the stakes were too high to allow the inquiry process to underuse their expertise by relying on simplistic questions and answers. Nor could the inquiry ignore their sense of urgency by indulging in complicated and protracted research that was not immediately useful. Action and inquiry had to come together in a process of purposeful and rigorous engagement, where the 'so what' and 'now what' questions were never left unasked by the Katkari themselves, or by the research team. In this book, the depth and thoughtfulness of the analysis and actions emerging from the Katkari communities illustrate what we consider to be the power of collaborative inquiry and communicative action as science, understood as 'truth telling' and 'trustworthiness' in a Habermasian sense (1984). This goes well beyond the toolbox approach to problem solving and the tendency in PRA to avoid both complexity and methodological rigour.

A second challenge was that the inquiry had to adjust constantly to situations of relative chaos and complexity. While it is now commonplace to say that our world is complex to the nth degree, it is another thing to come face to face with the unexpected and unpredictable in a particular situation. The habit of simply following a well-defined blueprint for social change is deeply ingrained. For instance, our initial reading of the eviction threat faced by the Katkari was that an administrative solution was possible and that clear planning to achieve that solution was in order. The legal rights of longstanding inhabitants of a piece of land are well established in state and central government laws and policies on land tenure, village development and rural housing. Mechanisms exist to compensate landholders for properties converted into village sites and officials in Maharashtra have issued specific directives to this effect at various times. Furthermore, the Katkari are formally recognized as a 'particularly vulnerable tribal group' and in need of immediate attention from officials charged with their protection (Ministry of Tribal Affairs 2011). What seemed like a straightforward path, however, led into a tangled briar patch. Unknown factors and unforeseen events forced many changes of course in the action inquiry process and demanded skilful means of navigating through messy, real-life conditions. The inquiry had to acknowledge and respond to the many twists and turns of the social and political forces at play. We did this, to the best of our abilities, by selecting, combining and adapting methods from different disciplines and theoretical perspectives with the goal of strengthening stakeholder decision making and action. The process of navigating through methods of data gathering and analysis that can deal with complexity contrasts sharply with conventional studies of planned change and community development, where fixed goals and methods are defined in advance. It also differs from ethnographies of micro-level responses to social change, approaches that typically fail to integrate the three fundamental concepts of participation, action and research.

The task of engaging people and mobilizing evidence in a complex world, while it was pursued systematically and sincerely, did not bridge fully the differences in gender perspectives or address directly the issues related to the status of women within Katkari society. The research team was composed entirely of men – gendered, interacting individuals with varying skills, inclinations, values and time constraints of our own. The small group discussions always involved and welcomed participation by Katkari women, but Katkari men and male youth were in the majority. While rights to a village site can reasonably be seen as a common concern within households and entire communities, gender bias was undoubtedly at work. The research team tried to manage this source of bias by actively soliciting the views of women and welcoming their ideas when they spoke up spontaneously in meetings. It is difficult to know what impact the presence of husbands, fathers and sons had on the stories women shared about the gaothan problem. We observed that Katkari women were by no means quiet or reluctant to express themselves. Women intervened regularly in discussions to challenge or sharpen the points being made. On various occasions, they brought disagreements among the men to an end through the force of their own arguments. Also, separate women's meetings were successfully convened on occasion, for example, with respect to livelihood priorities. While earlier anthropological research by Heredia and Srivastava (1994) and Gaikwad (1995) suggests that the anti-female bias that characterizes the wider Indian society is less pronounced among the Katkari, the power and roles of women in Katkari society did not receive direct attention through the inquiry, and remain largely untouched by it. This limitation is one readers should keep in mind as they explore the text.

Book Outline

Chapter 1 introduces the reader to the Katkari and the complex history of insecure village sites (lack of gaothan) that launched the inquiry. It traces the movement of Katkari settlements from the hills of the Western Ghats to the outskirts of caste (Hindu) agrarian communities on the plains of Maharashtra. Once settled, the Katkari became bonded workers on the farms of the region and in brick kilns and charcoal operations serving the urban and industrial interests of Greater Mumbai. These forces are described in detail, drawing on Katkari accounts, a formal survey, secondary sources and insights in the literature on the evolving relationship between Adivasi and caste-based agrarian societies in modern India. The chapter also examines expressions of 'untouchability' that excluded the Katkari from representation, participation and communication channels normally available to members of a village society. The history of migration, integration into bonded labour and social exclusion help explain why the Katkari have been unable to exercise their rights to land, and why they are currently so vulnerable to eviction and exploitation.

The Katkari perspective on enclosure and eviction from their hamlets is assessed in Chapter 2, as are the surprises the research team encountered when it first engaged with hamlets not facing the immediate threat of eviction. The difficulties of engaging the Katkari in exploring the gaothan problem from various perspectives provoked several shifts in the planning and inquiry process. The responses to complexity and uncertainty documented in the chapter include efforts by the Katkari to strategize in light of power dynamics, to empower themselves through information, to engage with village authorities and to appeal to public values of justice and the common good.

Chapter 3 seeks to understand the complexity of Katkari and landholder responses to insecure village tenure. The forces at play and the dynamics of fear and vulnerability experienced by the Katkari and analyzed by them through various advanced analytical tools provided new directions to the inquiry. These were formulated by the research team as working hypotheses and grounded in ongoing efforts to increase knowledge about the conditions and factors affecting the gaothan situation. The chapter illustrates the risks of rushing into action without understanding and, paradoxically, the need to act on the world in order to understand it. We suggest that the tension can be resolved, at least in part, by attention to continuous planning 'in the middle' of uncertainty and complexity.

Chapter 4 focuses on how the inquiry explored and addressed government neglect. It begins with a review of previous government responses to insecure village sites. Efforts to scale up the process of engagement with government officials and the Katkari's use of legal countermeasures under the Prevention of Atrocities Act are described in detail. This provides a grounded understanding of a sensitive and complex legal process that is drawing increasing national attention. The chapter chronicles and examines the reasons for systemic government neglect, the role of legislation in the past, and successful strategies developed with the Katkari to reduce the risk of eviction in more than 200 communities.

Chapter 5 delves into Katkari perspectives on bonded labour and alternative livelihoods. We provide readers with detailed assessments of a conceptual model that some Katkari use to think about their livelihoods and how this informs their efforts to break the bonds of migration to brick kilns. These efforts include the development of new local economic opportunities, collective bargaining on wages and acquiring land assets through the Forest Rights Act. The account of Katkari struggles to regain access to forest lands also sheds light on the contradiction that exists between forest rights legislation grounded in definitions of settled agriculture and the reality of a forest people such as the Katkari who practise shifting cultivation. It also points to the relevance of the National Rural Employment Guarantee Act (NREGA) as a bridge to eliminating bonded labour in India.

The role of collective organizations in renegotiating the place of the Katkari in the broader village and regional society is examined in Chapter 6. Katkari efforts to revitalize traditional political organizations, define future collective directions and select among ongoing priorities for collective action are discussed in the context of the organizational challenges facing many rural communities in India, and the Adivasis in particular. For the Katkari, these challenges include the fragmentation of their political voice and social dysfunction resulting from the abuse of alcohol.

The book concludes with a summary of what the inquiry achieved, particularly with respect to the security of Katkari hamlets and the resolve of the Katkari population to take a stand in their communities. It also reflects on the research process and the methods ('skilful means') used to engage the Katkari in an authentic process of reflection grounded in action. Throughout the book, readers are referred to a website (www.participatoryactionresearch.net) for detailed information and guidance regarding the tools selected, mixed and adapted along the way to fit the questions that emerged in the complex world of the Katkari.

Our goal in writing this book is to engage readers simultaneously in the ongoing struggle of the Katkari and in a process of reflection on what research and the making of knowledge are all about. As proposed by Kurt Lewin (1948), we have tried to gain a better understanding of the Katkari world by trying to change it. This strategy builds on the pragmatism found in Lewin's commitment to 'action research'. It also builds on Jürgen Habermas's (1983) critical appeal to human emancipation through dialogue and recognition of the intrinsic value of people-based and evidence-based thinking and decision making. Both the inquiry and its retelling in a book are based on intersubjective reasoning as well as fact finding – principles of radical democracy that can be applied to the pursuit of freedom and equality, difference and dissent. These two threads are woven into the spirit of this book and informed its writing. Doing engaged research is not easy and our journey with the Katkari reflects the difficulties, and opportunities, inherent in such an undertaking. It is our sincere hope that this book will prove useful, not only by illuminating the gaothan problem, but also by showing that meaningful dialogue with Adivasi people in complex settings and trying circumstances is both possible and necessary.

Annex I: Tools used in the course of the study[1]

Planning systems that learn

Process Mapping: helps you support planning, evaluation and research at the right time, and at the appropriate level of detail, in light of new information and unforeseen events. Plan and manage an action learning system.

Order and Chaos: helps you decide on the planning approach needed by answering two questions: what are the chances of achieving project or program goals and how certain or confident are people that the information and knowledge they have is complete and reliable?

What's the problem?

Timeline: helps you tell a story of changes over time, significant events of the past or the chronology of steps in a current or planned activity. Use this story to find ways to overcome barriers of the past and apply lessons learned.

Problem Tree: helps you assess the hierarchy of causes and effects of a core problem and look for root causes that if addressed will stop the problem from reoccuring.

Force Field: helps you understand the factors that contribute to a problem, a situation or a project and those that counteract it. Discuss ways of achieving key objectives by strengthening or reducing the factors at play.

Gaps and Conflicts: helps you identify the issues underlying a core problem and find out if these issues are mostly about gaps or conflicts in power, interests (gains and losses), moral values, or information and communication.

How good is your analysis?

Validation: Helps you validate the results of an inquiry and decide whether more evidence and/or consensus is needed before action can be taken based on the results.

---

[1] For detailed instructions on these and many other tools, see Tools and Software at: www.participatoryactionresearch.net and Chevalier and Buckles, 2012.

Who are the Stakeholders?

Stakeholder Analysis CLIP: Helps you create stakeholder profiles and build a base for advocacy and strategic action, especially in complex settings involving strong conflicts of interests or histories of conflict.

What are the Options and Scenarios?

Disagreements and Misunderstandings: Helps you rank stakeholders' goals in order of importance and review disagreements and misunderstandings people may have about these goals.

Tree of Means and Ends: Helps you identify the means (steps) to achieve on ideal scenario and related ends (goals).

The Socratic Wheel: Helps you evaluate and rate one or several elements or alternatives (current project goals, options to choose from, individual skills, leadership styles, products, events, etc.) on multiple criteria.

Previous Responses: Helps you assess past responses to a given problem or situation by answering two questions: are past response task oriented or people oriented and, how is the conflict being managed (distinguishing between force, concession, accommodation, negotiation and consensus and also between customary, legal-administrative and Alternative Dispute Resolution (ADR) responses to conflict?)

Understanding Systems

System Dynamics: Helps you assess how elements in a system (causal factor, activities, actors) interact with each other. It also helps you decide whether you should act directly on an element or through the other elements affecting it and the order in which you should act on certain elements.

Domain Analysis: Helps you describe how people view a domain or topic area, using their own words and concepts (local knowledge). Create new learning opportunities based on this understanding.

1

Origins of the Gaothan Problem

We put our hands in the mouth of the tiger, open the jaws, and count the teeth of the tiger. We are the Katkari. [Waghachya jabdyat, ghaluni haat, mojite daat, jaat aamchi, Katkaryanchi!]

– A Katkari saying

The origins of the gaothan problem are embedded in a complex historical process involving three main threads: Katkari migration from forested hills to the outskirts of caste villages on the coastal plain, integration into rural and migratory livelihoods where the Katkari could be easily bonded and systematic exclusion from the caste communities where Katkari hamlets are now located. The dual process of integration and exclusion (Kela 2006) sheds light on how and why the Katkari came to be so vulnerable to enclosure and eviction from their homes. This chapter traces the intermingling of these historical forces and concludes with a description of the Katkari's living conditions observed by the research team at the launch of the inquiry.

Our historical reconstruction of the gaothan problem also illustrates the evolving relationship between the Katkari and the caste-based agrarian societies of the coastal districts of Maharashtra. We argue, as Heredia and Srivastava do in their 1994 study of the Katkari, that their vulnerability to external exploitation is not due to some inherent characteristics of their culture and communities. The Katkari, and for that matter other tribes of India (Béteille, 2008), do not have a fixed cultural identity linked to an unchanging past that can be labelled as primitive and backward. Rather, their identity, and the strong negative attitude towards the Katkari prevalent among the communities with whom they interact, is the result of interaction with both local and global forces. The Katkari have been buffeted and transformed by these interactions, but have also acted on them through their own efforts to adapt and change. This book is consequently a partial retelling of an ongoing history that is multi-faceted and open-ended. While much of that history is characterized by social exclusion and the loss of land and livelihood, as subsequent chapters will show, courage and determination are also present.

Migration from Hills to Plains

The Katkari were at one time a forest people, with a special relationship to forest creatures such as the tiger or *waghmare*, a common Katkari surname. The name Katkari is derived from a forest-based activity[1] – the making and barter or sale of catechu (*kath*) from the *khair* tree (*Acacia catechu*). Catechu is produced by boiling wood from the khair tree in water and evaporating the resulting brew. This makes an astringent used in Ayurvedic medicine and in mixtures chewed with betel leaves. While few Katkari continue to produce catechu, their knowledge of forest resources remains with them; Katkari living close to forested areas still consume over 60 different uncultivated plants and over 75 different animals and birds, gathering these with incredible ingenuity and skill (Khedkar et al. 2002). For example, Katkari women can draw crabs from their holes during the summer months by rubbing two stones to imitate the sound of thunder showers. Crabs think it is about to rain and leave their holes only to be grabbed by the human thunder maker! Ironically, the brilliant understanding of nature and associated technologies used by the Katkari and some other tribal groups have in the past been construed by officials as an indicator of 'primitiveness'.[2] The Katkari are flagged in state government documents as primitive tribal groups (PTG) along with two other tribal groups: the Kolam in Yavatamil district and the Madias in Gadchiroli district, both in eastern Maharashtra (Tomar and Tribhuwan 2004).

---

[1] The Katkari are also known as the Kathkari, Kathodi, Dhor Kathodi, Dhor Kathkari, Son Katkari, Son Kathodi, Kathodia (cf. Karade 2008; Ministry of Tribal Affairs 2011; Sanyal 2006; Sarkar and Dasgupta, 2000).

[2] In addition to a pre-agriculture level of technology, three other criteria are used by government agencies and many academics to identify former 'primitive tribal groups', now called 'particularly vulnerable tribal groups': a very low population growth rate, very low level of literacy and a subsistence level of economy (Ministry of Tribal Affairs 2011). While the new term for these groups (particularly vulnerable tribal groups) is an improvement over the previous one, in our view there is nothing primitive about technologies based on a profound understanding of nature. Furthermore, a subsistence level of economy is not inherently backward either (cf. Mies 1999).

The Katkari were described by Heredia and Srivastava (1994) as 'nomads in transition', in reference to their hunter-gatherer lifestyle in the forests of the colonial period. Documents reviewed by Heredia and Srivastava, and references to Katkari myths of origins, also link the Katkari to forests and forest-based livelihoods. Even as they migrated over time from one area to another, forests were their home and main source of livelihood. Weling (1934, 2), drawing on census data from 1901, notes that the Katkari were 'thickly scattered' in small communities throughout the hill ranges and forests of Raigad and Thane districts in the present-day state of Maharashtra. Some also lived in hill areas in the southern part of the current state of Gujarat and in the forests of what are now Nasik, Pune and Dhule districts. The Katkari population, numbering some 80,000 in 1901, engaged in a wide range of livelihoods including the production and sale of catechu, charcoal, firewood and other forest products, freshwater fishing, hunting of small mammals and birds, upland agriculture and agricultural labour on the farms of both tribal and non-tribal farmers. While by no means isolated from other communities and the wider market, the Katkari's access to forests and forest resources provided them with a degree of autonomy and a source of identity (Heredia and Srivastava 1994, 72–73).

The Katkari of today are a fragmented and very scattered community, highly dependent on others for their livelihoods and for a place to live. Beginning in the 1950s, Katkari families began to migrate permanently from ancestral areas in the hills to areas on the plains near tiny hubs of economic activity associated with non-tribal agriculturalists. Many very small Katkari hamlets are now spread throughout the region, including Khalapur, Sudhagad, Karjat, Pen and Panvel talukas in Raigad district and various talukas in Thane district, right up to the outskirts of Mumbai. The The Census of India 2001 (GOI 2012a) indicates that the state is home to 235,022 Katkari, mainly in Raigad and Thane districts.

Our survey of Karjat, Khalapur and Sudhagad talukas of Raigad district, initiated in 2006, found 313 Katkari hamlets with a total population of approximately 39,000 people. We believe this accounts for all Katkari communities in the three talukas, although the communities are so small and scattered that some gaps may remain. Among the communities identified, 127 hamlets are located in Khalapur (40.7 per cent), 104 in Karjat (33.3 per cent) and 81 in Sudhagad (26 per cent). On average, these hamlets have existed for 55 years or so. Most of the hamlets are quite close to major roads and railways between Mumbai and Lonavala on the way to Pune and along the main roads connecting Karjat, Chowk,

Khalapur, Khopoli and Pali. The vast majority are quite some distance from the higher hills and forests of the district where most Katkari once lived. The hamlets range in size from as few as five up to 116 families. The mode is only 15 families. This very small size reflects the settlement pattern that led to the creation of the hamlets – a few households invited by landholding farmers to settle on the outskirts of non-tribal villages to serve as a pool of agricultural labour.

Katkari elders created timelines of the major events in the history of individual hamlets;[3] these timelines show common cause leading to the relocation from remote hillsides and forested areas to the outskirts of non-tribal villages on the plains. For example, people in Mohmalwadi trace their place of origin to an area in the 'Old Mohol' forest where five families lived before independence (Table 1.1). The hamlet was located near a *dalhi*[4] plot granted to them on lease during British rule. This was a time when the Katkari were allowed to grow crops on the dalhi plot and were in turn expected to protect the nearby forest. They lived by selling firewood, hunting, gathering non-timber forest products and cultivating upland crops on small agricultural plots. Shortly after independence, a farmer from the non-tribal village of Potal Pali near Kadav in Raigad district asked them to set up their homes near his paddy fields on the edge of the forest. He needed their labour and assistance to protect crops from wild boars living on the forest edge. The farmer helped the Katkari rebuild their houses on a part of his land not used for agriculture.

The creation of Nadode Katkarwadi, a hamlet associated with Nadode village near the current Mumbai–Pune highway, follows a similar pattern. According to Katkari in the hamlet, two non-tribal farmers from Nadode village invited 12 Katkari families to settle on their land. The landholder-farmers benefited from access to the Katkari's labour, while the Katkari families got jobs and a place to stay close to the village. A variation on this theme emerged from Wavloli hamlet in the Sudhagad taluka. The event that precipitated settlement in their current hamlet was a violent break between two groups of Katkari families in their home village.

---

[3] For detailed instructions and adaptations of the timeline method, see 'Tools and Software' at www.participatoryactionresearch.net. A table showing all of the participatory methods used in the study appears in Annex I.

[4] Dalhi or dalli is a word in Marathi. Dalhi now generally refers to a system of collective lease of forest land granted to Adivasi families for cultivation of crops. The word dalhi was also used to refer to a system of cultivation of millets on uplands (as opposed to aalhi, which is paddy cultivation on the lowlands).

Table 1.1: Timeline of major events in the history of Mohmalwadi and outcomes from the point of view of Katkari elders

Period	Events	Outcomes
Pre-independence	• Five Katkari families live in the 'Old Mohol' forest area, close to their dalhi plots.	• Katkari families cultivate the dalhi plot and protect the forest for the British. They also sell firewood and fish.
Around 1950	• A non-tribal farmer from Potal Pali offers wage work to the five Katkari families and asks them to shift their houses from the forest area to his private land. • The landowner helps the Katkari families rebuild their houses on his land. The new hamlet is called Mohmalwadi, from the name 'Old Mohol'.	• The landowner gets cheap, bonded labour to work on his land. • The Katkari get a place to live, employment and easier access to a village market. • Katkari families continue growing crops on their dalhi plot during the monsoon.
Around 1960	• Water from the Tata hydroelectric station at Bhivpuri is diverted into the region through an irrigation canal (Raj Nala). Land in the area is now irrigated and farmers start taking two or even three crops per year. • Employment is available throughout the year in the irrigated area.	• More Katkari families settle in Mohmalwadi, including sons-in-law. The number of houses increases but the landowner does not object because he needs the cheap labour. • Some of the Katkari families from the neighbouring Ambewadi village also work for the Mohmalwadi landowner. • Katkari families look on the landowner as their benefactor.
Around 1980	• It becomes more difficult to find full employment on farms. • The landholder restricts the expansion of houses.	• More Katkaris in the hamlet migrate seasonally to brick kilns. • Basic amenities in the hamlet are very poor.
Around 1990	• Farm houses start appearing in greater numbers. • Land prices increase substantially.	• Local farmers and real-estate brokers start selling land to outsiders. • The landowner of Mohmalwadi is tempted to sell his land. He contacts land agents to negotiate with outsiders.

Contd.

Contd.

Period	Events	Outcomes
2003	• The landowner sells the land on which the Katkari hamlet is located to a person from Mumbai. • The new landowner does a survey and takes legal possession of the land. • A barbed wire fence is erected all around Mohmalwadi. The approach road to the hamlet is completely blocked by the fence.	• Ten Katkari families are forced to remove their houses. • People do not file a complaint because they do not want to offend the old landowner. • Katkari families in Mohmalwadi are divided about what to do. • Katkari families are afraid and insecure.

A landholder,[5] who wanted the Katkari to labour in his fields, facilitated the resettlement of one group.

While the active solicitation of Katkari workers by farmer-landholders underlies the creation of many of the current Katkari hamlets, other factors were also at play. Heredia and Srivastava (1994) argue that from colonial times the Katkari were pushed into migratory wage labour as control of the forests shifted to the British rulers and to non-tribal moneylenders, traders and landlords. This process of land and livelihood alienation has been documented for many Adivasi populations in India (Bose 1967; Gadgil and Guha 1992; Roy Burman 1983; Singh 1983; von Fürer-Haimendorf 1982) and the Katkari are no exception. Older Katkari interviewed still have memories of how their ancestors cut trees for the British and were in turn provided with dalhi plots near the areas being deforested. They also had to shift their homes from time to time in search of work. They noted that the making of catechu declined sharply after independence when the felling of khair trees was banned by the Forest Department. Later restrictions by the Forest Department on the cultivation of dalhi lands undermined the forest-based livelihoods of the Katkari (Dalvi and Bokil 2000). These interventions left the Katkari with few options but to migrate in search of employment and new places to live.

---

[5] We have used the term 'landholder' throughout this book, instead of the term 'landowner'. This reflects our decision to emphasize the social and transient relationship all people have to land, as opposed to conventional notions of land that emphasize private and fixed property in perpetuity.

The timelines that Katkari produced show that many communities initially responded to constraints on their use of the forests near their villages by collectively shifting into the production of charcoal for traders and merchants. Before 1965, charcoal making in Maharashtra was concentrated in parts of Nashik, Dhule, Jalgaon and Pune with sizeable forests (Sathe 1988). These areas were eventually denuded to supply the carbon needed by industries near Mumbai that produced rayon, rubber tyres, textiles and carbides. By the 1970s, production had shifted to the central and southern parts of the state including Raigad, Ratnagiri, Sindhudurg and Satara. Sathe reports that between 4,000 and 5,000 families, 90 per cent of them Katkari from Raigad and Thane districts, were engaged in charcoal making during this period (ibid.). Details from Sathe's survey of workers suggest that this seasonal migratory work was combined with agricultural wage work, a pattern reflected in the hamlet histories that the Katkari developed.

Agricultural investments on the plains of Raigad district increased steadily throughout the 1960s and 1970s, stimulating demand for agricultural labour. In Karjat, some 25 Katkari hamlets were established as satellites to non-tribal villages benefiting from the creation of the Raj Nala canal. The canal provides irrigation water from the Tata hydroelectric station at Bhivpuri, making it possible for farmers there to grow two crops in a year. Other small irrigation projects here and there in Khalapur and Sudhagad talukas also stimulated demand for agricultural labour, filled largely by the Katkari.

While the growth of the agricultural sector was steady from independence to the late 1970s, the main factor driving demand for agricultural labour in Raigad district was a sharp decline in the availability of labour from the younger generations of non-tribal farming families living in the area. Education and shifting employment preferences among the sons and daughters of landholding farming families led to severe labour shortages, as many moved into white- and blue-collar jobs in the growing towns and cities. The farmers who continued farming drew on Katkari hamlets to meet their labour needs. Farmers needed help during the pre-monsoon period for *raab* (the burning of paddy nursery areas with cow dung and other biomass); this involved collecting cow dung, leaves, twigs and grass to spread and burn in the field. They needed help to sow seeds at the start of the monsoons and, during the monsoon, they required labourers for ploughing, transplanting, weeding, harvesting and threshing.

The Katkari were, and still are, well known for their physical strength and endurance. Landholders valued them as hard-working, cheap labour that could be easily bonded through debt. Landholders even competed with each other for access to Katkari labour, using a system of advances called the *khannuk* in the Karjat–Khalapur talukas and *varka* in Sudhagad taluka. During the pre-monsoon period, often a time of food shortage, a pig or one or two goats would be given to a group of 10 to 15 Katkari men and women. Katkari that accepted the meat were bound by this advance on their labour to do the paddy transplanting of the landholder on a priority basis. No additional compensation or wage was offered or expected. For landholders, the arrangement cost them only two-thirds of what they would normally have paid for agricultural workers and guaranteed their labour needs.[6] The Katkari elders we interviewed said that they accepted these arrangements, even though they knew they were being under-paid, because they needed the food during times of scarcity, enjoyed eating the meat, and appreciated the trust shown by this form of advance. The Katkari accounts also reveal that during this period, the Katkari began to look upon the landholders as benefactors. In addition to doing agricultural work, they gathered firewood for the landholders and other villagers and did the heavy work involved in plastering floors with cow dung, repairing walls and building approach roads. In exchange they received small cash and in-kind payments and a place to live on the outskirts of the main village.

Throughout the 1960s and 1970s, landholders actively promoted the settlement of Katkari in existing hamlets, or encouraged new hamlets on marginal corners of their land. Tiny Katkari hamlets initially set up in the 1950s grew significantly during this period and others were established. For example, in the late 1970s, a dozen more Katkari families settled in Mohmalwadi and the neighbouring Ambewadi hamlet with the support of the farmer-landholders. Landowners found it possible to accommodate small numbers of Katkari because only marginal, rocky knolls and sloping areas were needed for Katkari settlements. Also, land was relatively inexpensive and landholdings fairly large. The fragmentation of agricultural land through transfers to the sons and daughters of farmers was proceeding slowly during this period, in part because younger people were seeking employment in nearby urban centres such as Mumbai.

---

[6] In today's context, two goats are worth about 2,000 Indian rupees and three days of work by 15 people about 3,600 Indian rupees.

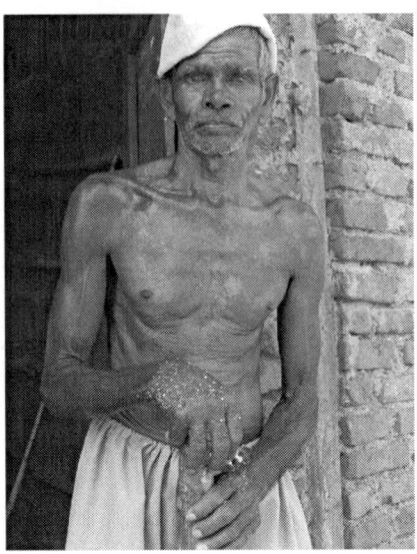

Image 1.1: Shripat Waghmare rests after threshing rice for a landowner in Sudhagad. *Waghmare* (tiger) is a common Katkari surname

Some Katkari also settled on small sections of land owned by the Forest Department. Our survey data indicates that about 17 per cent of all Katkari hamlets in the three talukas covered by our survey (Karjat, Khalapur and Sudhagad) are located on 'forest lands' owned by the Forest Department. Surprisingly, these lands are not contiguous areas in the higher hills where one might expect forests, but rather consist of many small hillocks and forest fragments scattered along the lower slopes of the Western Ghats and now near towns, highways and major roads. For example, Vakanwadi in Sudhagad taluka is located on a fragment of 'forest land' surrounded by private lands and quite close to a major road. A possible explanation for Katkari settlement on these lands lies in the Maharashtra Private Forests (Acquisition) Act, 1975. This act came into force with the intent of acquiring private forests larger than the 30 acres allowed under land legislation. Surveys called for by the act were not generally implemented until 1998 when the Forest Department was deeded the lands. It seems likely that many of the Katkari hamlets now located on forest lands were created when the lands were in private hands and that they remained there while the legal status of the lands was in limbo. Thus, the factors leading to Katkari settlement on private lands and forest lands were probably the same in most cases – the need to draw agricultural workers to the paddy fields of non-tribal farmers.

By the early 1980s, the active creation of new Katkari hamlets on the plains stopped as the demand for agricultural workers stabilized. The survey data indicates that the vast majority of the hamlets in the three talukas (97 per cent) were established before 1980. Since that time, Katkari communities have increased in population and density, but few have emerged in new locations: only 10 out of 313 Katkari communities surveyed in these three talukas were created after 1980. According to the Katkari's own assessments, by the mid-1980s it became more difficult to find work with local farmers. Landholders no longer needed to go out of their way to find the workers they needed, but rather could draw from the pool already there. The ramshackle huts and hamlets of the Katkari near established non-tribal villages provided a base from which to migrate in search of employment. Thus began a time when the Katkari combined agricultural work with bonded labour in other sectors of the rural economy, such as brick making and charcoal production. The traditional agricultural employers of the Katkari raised no objections to their seasonal migration so long as enough workers were available to meet their needs during both the pre-monsoon and the monsoon periods.

Tensions between landholders and the Katkari over settlement on private lands began to emerge in the 1990s, decades after most Katkari hamlets were established. The booming Mumbai economy, flush with cash, drove up land prices all along the highways and byways of Raigad district, including areas in Karjat and Khalapur talukas near the Mumbai–Pune express highway, the Karjat–Panvel railway line, the Morbe dam and the proposed international airport at Uran. Planning for the special economic zone in Navi Mumbai, eventually approved in 2002, also fuelled land speculation that drove land prices up dramatically between 1992 and 1996 and then again between 2002 and 2008.[7]

Karjat taluka, while formally a 'green zone' with restrictions on industrial and urban development, was subject to fierce land speculation by a new kind of land developer. Karjat's ample water, greenery and scenic qualities, given its situation in the shadow of the Western Ghats, were seen as the ideal location for so-called 'farm houses'. In the 1990s, these became a popular purchase for the emerging upper middle classes of Mumbai in search of weekend respite from the hustle and grime of the city. A leading film studio was also established in Karjat, followed

---

[7] Newspaper reports throughout this period, in the *Indian Realty News, Express India* and other local papers, provide details about the booming real-estate market.

later by other studios serving Bollywood. Tax and educational incentives associated with the ownership of agricultural land unintentionally facilitated this boom. Karjat is reported to have one of the largest real-estate chains of 'farm houses' in Asia.[8]

Image 1.2: Real estate agents lure Mumbai elites with advertisements like this one along Highway 17 near Nagothane

Ironically, the tiny hilltops where most of the Katkari settled, at one time considered useless land by the local farming population, became prime land for 'weekenders' seeking windy areas, dramatic views and lands free of stagnant water. Landholders began to worry about possible Katkari claims to the land and took various measures to discourage further settlement and any formal obligations. For example, the timeline created by Katkari in Ambewadi in Karjat taluka showed that in the 1990s the landholder arranged for the *sarpanch* (chair of the *gram*

---

[8] http://en.academic.ru/dic.nsf/enwiki/652077 (accessed on 7 October 2010). Gaikwad (1995) also notes the emergence of the farm house as an occasional employer of Katkari.

panchayat[9] to waive the house tax that the Katkari had been paying to the local government. The landholder was concerned that this payment might provide the Katkari with a claim. He also convinced other non-tribal farmers not to provide the Katkari with local employment. This action, while difficult to enforce widely and consistently, sowed fear and uncertainty among the Katkari in Ambewadi. Threats of eviction in other communities also began to emerge after the turn of the millennium. These reflected a break in the patron–client relationship that had once provided some security to the Katkari. It also signalled the end of the pattern of resettlement that had brought the Katkari from their ancestral forests to the plains in the first place. Meanwhile, most of the old abodes had been abandoned and now there is hardly any evidence that they existed in the first place. There is no going back to the forested hills, as any pieces of wood or *karvi* (*Callosa carvi*) sticks[10] that may have been left behind have either decomposed or merged with the vegetation.

From Forest to Mud Pit

Today, the Katkari are a pool of inexpensive and highly mobile labour bonded to farms and rural industries supporting the growth of Greater Mumbai. They comprise a large part of the workforce in the regional brick-making industry, contributing literally brick by brick to the rising cityscapes of Mumbai, Panvel, New Mumbai, Pune, Thane and Kalyan. The Katkari feature prominently in sand-dredging operations and stone-breaking work associated with the construction industry and in the production of charcoal used mainly by small industries. This work, the most physically demanding and lowest paid in the entire region, occupies

---

[9] The gram panchayat is the local governing body at the village and small town level. It is responsible for numerous local matters including village streets, village markets, village festivals and celebrations and implementing development schemes for agriculture and animal husbandry. It comprises seven or more representatives elected for a term of five years by the *gram sabha*, an assembly of all male and female village residents above the age of 18. A sarpanch (chairperson) selected from among the elected gram panchayat members oversees the gram panchayat, assisted by a *gram sevak* (secretary) who draws a salary from the Revenue Department.

[10] Karvi (Carvia callosa or Strobilanthes callosa) is a plant that grows on the slopes of hillsides. Long sticks of Karvi are collected, usually by women, for making the walls of houses using the wattle and daub method. The Karvi sticks are woven with horizontal twigs and then daubed with cow dung and mud.

about 60 per cent of the Katkari families in Karjat, Khalapur and Sudhagad according to our survey data. Katkari men, women and children migrate to work sites throughout Raigad and Thane districts, often for six to eight months each year, leaving their homes unattended and hamlets virtually abandoned. This creates a gap in residence that landholders use to justify enclosure and eviction when it suits them.

Brick-making kilns operate in close coordination with farmer-landholders. After five to six years of flooding a paddy field, farmers find that sediments build up unevenly, making water retention and seed germination more difficult to manage. Brick making lowers and levels the field, thereby reducing farm management costs and improving production in the short term. (In the long term, however, this practice may deplete top soil and soil nutrients.) Kiln operators typically rent and excavate the sticky soils of paddy fields that have a nearby water source and an approach road. Farmers agree to rent out their fields because it brings some benefits to their land, in addition to the rental income. These arrangements between farmers and brick operators are, for the most part, mutually beneficial. On the other hand, the Katkari become tied to the kiln masters (*sheth*) by debt and various acts of coercion.

The organization of work at brick kilns sets the tone for bondage. Typically, a Katkari husband and wife work as a couple, with a younger brother or sister as a reliever and assistant. A team of three people uses one metal mould or *patli* for making bricks and so the team itself is also called a patli. Brick-making operations engage a patli to manage a set of three pits (an *ara*) where mud is soaked, excavated, made into bricks and stacked for drying. Larger operations of 40 or more people are also divided into patlis of three members each. Each patli works independently, creating 1,000 to 1,300 bricks per day once they are set up and fully operational. During a season that lasts five to six months, one patli produces about 100,000 bricks.

Work on brick units usually begins between 5:30 and 6:00 a.m. and goes on until 7:00 or 8:00 p.m. Much of the season coincides with the summer, when day-time temperatures reach 40 degrees Celsius or higher. People work in the brutal sun six days in a week, the weekly market day generally being an off-day. One Katkari worker noted:

> If we fall ill, the sheth gives us some money so we can go to the doctor, but we can't stop work. The work goes on. Even if we do stop for one day then we lose two to three days of pay to get back on the cycle of soaking mud. If one person in the patli falls ill, the other two have to manage somehow.

Living conditions at the brick kilns are squalid. Upon arrival at the brick kiln, each family is allowed to build a small, makeshift hut next to the kiln. There is often no safe drinking water: the same water pumped from an open river or lake to mix with the mud is used for drinking and bathing. Men, women (including those who are pregnant), adolescent girls and boys and small children work in the harsh conditions with no shoes, gloves or safety equipment. The survey data shows that 79 per cent of the families migrating to brick kilns take their children with them, making attendance at school periodic at best. Older youngsters carry water to the pit while toddlers play with the sand in imitation of their parents.

The arrangements between the Katkari and kiln operators fully deserve the term debt bondage: forced advances, unpayable debts, cheating on wages, not keeping accounts, making people work excessive hours in extremely difficult conditions, casual treatment of serious injuries and illness, confiscation of identity papers, confining people who want to leave, exploiting women sexually and beating men, sometimes to death.

The cycle of bondage begins with a visit from a sheth just before the Ganesh Chaturthi festival (in August–September) or prior to the Pittar Amoshya festival for the souls of the elders of the home. Families are given an advance (*uchal*) on the upcoming season, typically of the order of Rs 10,000 to Rs 20,000. This is then deducted at the end of the season from the total wages earned. In the meantime, each Katkari family is given small weekly payments (*kharchi*) of Rs 500 to Rs 750 per week to cover subsistence needs during the time they are working on brick units. This is also deducted from wages at the end of the season. Any remaining debt is carried forward to subsequent years, thereby creating an obligation borne by the entire family.

The system of payment is riddled with opportunities for unscrupulous accounting practices. Workers are paid for only 1,000 bricks when they actually produce 1,100 bricks. The surplus bricks are treated as interest on the uchal. Prevailing rates are Rs 300 to Rs 350 per 1,000 bricks, but in reality wages are rarely calculated and paid precisely. Rates of pay per 1,000 bricks also tend to be lower when larger advances are given. As most Katkari are not literate or numerate, it is difficult for them to calculate the number of bricks made, the wages earned and expenses deducted. The work itself is so demanding that people have little energy or time left to pay attention to accounts and most operators do not keep records of their own, let alone share them with the workers. On the contrary, the sheth does all that he can to keep the Katkari uninformed and confused. Concerns about improper accounting by the contractor were reported by 30 per cent of all surveyed families working on brick kilns.

Most families return from the brick units empty-handed, or in debt for both past and future seasons. According to the survey, some 83 per cent of families who migrated to brick kilns the previous year were unable to repay their debt completely by the end of the season and therefore started the new season in debt. Some 53 per cent had not saved any money at all by the end of the season, returning with the full debt (plus interest) they had started with. This cycle of Katkari indebtedness is repeated year after year. Gaikwad (1995) finds a similar pattern of forced advances, debt, accounting abuses and severe back and joint pain among the Katkari working on brick kilns.

The reasons for taking an advance, and the implications or effects of doing so, were explored with Katkari families using the 'problem tree' method.[11] For example, in Asra Katkarwadi, families indicated that they took the advance to celebrate during festivals, to pay for marriages, to purchase a grain supply or to make improvements to their homes. They turned to the advance because they had no savings or alternative sources of income with which to undertake these social obligations or subsistence activities. They also noted that some contractors gave them an advance forcibly (literally putting money in their hands or in the hands of older children when parents were absent) to create an obligation. Some families also said that they would take the advance out of fear that the contractor would not pay their full wages – the advance was at least a guarantee of some income for their labour.

A survey of several hundred families engaged in brick making validated and extended these observations. It found that only 8 per cent took the advance for house repairs, house construction or to purchase a grain supply. The majority, 77 per cent of the families surveyed, took the advance to celebrate festivals. These funds were spent primarily on gambling and drinking, in which men and women alike participate. According to the Katkari involved in these discussions, the annual uchal leads many to debilitating alcohol and gambling addictions. Only 15 per cent of the households in the survey funded a marriage from the advance. Among the Katkari, marriage involves a bride price paid by the father

---

[11] For detailed instructions and adaptations of the problem tree method, see Tools and Software at www.participatoryactionresearch.net.

of the groom rather than a dowry provided by the bride's family. The advance provided for this purpose is inevitably much larger than regular advances on wages and often leads to a cycle of debt lasting 15 to 20 years and passing from father to son.

Identity papers are often seized by the brick contractors as a way of holding workers at the site and making them dependent on contractors for access to medical or other government services. The survey found that most Katkari had documents seized at the beginning of the season and some did not get them back when the season ended. When Katkari try to protest against the exploitation, kiln masters are known to file cases of robbery and theft against them at the police station. During the brick-making season, they are confined and beaten if they try to leave for any reason, including a death or illness in the family.

> If there is a disagreement, and we say something, the sheth abuses us verbally and hits us below the ear [considered a degrading blow]. This year the contractor came to my village, tied up my brother-in-law and took him away. My brother-in-law had run away, leaving a debt of 7,000 rupees. The contractor said his debt was now 14,000 rupees for having run away and then started beating him. I tried to stop him but the contractor asked me if I was going to pay the amount and threatened me. He called me *bhadvya* [a pimp]. Then he tied my brother-in-law and took him to Panvel. While travelling to Panvel there was an accident on the road. The contractor fractured his hand and got very angry. When they arrived at the brick kiln they tied and beat my brother-in-law again very badly. He is working with him still. He has 'eaten' the money so he has to go. I don't know when he will return. How can I file a police case against the contractor? He will come back and beat me too. (Katkari man in Sudhagad, author's field notes, March 2, 2009)

While the men are beaten, the women face the risk of sexual exploitation. The Katkari surveyed reported 23 cases of physical violence and three cases of rape while at the brick kilns the previous year. Interviews suggest that the incidence of sexual abuse is much greater: operators, or managers employed by the operators, are known to demand sexual favours when problems arise or an extra advance is needed for one reason or another. Sex has even been claimed as a right for giving the Katkari employment in the first place.

These stories are commonplace. Members of the research team have recorded and reported to the police 12 deaths due to beatings on brick kilns over a five-year span. On one occasion, a member of the research

team was asked to deliver the body of a murdered man to his family. In
another case witnessed by members of the research team, an elderly
Katkari brick worker was hit at the site by a motorcycle driven by a
friend of the sheth, severely breaking his leg. The man was dumped
unceremoniously at a hospital and left there without money or the identity
papers he needed to access medical treatment. The leg never set properly,
leaving him crippled and him and his wife destitute. Neither of these
cases was thoroughly investigated by police and no charges were ever
laid. Gaikwad (1995, 29) reports cases where Katkari labourers have been
'burnt alive in the coal kiln furnace due to differences or refusal to comply
with the master's expectations'. Abuses like this happen periodically on
the larger operations from Panvel to Pen and all the way up to Mumbai.

Brick making is common among the Katkari in Karjat and Khalapur,
while in Sudhagad both brick kilns and charcoal operations draw Katkari
families away to work. Families in this taluka have engaged in charcoal
production for decades, even as production shifted from one area to
another. Labour agents and contractors who shifted their operations to
new areas continued to seek out Katkari from Sudhagad because the
Katkari are expert in this occupation and can be easily bonded.

Image 1.3: An injury at a brick kiln crippled this Katkari man in Sudhaghad. The kiln
operator kept his identity papers, making it difficult for him to access medical assistance

The charcoal-making process provides contractors with two ways of making money: removing trees and making charcoal. Contractors make arrangements with private landholders who want their land cleared of vegetation, employ labour agents to collect workers and then ensure that all the trees are cleared. Five or six Katkari families per contract are hired as a unit to cut all the trees and brush, transport the material to a central location, build a furnace and make the charcoal. Wages are set according to the quantity and quality of charcoal produced, not the number of trees felled, so little management is needed. Much larger advances – typically Rs 25,000 – are provided to Katkari families engaged in charcoal making compared to brick making. Supervisors also provide food and money for weekly expenditures, resolve disputes and arrange for medical assistance as needed. The Katkari often spend seven to nine months making charcoal, returning to their villages well after the start of the monsoon. This makes it impossible for them to do any agricultural work of their own, leaving them entirely dependent on agricultural wage work until the next charcoal season begins.

Usually, the Katkari working on charcoal operations are treated as a valuable resource. The work is very demanding physically and, because of its decentralized nature, it requires a motivated and relatively independent workforce. This creates an incentive for operators to be careful not to exploit the Katkari excessively. Bondage is usually less severe compared to brick operations. According to the livelihood survey, families that migrate to charcoal operations are significantly less likely to start their season already indebted, compared to families who migrate to brick kilns.[12] They are also much less likely to be subjected to various forms of abuse, including harassment, physical violence, sexual violence, improper accounting by their contractor and having their important documents seized. The situation is only relatively better, however. Workers on charcoal-making units are still bonded by debt and subject to other forms of coercion. They are also poorly paid. According to a detailed study by Sathe (1988), the income earned by Katkari and other workers from charcoal making during the 1980s was lower than their subsistence needs. It seems unlikely that this has changed much in the intervening years.

---

[12] Statistical measures of significance for the livelihood survey and general survey referred to throughout the text are for correlations with a p-value of 0.10 or less.

Exclusion from the Caste Community

The fragmentation and scattering of the Katkari community from hills to plain areas and their integration into highly exploitative, migratory livelihoods has left the Katkari with a very tenuous connection to their homes and hamlets. To other members of village society, the Katkari appear to be vagabonds and tramps with no ties to village life or claims to village land. The resulting vulnerability to enclosure and eviction is greatly compounded by a long and dramatic history of social exclusion and active prejudice against the Katkari going back to the British Raj. Written references to the Katkari from the nineteenth century are replete with derogatory and bigoted language more extreme than that used by the British to describe most other segments of Indian society.

> At the beginning of British Rule [1818] the hill tribes, among whom Kolis, Bhils, Kathkaris, and Ramoshis are mentioned, the Kathkari [sic] were most degraded. They gained a scanty living by tilling forest glades and by hunting. But their chief support was plunder. They lived in small cabins in the heart of the forests, and were not only wretched themselves but kept the villagers in a state of alarm... .
>
> In 1825, according to Bishop Heber, who had his information from Mr. Elphinstone, the charcoal burners of Salsette, probably Kathkaris, were so wild that they had no direct dealings with the people of the plains ...
>
> About 10 years later Major Mackintosh [1836] described the Kathkaris as great thieves, stealing corn from fields and farm yards, committing robberies in the villages at night, and plundering lonely travellers during the day. Their circumstances were often desperate. (Gazetteer of the Bombay Presidency 1883)

Weling, a British anthropologist who published a book on the Katkari in 1934, wrote that the police department informed him 'about the Katkari having a peculiar odour: a Katkari stick has a particular smell and that gives a clue for the detection of crime' (1934, 36).

Colonial perspectives on forest peoples like the Katkari were codified through the Criminal Tribes Act of 1871 and successive pieces of legislation enforced in India during British rule. The Criminal Tribes Act was in part a response to the mutiny of 1857 and efforts of the British administration to retain law and order (Bokil 2002). It also sought to control 'hereditary criminal' sections of Indian society, reflecting the British social policy of the time that held that 'crime was a genetic trait transmitted over generations in a family through parents or ancestors' (Radhakrishna 2008, 2). The concept of a 'criminal tribe' extended this notion of the causes of individual criminality to entire communities or caste-based collectivities: 'Like a carpenter would pass on his trade to the next generation, hereditary criminal caste members would pass on this profession to their offspring' (ibid., 5).

The notion of crime as an inherited profession was initially applied to the so-called 'wandering tribes' of northern India, and then broadened in 1911 to cover gypsies, nomads and migrating peoples all over India. These communities were seen by the British authorities as a lower race with unusual occupations and skills of no use to the Empire (entertainers, petty traders, traditional craftspeople, hunters and gatherers, etc.). The legislation provided district magistrates throughout British India with the power to specify as a 'criminal tribe' any community he had 'reason to believe to be addicted to the systematic commission of non-bailable offences' (section 3 of the act, quoted in Radhakrishna 2008, 38). Identification of a particular population as a 'criminal tribe' was done by issuing a notification to that effect. The act gave local governments wide-reaching powers over 'criminal tribes', including the ability to

> deport any number of persons any distance from their homes, employ them in any form of labour, hire them out to employers, punish them with fine and imprisonment if they refused to work, bring them back if they attempted to escape, and subject them to additional disciplinary measures ... . These measures applied to all members of the group concerned – men, women and children. (Ibid.).

In name alone, the act clearly demonstrated the desire of its drafters to assert the social inferiority of particular populations and traditional livelihoods. In fact, it did much more.

Whether or not the intention of the act extended to an imposition of economic sanctions on certain peoples, its effect was to allow for the enslavement of labour. Radhakrishna (2008) shows that the procedures for notification of a community as a 'criminal tribe' were used systematically by landlords-cum-headmen (who acted as revenue officers), the junior police administration and British financial interests to mobilize certain populations for their own profit. She notes, for example, that when the Kathiars, a tribal community in eastern India, refused to work voluntarily in the mica mines owned by Brandt and Company, they were declared a 'criminal tribe' and rounded up to work in the mines.

When this pool of labour proved to be insufficient, a Telugu branch of the Korava tribe was also notified as a 'criminal tribe' and forced to work in the mines. Notification of a community as a 'criminal tribe' was also used by British administrators, with the assistance of the Salvation Army in India, to settle people on unproductive lands or recruit them into industrial activities that could generate revenue for the government.

Research on the Katkari experience under the Criminal Tribes Act has not been undertaken, although it is known that they were among the first tribes included in the original version of the act in 1871 (Kennedy 1908, cited in Bokil 2006). Weling wrote in 1934:

> It is a known fact that the Katkari, perhaps for purely administrative purpose, are included in the category of criminal tribes. From an Anthropological standpoint, the case where a certain class of people is stamped as criminals continuously for a number of years and is governed under this condition is highly interesting. But my attempt to study the case by collecting reliable data from official records could not succeed [in demonstrating criminality]. (Weling 1934, 56).

The Criminal Tribes Act was repealed by the Government of India after independence. Members of the 'criminal tribes' were 'denotified' and many were re-listed as denotified and nomadic tribes (DNT). They were subsequently included under the Habitual Offenders Act, 1952. At present, the 'denotified and nomadic tribes' listed under the act comprise some 60 million people in India. Radhakrishna argues, however, that 'the Habitual Offenders Act replicated all the victimizing sections of the colonial Criminal Tribes Act, showing that the legal edifice of the independent Indian state did not treat the concerned marginalized people any differently' (2008, 174). She goes on to show that under the Habitual Offenders Act, the DNTs have been treated under law as vagrants and as beggars on the assumption that they are lacking an occupation, shirking honest work and prone to criminality (see also D'Souza 2001;). Bokil (2002, 150) also notes that, despite the intentions of the act, 'in actual practice, the police department, still moulded in the colonial mindset, follows the same old practices'. Recently, the United Nations Committee on the Elimination of Racial Discrimination has called on the Government of India to repeal the Habitual Offenders Act and address the systematic discrimination faced by the 'denotified and nomadic tribes'.[13]

---

[13] http://www.asiantribune.com/index.php?q=node/4972 (accessed on 12 June 2010).

The Katkari, while listed among the criminal tribes in the British period, were not included among the list of DNTs created through the Habitual Offenders Act. Instead, they were listed at the state level as a scheduled tribe, and, within that category, as a 'primitive tribal group' in need of the greatest attention. This is a formal advantage for the Katkari as it gives them access, at least in theory, to affirmative action programmes that DNTs are still struggling for (Bokil 2002). In fact, however, the legacy of being a 'criminal tribe' and the pejorative label 'primitive' still defines the Katkari identity today and underlies the extremely marginalized position they occupy in the social structure of the communities in which they live.

The most apparent implication is harassment of the Katkari by the police, and the deep-seated fear of the police widespread in the Katkari community. Years of work by ADS and SOBTI with Katkari involved in police cases suggest that even today, when a crime is reported, police will pick up Katkari at random from the street, beat them up and force them to admit to the crime (also reported by Gaikwad 1995). As a result of this long history of abuse, the Katkari have become extremely frightened of the police. It is a common reaction in Katkari villages that when a family receives a notice from the police *patil* (chief) to report to the police station, the affected person immediately takes an advance of between 600 and 700 rupees from a moneylender and goes to the station with the money in hand (to pay the required bribe). This visceral fear is a great tragedy for a people who saw themselves as a courageous people like none other, 'counting the teeth of the tiger'.

The marginalized position of the Katkari within the village society is reflected as well in the naming of Katkari individuals and families. In government records, most Katkari have the general surname 'Katkari', even though people have their own clan names: Waghmare, Jadhav, Wagh, Pawar, Mukne, Hilam, etc. Gaikwad (1995, 35) notes that the 'Katkaris are not listed as residents in many villages by the local gram panchayats, which makes it easy for the establishments to make them vacate the area whenever required'. The censure implied by this naming and non-registration practice extends as well to the naming of their hamlets. In the vast majority of cases, Katkari hamlets are named after the revenue village they are associated with, with the suffix 'Katkarwadi' (Katkari hamlet) or just 'wadi' (hamlet) added. Examples are Nadode Katkarwadi, Sarang Katkarwadi and Siddheshwarwadi. This naming practice is unusual for both tribal and non-tribal communities in various parts of the state; most communities have distinct names. The Thakur

and Mahadev Koli, two other prominent tribal communities in
Maharashtra, have distinct names for most of their hamlets and villages,
even when these hamlets are associated with non-tribal revenue villages.[14]

Heredia and Srivastava (1994), in their study of the Katkari in Raigad
district, found that both caste communities and other Adivasi communities
consider the Katkari inferior to themselves and to all other communities
in the area. Dominant caste communities, including the Marathas and
the Agris, generally consider the Katkari a primitive and drunken society,
who are beyond redemption. They also recognize the importance of the
Katkari as a source of labour and seek to reproduce the relationship of
exploitation they once had with the Dalits living in the area. The Dalits,
for their part, look upon the Katkari as an economically backward people
in the same position they had occupied some decades before. Even among
other Adivasi communities such as the Thakur, the Katkari are considered
inferior due to their propensity for drink as well as their food habits,
strongly rejected by both Hindu and other Adivasi groups.

The food habits of the Katkari are particularly problematic for other
communities. The Katkari are one of only a few tribal groups in India
that eat rodents, including the Little Indian Field Mouse (*Mus booduga*),
the Servant Mouse, the Black Rat (*Rattus rattus*), the Brown Rat (*Rattus
norvegicus*) and the Greater or Indian Bandicoot (*Bandicota indica*). In
Hinduism, eating rodents is considered extremely inauspicious and people
who do so are seen as dirty and socially inferior in the extreme. For the
Katkari, however, eating rodents is a cultural practice. They believe that
their strength and long life comes from eating the meat of rodents. They
have even created a cultural festival, the Undir Navmi, dedicated to the
rodent.

The Undir Navmi takes place in October or November after crops
are harvested. On the appointed day, the *naik* or traditional leader of
the Katkari community gives a call to the people to come out for a
rodent hunt. A group of Katkari people go to nearby paddy fields where
they have been given permission to hunt. They identify a burrow where
rodents have deposited mud at the entrance. They then burn dried cow
dung and hay inside one of the openings and watch for smoke emerging
from other openings of the burrow. Immediately, people go and stand
outside each of these openings. Unable to breathe in the smoke, the

---

[14] Thakur and Mahadev Koli village names are often based on the names of trees,
rivers, mountains or animals found in the area.

rodents rush out and are killed by the Katkari standing outside. Some rodents die of suffocation within the burrows. The Katkari then dig all the channels of the burrow, collect the dead rodents and along with them the panicles of paddy that have been collected and stored by the rodents. They can get as much as 12 to 15 kilos of paddy from the burrows. A complete meal from the rodent hunt!

The meat is shared equally among all the participating families. A single bandicoot weighs as much as 1.4 kilograms and measures 30–40 cm in length not counting the tail. Smaller young rodents are roasted immediately and eaten in the field, while the larger rodents are taken home, roasted, cooked in the form of curry (with spices) and eaten with rice or bread (*bhakri*). The rats' intestines and liver are cooked separately with salt and turmeric and consumed as a tonic for stomach ache. The older Katkari say that rodent meat is the main source of health, vigour and vitality among the Katkari people. That is why they are long-lived and have a lot of strength.

Despite the social censure against eating rodents, hunting rodents is actually encouraged by landholding (Hindu) agriculturalists. Rodents are found in fields and gardens throughout western India and are major agricultural pests. After catching the rodents, Katkari leave the dug up burrows and go back to their hamlet. The farmer who owns the paddy field then comes and fills-in the dug up burrows with mud, thus closing channels that siphon water from the paddy fields. The rodent hunt is thus a win–win proposition for the Katkari and for the paddy field owners, since the Katkari get food grains and meat while the farmer benefits by way of vital (and free) repairs to the paddy field. Similar arrangements exist with respect to monkeys, another agricultural pest and much-revered by the Hindus. While farmers would not themselves kill monkeys, they will pay the Katkari to kill monkeys that threaten their fields. In Sindhudurg, a district in southern Maharashtra, the Katkari are called *wanarmare*, a Marathi term for a community that kills monkeys.

Acknowledgement of the subordinate economic and social position the Katkari occupy in the region, and strong negative reactions to their food habits and related cultural practices, reinforce active prejudice against the Katkari in the broader society, including exclusion by other tribal groups. The Thakur, for example, use the word 'Kathodi' as a term of abuse and disrespect. In these direct or subtle ways, the distinctiveness of the Katkari collectivity is used to exclude the community utterly, leaving them in a position even more vulnerable than the lower castes and other tribal groups who have some form of membership in the village system. Although Srinivas (1987), in his landmark studies of the caste system in India, argues that even the lowest castes are members of the village community, Katkari communities have no place in any village hierarchy. Instead, they are treated as an illegitimate community and banished to an ambiguous social space where exploitation and subjugation can occur with impunity. Ideas of common good and the emergence of public action possible in many Indian villages (cf. Brara 2006) have little scope in this context. Exclusion from the basic rights of residence and participation in village life is a source of enormous physical and psychological hardship for Katkari communities, and a significant burden for a people already on the brink of both physical and cultural annihilation.

Katkari Livelihood and Living Conditions

A survey of Katkari hamlets conducted in 2006 paints a bleak picture of the livelihood and living conditions of the community. Descriptive data dealing with a range of hamlet-level and household-level characteristics was collected by convening a meeting in each hamlet and administering a structured interview with the assembled group. All questions were of a descriptive nature, such as 'how many households are there in the village' and 'how many children go to school'. Participants discussed and clarified each question and formulated a response reflecting the group consensus. This group process provided a means to pool knowledge about the hamlet and compare and verify responses through discussion, thereby reducing some measurement errors. It also provided a sensible alternative to a randomized survey of individual households, an impractical undertaking in communities with very high rates of migration. The large number of hamlets included in the survey, representing perhaps all Katkari hamlets in the three talukas, and systematic attention during the interviews to absent families, also helped to reduce both coverage and non-response errors common in surveys. While still subject to sample bias, the data provides a careful estimate of key demographic characteristics of the Katkari population in the three talukas.

Findings related directly to Katkari living conditions are presented in the remaining part of this chapter. These are compared, when relevant, with findings from a random sample of two Katkari hamlets in Pen taluka analyzed by the Tribal Research and Training Institute (Tomar and Tribhuwan 2004); with demographic information on tribals in Maharashtra (Jain et al. 1995); with aggregate data on scheduled tribes from the Census of India 2001 analyzed by Maharatna (2005); and with the Census of

India 2011 data on houses, household amenities and assets (GOI, 2012b). By all measures, the Katkari are exceptionally deprived in relation to land rights, employment, basic amenities, education and health-care provisions normally available to Indian citizens.

Agricultural Land Rights

While farmers depend on the Katkari for farm labour, the Katkari are effectively blocked from being farmer-proprietors. Only about 13 per cent of the Katkari families in Karjat, Khalapur and Sudhagad talukas have agricultural land, mainly dalhi land on higher hills far from where they currently live. The landless rate of 87 per cent among the Katkari is much higher than the 48 per cent rate for rural households in India as a whole. A history of land alienation, and failure on the part of government officials to implement policies on land reform and tribal land rights, are the main reasons why the vast majority of Katkari remain landless to this day. At present, only about 10 per cent of the Katkari households in the three talukas surveyed have rights to dalhi plots granted to the Katkari during the British period. Most of these households have not received the secure titles they are entitled to, leaving them vulnerable to harassment and eviction by the Forest Department under the pretext of 'forest encroachment'. Gaikwad (1995) reports that Katkari that do have these rights say that cultivation is impossible due to grazing of cattle by the upper castes. Even fewer Katkari households, some 3 per cent of the population surveyed, received ceiling lands acquired and redistributed under the Maharashtra Agricultural Land (Ceiling on Holdings) Act 1961. This legislation was developed as a way of limiting the amount of land any individual could hold, and to acquire surplus land for redistribution among landless families, including members of scheduled tribes. The Bombay Tenancy and Agricultural Lands Act, 1948, and the Maharashtra Land Revenue Code, 1966, have not benefited the Katkari in any substantial way; only 6 per cent of Katkari families in the three talukas currently have tenancy land, another form of land tenure distinct from private property titles. These tenancy rights are also vulnerable, as most of the tenant households have not registered their land under the appropriate legislation, a process that is bureaucratic and difficult to navigate or accomplish for non-literate people such as the Katkari.[15]

---

[15] Some of the households in hamlets have ceiling land, dalhi land and/or tenancy land, an overlap that accounts for the percentage difference between landownership overall (13 per cent) and percentage ownership of each type of land.

Employment

Virtually all Katkari households combine various sources of employment throughout the year. While agriculture is the primary economic activity in areas where the Katkari have settled, the vast majority engage in agriculture as labourers, not as cultivators and proprietors. Some 90 per cent of all households surveyed reported that they worked for three to five months of the year as agricultural workers, typically on the farms of non-tribal farmers close to their homes. This is poorly paid work and periodic at best. Our discussions with the Katkari described the yearly cycle as follows. Agricultural wage work begins in April with raab. Later, labour is contracted for land preparations, and paid a lump sum (Rs 1,500 to Rs 2,000) for ploughing, levelling of the paddy field and repair of field bunds. Once the rains begin, day workers are contracted to uproot the paddy seedlings and transplant them to the paddy fields. This work is generally done by women. Weeding, harvesting, threshing and storage follow as the season progresses, work undertaken by both men and women. Workers are paid Rs 120 per day, or Rs 100 if food is offered. Labourers working 'with food' get one meal, tea (twice a day), some tobacco and half a bottle of raw alcohol in the evening. Wages for threshing of paddy fields are paid based on the number of bundles threshed, at a rate of Rs 10 per bundle. In the study area, both men and women receive the same wages for this general agricultural work, unlike the gender pay inequities prevailing in other parts of India.

The cultivation of millets and pulses on small plots of sloping lands in forested areas was an element in the traditional livelihood strategy of the Katkari and is still practised to some extent. The survey data shows that 10 per cent of households in the three talukas periodically grow upland crops, mainly on dalhi lands. These can meet food needs for three to four months in a year. As discussed in later chapters, the Katkari were never resolute agriculturalists like the Thakur and some other Adivasi communities in Maharashtra. Their connection to upland agriculture has also been systematically eroded by decades of harassment by Forest Department officials bent on displacing people from forested areas managed using traditional methods of shifting agriculture. The Census of India 2001 (GOI, 2012a) shows that only 6 per cent of the total Katkari working population in Maharashtra are classified as 'cultivators'.

River fish and fishing are dear to the Katkari and represent a tangible connection to their earlier, forest-based livelihoods. Today, fishing, hunting small animals and gathering forest plants for food and sale supplement other kinds of work grounded mainly in wage labour of various kinds. Some 7,970 families in the three talukas, or 90 per cent of the families in the three talukas, have family members that regularly dedicate some time to these traditional livelihoods. These activities play small but strategic roles in ensuring food security during particular seasons and when no other options are available.

The collection and sale of firewood is a daily activity for many Katkari women and girls. The majority of Katkari households reported that family members collect fuel wood from the surrounding forests and forest fragments and carry the bundles to towns and larger villages, where they sell it house to house or in the common market. Husbands help when they are not involved in other work by collecting and carrying larger bundles into town, then splitting those up into smaller bundles that women and girls sell. Goat rearing is less common, but is a livelihood highly valued by women who have managed to acquire local breeds of goats. It involves taking the animals out to fallow areas, roadsides and other open lands where they can graze and watching over them to protect the animals from stray dogs and other dangers. Goats are vulnerable to various health problems, especially during the monsoon, so great care is taken to provide them with shelter and to treat sick animals with medicines the Katkari make themselves from medicinal plants.

Landlessness, the decline of forest-based livelihoods and insufficient employment in the agriculture sector underlie the dependence of Katkari families on migration for year-round livelihood. As discussed earlier, some 60 per cent of the Katkari families in the three talukas migrate seasonally for six to eight months to work on brick kilns or charcoal operations owned and controlled by non-tribal operators. Employment with the government or the private sector is extremely rare among the Katkari, with only a handful of families reporting working members with permanent jobs.

Village Sites and Housing

The survey data shows that 212 Katkari hamlets, or 68 per cent of the total in Karjat, Khalapur and Sudhagad talukas, are without title to a village site. Most of these hamlets (73 per cent) are on privately owned land adjacent to non-tribal villages, while 25 per cent are on forest lands now held by the Forest Department. Some 2 per cent of the Katkari villages without a gaothan are located on common grazing lands (*gurcharan*) or temple lands (*devsthan*). Uncertainty over the tenure and security of Katkari homes and hamlets affects approximately 25,010 people in the three talukas. Figure 1.1 shows the location of these hamlets. About 101 other Katkari hamlets in the three talukas are secure, typically because

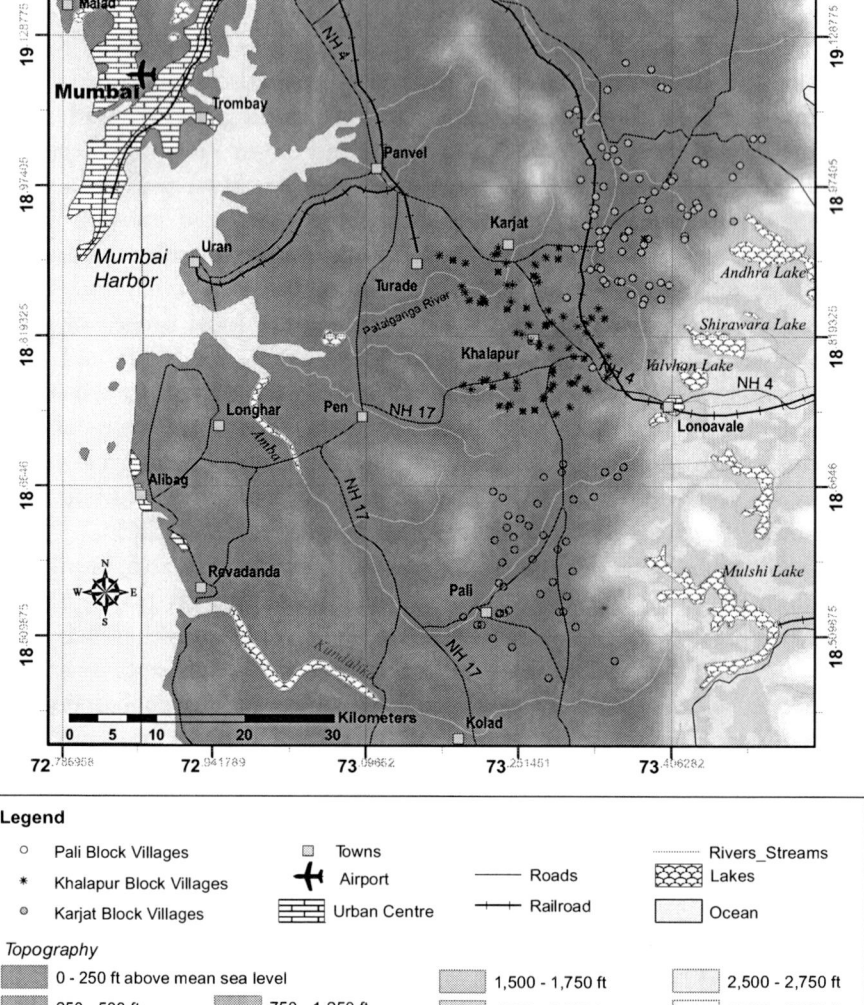

Figure 1.1: The location of 212 Katkari hamlets that do not have title to a village site, in relation to three talukas (Sudhagad-Pali, Khalapur and Karjat) and the Mumbai Metropolitan Region

Source: Author's field notes, April 2006 to December 2010.

their site has been incorporated into the gaothan of the neighbouring non-tribal village. Only a handful of communities have free-standing village sites of their own, corresponding mainly to the few remaining ancestral communities of the Katkari in the upper hills of the Western Ghats.

The houses in Katkari communities are very small and usually dilapidated. The majority (75 per cent) are *kuchha* (temporary) houses in the sense that they need to be repaired or rebuilt periodically. Only 11 per cent of households in Maharashtra are of this type. A well-built kuchha house consists of a wattle-and-daub structure built on a raised stone foundation. Walls are made from woven sticks of karvi, with a tiled or thatched roof supported on a wooden frame. The wattle-and-daub walls of a kuchha house need to be replaced once every three or four years. It has become increasingly difficult for tribal families to collect enough karvi from mountain slopes. As a result, the walls of many kuchha houses are not in good condition and offer little protection from rain or cold. A poorly constructed kuchha house, accounting for the vast majority of houses in Katkari hamlets, does not have a stone foundation or any foundation at all. This allows moisture and water to seep into the house during the months of monsoon. The wooden elements and thatch of most homes are of extremely poor quality and the walls are partially open to the elements. Dampness and moisture in the home lasts for two or three months during the monsoon, making the living space miserable and inhospitable. Homes of this quality last only five years or less before they need to be rebuilt entirely.

Pucca houses, or permanent houses, are made from bricks and a tiled roof on a stone foundation, making them more durable and offering better protection from the elements as well as better physical security. Only 25 per cent of the homes surveyed are of brick, even though more than 60 per cent of Katkari households labour at brick-making kilns. Typically, the brick houses are not plastered, and mud is used instead of cement to bind the bricks. Mud is cheaper and it also helps keep the houses cool during the hot season. Doors and windows are made with wood. These houses, by virtue of their sturdier build, are very expensive to dismantle and rebuild elsewhere.

Building a house is a once-in-a-lifetime activity for most Katkari families and is done in stages over two or three years, depending on the financial capacity of the family. While families try to account for space requirements based on family size and space for keeping livestock in the house during the monsoon, most homes are less than 200 square feet and very crowded.

The data shows that while 8,841 families live in the hamlets studied, there are only 7,735 houses, an average occupancy rate of 1.2 families per house. This is a slightly higher density than the general rural population in Maharashtra, which stands at about 1.1 married couples per household (GOI, 2012b).

Access to Civic Amenities

Katkari hamlets in general do not have the most basic civic amenities provided by governments for common people. For instance, only 13 per cent of the houses in the three talukas have electricity as a source of lighting, in stark contrast to much higher rates (65 per cent) for the general population in rural areas of Maharashtra (GOI, 2012b). This is even lower than the rate for the scheduled tribes of India as a whole, 22.8 per cent of whom use electricity as a source of lighting (Maharatna 2005). Electrification is completely absent in most Katkari hamlets and insecure in others, even when neighbouring communities have electrical power. While some Katkari households use electricity tapped illegally from power lines that pass through a Katkari hamlet on their way to neighbouring villages, many Katkari congregations are located on hillocks above the non-tribal village or fully outside the village limits, too far from the power lines servicing these communities.

Wells supplying drinking water are located in 58 per cent of the communities in the three talukas, compared to 83 per cent of rural households in Maharashtra. Even when wells exist in Katkari hamlets, periods of water scarcity are considerable – 45 per cent of all hamlets experience severe water scarcity at least three months a year. The situation is even more severe in Karjat compared to the other two talukas. Here, the average distance to a river or other natural water source is 2.4 km, and many of these sources are dry during the pre-monsoon period.

Other civic amenities are also rare in Katkari hamlets. Only a handful of the hamlets in the three talukas have a health depot and the majority are more than 10 km from the nearest primary health subcentre. This compares to about 13 per cent among 'non-tribal' villagers (Maharatna 2005, 70). Even an approach road to the hamlet is absent in 18 per cent of the hamlets, increasing the physical and psychological isolation of the Katkari from surrounding communities. Only 13 per cent of all Katkari hamlets have a community centre, a void felt intensely by a community in desperate need of ways to organize and represent itself in public and cultural life.

Literacy and Basic Education

While education is often seen as the most important means of social mobility in India, people in Katkari communities face severe constraints compared to other populations in the relatively prosperous state of Maharashtra, and even to scheduled tribes as an aggregate population. On average, only five men and one woman are literate in each of the Katkari communities of the three talukas – an adult literacy rate of only 16 per cent among men and 3.8 per cent among women. Literacy rates estimated by Tomar and Tribhuwan (2004) for Katkari hamlets in Pen taluka are even lower (9 per cent). This compares to a rate of adult literacy in a mother tongue of 92 per cent for the general population in Maharashtra and 64.8 per cent for the country as a whole. The literacy rates among the Katkari are also much lower than the 40 per cent literacy rate reported for males and 18 per cent for females aged seven and above among the aggregate population of scheduled tribes (GOI 2001; 2012a; Maharatna 2005).

Scope for improving levels of literacy and educational progress among younger generations through regular schooling is very limited in Katkari communities. In the three talukas, some 3,965 children between 6 and 14 years of age do not attend primary school. This is an average of 13 children per village, or 32 per cent of all children in this age group. By contrast, school attendance is very high for the state of Maharashtra as a whole, with almost 98 per cent of primary school age children enrolled (ASER 2007)

Maharatna (2005) points out that scheduled tribes on the whole have had the greatest educational deprivation among all social groups in India. While many factors are undoubtedly involved, he argues that 'this can largely be attributed to a relative dearth of educational facilities in tribal concentrated areas' (ibid., 59). Among the Katkari, only two hamlets in the three talukas have a primary school within the hamlet, and only 35 (11 per cent) have a nursery or day-care facility (*balwadi* or *anganwadi*). This compares very poorly to tribal majority villages where 36.6 per cent had a primary school within the hamlet even as early as 1980 (ibid.). Primary schools and nursery or day-care facilities located in non-tribal villages are open to Katkari children, but many do not attend. Those who manage to go to schools find the syllabus so demanding and unfriendly that they drop out at an early stage.

For children who do complete primary school, pursuing a secondary school education is almost impossible. The average distance to a secondary

school for Katkari in the three talukas is 3.3 km. This daily walk is
particularly stressful during the long hot season when school is in session.
The distance to a special residential school for tribal people (Ashram
Shala) is also significant, at 13 km. While the stay in residential schools
is free, most eligible Katkari youth do not attend. Discussions with Katkari
youth indicate that they feel very uncomfortable in these schools, in part
because they do not speak Marathi, the dominant regional language,
and because they find it difficult to leave their parents for extended
periods of study.

While the absence of schools in or close to Katkari hamlets and the
paucity of teachers that speak their mother tongue are profound gaps in
educational opportunities between the Katkari and virtually every other
social group in the state of Maharashtra, migration to brick and charcoal
kilns is an underlying constraint that deepens their educational deprivation.
As discussed earlier, more than half of the Katkari families in the three
talukas migrate for months at a time, typically taking their children with
them. There are no schools or facilities in their places of work and the
children are left to contribute what they can as child workers.

Access to Administrative Supports

The isolation and marginalization of the Katkari are also reflected in the
significant gaps in the paperwork affirming their identity as an Adivasi
people – the caste certificates needed to access administrative supports
from the government. The survey data shows that 81 per cent of Katkari
families in the three talukas do not have caste certificates, even though
they are eligible and it is a basic requirement for proving that one belongs
to a schedule tribe. A study in the Pen taluka of Raigad district found a
similar pattern: 96 per cent of the Katkari individuals surveyed did not
possess a tribal identity certificate (Tomar and Tribhuwan 2004, 61). By
comparison, some 67 per cent of Kolams and 48 per cent of Madias,
other PTGs in Yavatmal and Gadchiroli districts, respectively, did not
possess tribal identity certificates according to the same study. This means
that these individuals and families cannot avail themselves of benefits
and protections that are routinely available to other tribal persons and
marginalized communities.

Significant gaps also exist with respect to other rights as Indian citizens.
Some 15 per cent of Katkari families in the three talukas do not have a
ration card, a key part of the public distribution system in India. This
problem is more acute in Khalapur and Sudhagad, compared to Karjat.

The ration card, were it in hand, would allow some 1,329 additional families in the three talukas to access the public distribution system and fair price shops providing rightful citizens with subsidized food grains. Katkari participation in the Antyodaya Anna Yojana, another government food security scheme, is even lower. Under this scheme, the poorest families in India gain access through government stores to a monthly allocation of 35 kg of food grains (mainly rice and wheat) at a highly subsidized rate (Rs 2 to 3 per kg). While virtually all Katkari are eligible to register in the scheme, 65 per cent of the families in the three talukas are not registered. Registration in the Antyodaya Anna Yojana is lowest in Sudhagad, where only 21 per cent of the Katkari population is registered.

Some 75 per cent of the Katkari families surveyed in the three talukas are registered in the government census as below the poverty line (BPL), a figure much higher than for scheduled tribes as a whole (50 per cent in the early 1990s, according to Maharatna [2005, 51]). Many more Katkari families are not registered than probably should be. Some 2,289 families, an average of seven families per hamlet, are not included in the BPL census even though their incomes are extremely low. This non-participation problem is more acute in Khalapur, where 35 per cent of Katkari families are not registered. The registration could provide these families, typically living on the edge of survival, with special access to welfare and development programmes currently not available to them despite their eligibility and need. Data from Pen taluka shows that only one family of 46 interviewed had ever received benefits from a government scheme, while none had received any benefits in the last three years from the Integrated Tribal Development Project (ITDP), the agency responsible for tribal welfare (Tomar and Tribhuwan 2004).

Health, Birth and Mortality

The Katkari are known by local farmers and others to be physically the strongest among tribal groups in Maharashtra, an advantage that Katkari elders attribute to a forest-based diet, including the consumption of fish, leafy greens and rodent meat. Field-based evidence suggests that Katkari diets have worsened significantly over time (Khedkar et al. 2002). Resettlement in non-tribal areas has taken them far from the forests that traditionally provided diverse and nutritious food sources. This may be part of the broader problem of permanent undernutrition bordering on starvation reported by Radhakrishna (2009) for many PTGs in India.

Alcoholism is also taking a heavy toll on the Katkari and may be leading to a systematic decline in the health of the population. Whether due to a desire to enjoy the effects of alcohol, or to an effort to escape from the reality of poverty and social isolation, many Katkari spend whatever money they earn on gambling, drinking and watching Hindi movies. These are major obsessions for many Katkari. The research team estimated that a typical Katkari family spends between 50 and 55 per cent of its cash income on gambling, alcohol and entertainment. Barely 50 per cent is spent on food, clothing, schooling and other primary needs.

Many Katkari women drink regularly and are binge drinkers during festivals. While drinking by women is culturally discouraged during pregnancy, there is no awareness in the Katkari community of the serious health effects of this practice. It seems likely that drinking, including binge drinking, during pregnancy is much more common than it should be, and may be leading to permanent birth defects. Foetal alcohol spectrum disorder (FASD) is currently the biggest cause of non-genetic mental handicap in the western world and a serious problem in the rural areas of some developing countries (May et al. 2008). The condition leads to physical malformations and delays, intellectual and learning disabilities, as well as, very often, behavioural problems. While FASD is 100 per cent preventable – if women refrain from drinking while pregnant – it may be a significant factor in the lives of the Katkari community. Although beyond the scope of this inquiry, action research aimed at understanding more about and reducing Katkari's women's alcohol consumption during pregnancy would be a worthwhile effort with long-term implications for better health of the community.

Patterns of population change among the Katkari, reflected in birth and mortality rates, seem to coincide with the problems of the so-called 'vanishing' tribes in India. Maharatna (2005, 42) notes:

> The population of Katkari, an originally nomadic tribe of the Konkan region of Maharashtra, has, according to census counts, been almost stationary during 1961–71, as compared to the nearly 2.3 per cent average annual growth rate of the aggregate tribal population in the state. . . . Notable, in the following decade of 1971–81, the rate of growth of the Katkari population went up to about 2 per cent per annum, but remained far less than that of many other tribal communities and the total ST [scheduled tribe] population of Maharashtra [about 9 per cent].

Maharatna goes on to say that 'while this could well be related to a relatively acute (absolute) material deprivation, other possibilities (for example the effect of removal of area restriction) cannot be ruled out' (ibid.).

Under-enumeration, Katkari migration, a cultural preference for small families and comparatively low fertility rates may also be at play. Katkari typically have fewer children than other tribal communities in Maharashtra – two or three at most. Bonds within the family are consequently very strong; both male and female parents are usually tender towards their children, an attitude apparent to close observers. In addition, the Katkari have a relatively more balanced sex ratio than the norm in India – 983 females per 1,000 males, compared to 933 for the total population in India and 977 for scheduled tribes in the aggregate (State Primary Census Abstract, 2001; Maharatna 2005, 18).

This more balanced sex ratio is consistent with our observations regarding the relatively egalitarian family system of the Katkari, corroborated by similar observations by Heredia and Srivastava (1994), Gaikwad (1995) and Bokil (2006). Katkari husbands and wives work very closely together, as wage workers, as teams at brick kilns, when shopping in the market and even when collecting firewood and non-timber forest products. They watch Hindi movies and even drink together. While the Katkari have adopted many of the Hindu rites of the dominant society, the dowry system has not displaced the traditional practice of the man providing a 'bride price' to the woman's family. Newlyweds often settle in the village and even under the same roof as the woman's family. Divorce is allowed and women can remarry after the death of their husbands. Birth ceremonies are the same for both boys and girls, although the amount spent on the ceremony differs more now than in the past (Gaikwad 1995). Gaikwad reports that Katkari elders said 'they did not find much of a difference between a son and a daughter' (ibid., 26). The significance of these perceptions for understanding the evolution of women's status within Katkari society is nevertheless largely unknown. Significant gender inequalities remain with respect to political roles and the dominant societal views on property rights are also prominent. Deprivation in health, education and other material levels of living, acute among many tribal populations in Maharashtra (Gangopadhyay and Gangopadhyay 2006; Ghatage 2008) undoubtedly burden women even more profoundly.

2

Responding to the Threat of Eviction

Our engagement with the Katkari about village sites began in March 2005 when several Katkari women from Malegavwadi in Karjat taluka told a member of the research team that a barbed wire fence had been erected around their hamlet. A religious trust had recently purchased several properties to establish an ashram. The sale included title to land settled some 80 years earlier by about 20 Katkari families. The barbed wire fence was placed tightly around the irregular perimeter of the hamlet, within a few feet of each house. A single small gate was left for people to enter and leave the site. Inhabitants said they felt like prisoners in a space they considered the sacred home of their ancestors. Strife within the community grew as the new owner pressured some families to convince others to dismantle their houses and shift to another location. The trust offered the inhabitants an alternative site some 3 km away. Villagers were conflicted over what to do and some sought the advice and assistance of a member of the research team with whom they had a longstanding relationship.

This chapter describes initial Katkari responses to the threat of eviction, including efforts that our research team supported, such as developing and submitting petitions for assistance from village authorities and government officials. As this chapter will show, work on the various activities and objectives of the Katkari encountered many unexpected problems. These problems challenged our entire approach to planning the research and engaging with the Katkari. But before delving into these dilemmas, the following narrative, reconstructed from several conversations in the hamlet of Malegavwadi, reveals the strong emotions stirred up by the threat of eviction.

Marya Waghmare's Story

My name is Marya Naoji Waghmare.[1] I am a Katkari. My age may be somewhere around 60 or 65. I have lived all my life in Warghavne Katkarwadi. Before me, my father and before him his father also stayed in this *wadi* (hamlet). That is as far as I can remember. However, it is our belief that our deities (Satvai, Chedoba, Hirva Dev, Somjai and others) live with us in and around the wadi. They protect us from evil spirits, ill-will and calamities.

I live in a small hut of 10 by 15 feet. My hut is very simple and somehow I have never been able to build a good house in my life. This is a dream I could not fulfil. My wife, Rami, is also very old and she is often sick. I have three sons. My eldest son, Maruti, married and went to live in his wife's village, which is one or two hours from our village. My second son, Dehu, has built a small house next to my house. He has three children. My third son, Baban, and his wife Dharmi stay with us in our house. Baban has two children.

My wadi is located on the banks of the Veluk river and is surrounded by mountains and forests. We get firewood, vegetables, fodder, timber, karvi (a reed-like plant used for building the walls of houses), medicines, fruits and honey from the forest. I worked for a brick contractor for 15 or 20 years, but have stopped going to the brick unit since the time I became unable to do hard physical work. My sons Baban and Dehu now work with the brick contractor. Baban goes to the brick unit for six or seven months every year. Sometimes he leaves his children behind but they want to be with their parents and often accompany them to the brick unit. My children also grew up on brick units. The brick contractor is our protector. He had given an advance (a loan) of Rs 8,000 for Baban's marriage and he also gave me Rs 500 as a bonus when I could no longer work for him. I was the best brick maker in our group. I repaid most of the advance that I had taken for Baban's marriage by working with the contractor for seven or eight years. However, I still have to repay some amount. The contractor is now deducting the loan amount from Baban's wages.

There are 42 Katkari families staying in 35 houses in our wadi. Most of the families are landless. Sixteen families work on brick units while 10 families work for a sand contractor at Neral town. Others try to find wage work at farm houses or on farms in nearby villages.

---

[1] The names of people provided here are fictitious.

Our wadi does not have a gaothan (village site). The village land is owned by a non-tribal person from the revenue village. The landowner does not give us permission to build new houses and so two or three families have to stay in one house. There is no space to grow vegetables or to keep goats or cows around the house. The insecure gaothan forces us to stay in cramped and dirty conditions and puts a lot of restrictions on our livelihoods. We cannot access any government schemes for housing or schools.

Over the last 10 years, a number of rich people from Mumbai have purchased land around our wadi and have built big farm houses. The river, forest and mountains are a big attraction for city people. The prices of land in our area have gone up. Our landowner too has sold off the village land to a Mumbai party two years ago. The new landowner has built a religious and spiritual centre for people from Mumbai and other cities.

The first thing the new landholder did was to fence off our wadi totally with a barbed wire fence. He has sealed off all the roads coming into the wadi and has kept just a small gate for people to enter and leave. The fence is tight to the walls of the outer houses. A few families who own some goats do not have any space around the wadi for grazing

Image 2.1: Barbed wire fences erected in a village in Karjat in an attempt to intimidate and evict the long-time residents

their goats. Children do not have space to play. There is not even an inch of space to extend our houses. The question of building new houses does not even arise. Our insecure livelihoods and lives have been further marginalized because of the fencing off of our wadi. Suddenly we feel like we are living in a prison.

The new landholder has used a clever ploy by giving some money to four or five leaders in our wadi. As a result, people in the wadi are not at all organized to fight against the injustice. As a matter of fact, the new owner has started efforts to evict us from the wadi. He has promised to give alternative land for our wadi and Rs 5,000 to each family for rebuilding our houses at a new site. This is only a fraction of what it would cost and would leave us isolated and vulnerable.

How can we leave the land on which our deities reside and go to stay on a new plot of land? Several of our generations have lived in this wadi. We have a deep relationship with the village land. At this age, at least my wife and I do not wish to relocate to a new village. The future looks very uncertain and I do not know what will happen to our children and their families. We will not live long but we cannot see the suffering of those who have small children. The government does not do anything for us although we have been staying on this land for more than 80 years.

The Planning Process

The situation in Malegavwadi prompted the research team to raise the question of gaothan ownership in informal conversations with other Katkari whom we knew well through our previous work. The Academy of Development Science had been active for many years on land rights issues among the Katkari in Karjat, focusing primarily on dalhi (forest) and ceiling (surplus) lands. SOBTI had also worked for several decades with Katkari in Sudhagad, using a broad-based development and cultural approach to strengthening Katkari communities.

Inquiries by members of the research team about the legal status of hamlets and about hamlets threatened with eviction quickly revealed that Malegavwadi was not alone in its predicament. It seemed that many hamlets did not have legal title. Various tales of enclosure and eviction both past and present also emerged. In some cases, houses had been levelled and residents threatened with violence. In others, as in Malegavwadi, hamlets were enclosed and residents intimidated, causing extreme distress. While initially the scope and impact of the problem was unclear to us, the various incidents suggested that enclosure and eviction were an emerging problem in the region, one that had potentially devastating implications for many Katkari communities. This led the research team to decide to convene a planning meeting with Katkari men and women from various communities to discuss the initial steps of an inquiry into the insecure gaothan problem.

What emerged from the first meeting in May 2005 was a decision by those involved to assess the scope of the problem by conducting a survey of Katkari villages in three talukas (Karjat, Khalapur and Sudhagad) and to engage Katkari living in a subset of hamlets in detailed discussions. We also planned to meet with other stakeholders, including gram panchayat members, landholders, officials of the Revenue Department, and project officers with the Integrated Tribal Development Project (ITDP), to examine the rights and responsibilities of the various parties involved, and to outline the Katkari community's ethical claim. These steps, we thought, would launch a process leading to legal title for the hamlets involved.

As part of the initial planning process, the research team used the tool 'order and chaos' to reflect on the goal of the inquiry and what might be involved. The problem, we concluded, was well defined and clear-cut, with a strong body of land reform legislation and special constitutional rights to protect scheduled tribes and particularly vulnerable tribal groups such as the Katkari. The state government seemed to have a process and a source of funding for meeting housing needs in rural areas dating back several decades. A direct approach seemed possible, relying on the existing legislation, self-evident housing rights and established housing programmes. The political climate for addressing the most extreme cases of human rights violations also seemed to be favourable given the economic boom in Maharashtra at that time and the state government's apparent interest in projecting an image of prosperity for all. The financial cost seemed low as well. Katkari hamlets are very small, often only a few acres, and typically located on extremely poor lands of no agricultural value. Based on these considerations, we estimated that the chances of achieving the goal of securing title for Malegavwadi and other Katkari hamlets were relatively high (about 75 per cent probability).

We also discussed our level of certainty regarding our knowledge of the conditions and factors affecting the goal. We had on hand detailed information on the relevant land rights legislation and provisions regarding marginalized populations. Members of the research team had collected the information over the years while lobbying in support of tribal rights to forest land. We understood what was involved in making land claims in the state of Maharashtra. Both organizations (ADS and SOBTI) had been working with the Katkari and with local government officials for many years and had good knowledge of whom to speak to and how they might react. We also had good information on the location of Katkari communities scattered throughout three districts, based on many years of criss-crossing the area on motorbike and by vehicle. Relationships with the Katkari were personal and trusting in many hamlets. The strength of these various sources of information gave us confidence that we had a fairly complete and reliable picture of the conditions and factors affecting the situation. We concluded that our information and knowledge base also merited a relatively high score (80 per cent certainty that it was complete, accurate and reliable).

The assessment conducted by the research team using these two criteria (probability of success and sound knowledge of the conditions and factors for success) showed that not only were the chances of success good but also that we actually felt confident that we knew the situation well enough to justify our optimism. This conclusion, summarized by point 'A' in Figure 2.1, suggested to us that we could plan an action research process in detail and with considerable confidence, much like a blueprint for building a house. While it would involve a lot of work on everyone's part, and might take some time, one thing would lead to another until Katkari rights to the land were secured.

As readers might suspect, our experience was quite different from the plan, due to many problems that emerged along the way along with new information challenging the knowledge we had when we developed the plan. The imponderables and unknowns that played havoc with our plans were many. To begin with, engagement with Katkari in their villages was immediately interrupted by record rainfall and widespread flooding. These weather conditions cut many hamlets off from major roads and delayed a planned survey. When the survey was finally completed three months later, it showed that the scope of tenure insecurity was much greater than anticipated. We determined that 212 Katkari hamlets out of 313 in three districts, that is, 68 per cent, did not have title to a village site. It became evident to the research team that the risk of eviction was widespread. As small organizations, we could not engage with more than a few of the affected hamlets. We also realized that significant human and financial resources would be needed for the government to address the problem in all communities.

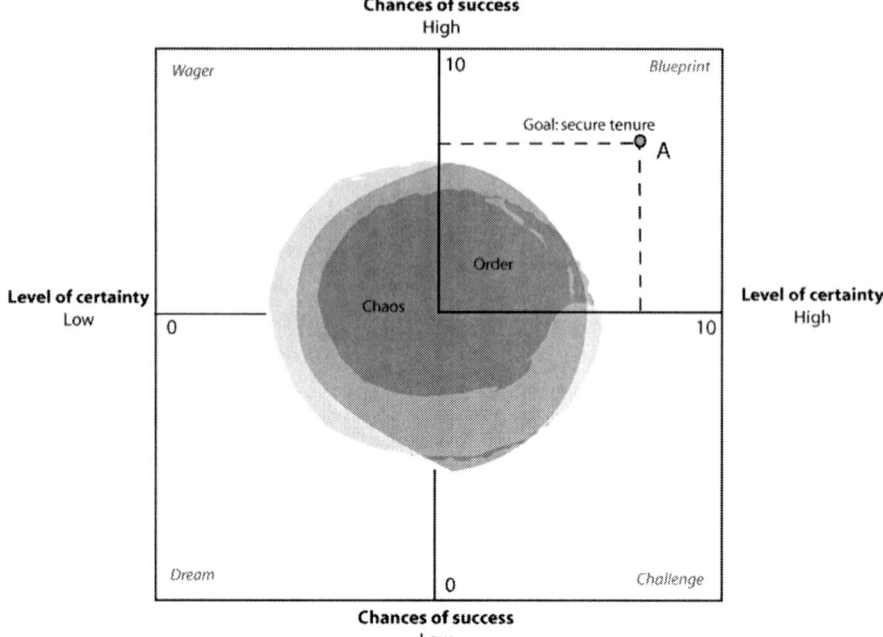

Figure 2.1: Assessment 'A', chances of success and level of certainty

Source: Author's field notes, May 2005, Pali, Maharashtra.

Notes: Point 'A' shows the interaction of two estimates. On the vertical axis, the chances of successfully securing village sites received a high rating. On the horizontal axis, the level of certainty regarding knowledge of conditions and factors affecting the proposed action also received a high rating. The point of intersection of the two ratings places the action research project in the upper right quadrant. This is the world of relative 'order', where plans can be made in great detail and implemented with confidence, much like a blueprint describing a methodical plan of action. The other quadrants refer to the world of relative 'chaos', where the chances of success are lower and/or the level of certainty and confidence is lower due to limited understanding of the conditions and factors influencing success.

It also became evident after the first few community meetings that working with the Katkari on this issue required a lot more time and skill on our part than we originally thought. Unlike cases of individual land rights addressed by team members in the past, mobilization around the right to a village site is a collective action. This means that high levels of community participation and agreement are needed. Given the extremely difficult living and livelihood conditions of the Katkari, full and immediate participation in a collective action by all or even a majority of residents in a hamlet was simply not possible.

To complicate matters further, the team discovered that very few Katkari households had any of the legal documents needed to support their claims. We learned that, unlike most other tribal groups in the state, a vast majority of Katkari did not have the basic documents of an Indian citizen, such as the ration card or voter's identification card. Nor did they have caste certificates identifying them as members of an ST and a PVTG. In many cases, households were not registered with the village authorities (gram panchayat) and had not paid house taxes even though they had been living next to established villages for generations. The houses of many Katkari are in such disrepair that any documents stored there are quickly destroyed or simply lost through neglect. Compiling the documents and legal proofs needed to support claims to a village site and registering households with the gram panchayat would be extremely tedious and time-consuming tasks.

The challenges of doing the hamlet-level work prompted the research team to reduce the number of hamlets involved in the research. The original hamlet prompting the study was not among the selected hamlets, because the community was sharply divided over what to do. Furthermore, the religious trust actively blocked the research team from entering the community. The sites eventually selected were well known to us as places where meetings could be convened peacefully. Our thinking was that an intensive effort in a few communities with good conditions would show that, with strategic assistance, Katkari communities could mobilize around the issue and secure their own village titles. This, we thought, would prove the concept and provide a model for a more comprehensive government response to the problem. We would later resume work in communities such as Malegavwadi, once successes could be seen.

In fact, challenges to our thinking about the action inquiry process had only just begun.

The Initial Hamlets in Our Study

Table 2.1 lists the hamlets where the inquiry started, followed by a description of the gaothan situation encountered in each. In Karjat and Khalapur talukas, where ADS had been active with Katkari for many years, five communities were selected. Sudhagad taluka, the work area of SOBTI, provided another five communities. None of the hamlets had a legal gaothan. Some were facing the threat of immediate eviction and others were not.[2]

Table 2.1: Katkari hamlets engaged initially in the study

No.	Village	No. of Families	Revenue Village	Taluka
1.	Mohmalwadi	36	Potalpali	Karjat
2.	Ambewadi	31	Potalpali	Karjat
3.	Nadode Katkarwadi	45	Nadode	Khalapur
4.	Asra Katkarwadi	72	Asra	Khalapur
5.	Sarang Katkarwadi	22	Sarang	Khalapur
6.	Narsurwadi	39	Narsur	Sudhagad
7.	Siddheshwarwadi	94	Siddheshwar	Sudhagad
8.	Wavloliwadi	33	Siddheshwar	Sudhagad
9.	Vakanwadi	29	Adulshe	Sudhagad
10.	Dhoklewadi	26	Khandpoli	Sudhagad

Source: Author's survey, May to November 2005.

Mohmalwadi is about 3 km from the revenue village Potalpali in Karjat taluka. There are 28 families in Mohmalwadi, who had relocated there from their traditional hamlet in recent memory. There is no approach road to the village, and although electricity poles pass through the hamlet none of the houses has a legal connection or metre. Water has to be brought from 2.5 km away. Several years ago, the landholder began telling the Katkari that they should relocate back to their traditional hamlet some distance away. Mango trees were planted next to the hamlet and many adjoining plots of land sold to outsiders. Fences were put in place, leaving one small gate through which people were allowed to enter and leave the hamlet. Some of the Katkari families work on the landholder's farm while others benefit from his sand contract. Many also migrate to brick units.

---

[2] The village in India takes two administrative forms: the revenue village and the village panchayat. Both build from the geographic units of village sites. Villages and hamlets are grouped together under the village with the largest population, and this is designated as the revenue village for the purpose of coordinating the collection of taxes in all associated villages and hamlets. The revenue village may or may not be the same as the village panchayat, the smallest unit of administration and governance within village-level groupings. A village panchayat comprises villages and hamlets with a total population of at least 300 people.

Ambewadi is a tribal hamlet located on the private land of an individual also from Potalpali. Over 45 years, the hamlet grew from the original 12 households that settled there at the invitation of the landholder to 42 families. All families have various proofs of residence including ration cards, listings on electoral rolls and receipts from the payment of house taxes. Five houses in the hamlet were constructed under a government housing programme (Indira Awas Yojana) and an informal school (Vasti Shala) was recently built in the hamlet by the government. These provide clear proof of residence. The landholder from Potalpali has let families stay on the land for many years because they provide him with cheap, bonded labour for work in his agricultural fields. The land in the area gets irrigation water from the Bhivpuri Hydro Electric Station (Raj Nala), making it possible for him and other landowners in the area to grow two rice crops annually and cultivate market vegetables during the summer months. Recently, however, land prices have increased substantially for lands with access to irrigation and close to growing urban centres. The landholder has identified a possible buyer for the land in Mumbai and has told the Katkari to leave. He erected a fence around part of the hamlet and sought assistance from local authorities to evict them. When this study was launched, the Katkari residents had begun to formulate plans to abandon the village.

Nadodewadi is about 2.5 km from the Mumbai–Pune National Highway No. 4 in Khalapur. It is located on land owned by three individuals from Nadode village. The ancestors of two of the landholders brought the Katkari families to settle here some 80 years ago, employing them for decades in their paddy fields. Living conditions in this hamlet are very cramped. Given the prime location of the hamlet, land prices have appreciated considerably, prompting one of the landholders to sell some of his adjoining land to a Mumbai party, including the area where the hamlet is located. The new owner fenced off the entire area and told the 58 Katkari families to relocate their houses to a small corner of the property. At the time of the initial study, most Katkari in Nadodewadi were mentally prepared to relocate their houses.

Asra Katkarwadi is located a half kilometre from Asre village in Khalapur. Like Nadodewadi, it is very close to the Mumbai–Pune National Highway No. 4. Some Katkari families settled on the land over 80 years ago and the number of families slowly grew to the present total of 56. The land is owned by one person from Asre village. Paddy fields in the area are irrigated with water from the nearby Kalote dam and were for many decades a source of employment for the Katkari. While 26 Katkari families engage in some agriculture of their own, on dalhi plots, purchased land or leased land, 30 migrate regularly to distant brick units for six or seven months each year. There is a nursery (anganwadi) in the village but no primary school and no approach road to the hamlet. Drinking water has to be fetched from a distance of 1 km. Asra Katkarwadi village is on a hillock and so women must climb the steep slope carrying water. Without notice, in 2006, the landholder sold the land to a person from Mumbai. The new landholder surveyed the land and immediately demolished three Katkari houses. A complaint filed by the Katkari at the local police station under the Scheduled Caste and Scheduled Tribe (Prevention of Atrocities) Act, 1989, required the owner to rebuild the houses. He did so, but enclosed the community within a barbed wire fence almost touching the walls of the Katkari homes. Katkari families who own livestock have very limited space in the village to keep their livestock. A market has also moved quite close to the village and so villagers now see different livelihood opportunities based on agriculture, livestock and trading. People desperately want a secure gaothan with more land for houses, civic amenities and livelihood activities like livestock and vegetable gardens. News that some of the land had been sold by the landholder to an outsider caused a near panic among Katkari families in the hamlet, who feared they would be evicted or forced to relocate onto a very small part of their village site owned by the Forest Department. Divisions then appeared within the Katkari community, since the families living on forest land were less concerned about the sale of land or about the demand for a legal gaothan.

Sarang Katkarwadi is a hamlet of 22 Katkari tribal families located a few kilometres from the Mumbai–Pune Express Highway. The hamlet has existed for more than 60 years on land owned by a non-tribal person in the nearby village of Sarang, a prosperous agricultural community with access to a perennial water source for irrigation. A number of Katkari households lease agricultural lands from non-tribal villagers in Sarang, but most people in the hamlet work as bonded labour on brick-making units in the region. A few households work at a sand-dredging operation for a contractor in Sarang village. At the time the study began, the landholder sold nearly 10 acres of his land, including the land where the hamlet is located, to someone from Mumbai. This action was prompted by the announcement in 1999 of plans for the Mega City Project, under which a township was to be established with residential, business and industrial units near Chowk in Khalapur taluka. The project was eventually cancelled due to stiff opposition from local people and political parties, but the Katkari remain vulnerable to eviction from a landowner who has no interest in their labour or any relationship with them. This created a great deal of uncertainty among the Katkari families about the future of their hamlet. They expressed fear that sooner or later they would be evicted by the new landholder or that the land would be resold to another.

There are 47 families and 39 houses in Narsurwadi, a Katkari hamlet in Sudhagad. The village has a primary school, which is an outcome of a non-formal education programme run by SOBTI for five years. Most families in the hamlet migrate seasonally to distant charcoal units and engage at other times in agricultural wage work or in collecting and selling fuel wood. The land where the hamlet sits is owned by three people from a nearby village. In the 1970s, 10 families were assisted by a civil society group to get ownership of house lots (*gharthan*) on this land, but were not able to establish a gaothan. The landholders had to part with small portions of their land to accommodate these transactions, and did not wish to part with any more land. At the same time, they are not trying to evict the Katkari families because they actively use them for agricultural work and benefit periodically from their labour on contracts to build houses and approach roads to the village, under government-sponsored programmes.

Siddheshwarwadi is located some 110 km southeast of Mumbai, near Pali, a religious centre and commercial town. It sits on parts of three properties owned by people in the nearby non-tribal village of Siddheshwar. Most healthy men, women and children in Siddheshwarwadi have worked as bonded labour at charcoal-making units in other states and brick-making kilns in different parts of Raigad district. They migrate to their work sites for seven or eight months during the dry season to find work, leaving their homes unattended. They have lived there for many generations and the village is so large that landholders have never dared to try and evict them. They were required, however, to work for free for the landholders and are prevented from expanding their homes or making significant improvements to the hamlet.

Wavloliwadi in Sudhagad taluka is a Katkari hamlet of 33 families crowded into 23 houses on a hillock without a drinking water source. Women from the village carry three or four pots of water daily on their heads from a well 0.5 km away at the bottom of the hillock. An approach road has been built recently. The landholder is a distant descendent of a local royal family (Bhor Sansthan) and is well known in the field of education. Because of his social standing, the landholder has not threatened the Katkari with eviction, but he will not allow them to expand their houses or use land around them for kitchen gardens and other livelihood activities.

Vakanwadi is located on a hillock surrounded by a forest where 29 Katkari families settled in search of a livelihood from the forest. The village does not have an approach road. Most of the houses in the village are huts. The village does not have a *samaj mandir* (community hall), anganwadi or primary school and the nearest ashram shala (tribal residential school) is more than 5 km away. Many children do not go to school, or they drop out at an early age. All families in the hamlet are landless and below the poverty line. Non-timber forest products (NTFPs) are an important source of livelihood for most families in the village, although 12 families also cultivate crops on forest land. Seventeen families migrate to brick kilns or to work with forest contractors in neighbouring Ratnagiri district. The Forest Department has been constantly harassing the Katkari families in Vakanwadi to discourage them from cultivating crops on forest land and staying on forest land. Forest Department officials have gone so far as to dig a trench all around the village to prevent the construction of new houses, or extensions to existing houses. They have also destroyed Katkari crops.

Dhoklewadi is an isolated community of 27 families. There is no approach road and all but three houses in the village are huts of very poor quality. The residents are very poor: only four have any land of their own and all are well below the poverty line. Because the village is located close to a forest, some families earn their livelihood by collecting forest products. The prices paid by local traders are very low, however. Most families (18 in all) migrate to brick units as bonded labourers. Alcoholism is very high among people in this hamlet. The village site is owned by a non-tribal man from Khandpoli. He does not allow any new construction or other land uses. Nor does he allow the Katkari families to pay the house tax to the gram panchayat, in case this could be used to generate a proof of residence. As a result, the Katkari families cannot get legal electrical service to their houses.

Recognizing the Gaothan Problem

People living in hamlets enclosed by barbed wire feel the bite of insecurity. They know that they do not have tenure of a village site (gaothan). Suddenly, they see eviction right in front of them. Communities in this situation are forced to act and to seek help from any quarter that will offer it. However, when we talked with people in Katkari hamlets not facing immediate eviction, many were puzzled by the question of ownership of the gaothan. They recognized that they did not have title, but did not think this was a key problem in their community. For them, the problem of ownership seemed remote, compared to more pressing matters such as hunger, water scarcity, sickness and the constant struggle to find employment.

At first we were uncertain how to respond to this apparent indifference. We had to admit as well that during the previous 10 years of working with the Katkari, neither ADS nor SOBTI had paid much attention to the scope or impact of an insecure gaothan on the life situation of the Katkari. The organizations had worked instead on addressing the lack of access to agricultural land, dalhi land rights, exploitation in the workplace, difficult living conditions and abuse by the police. Ownership of the hamlet site had rarely been mentioned by the Katkari themselves, or perceived by us and most outside actors, as a key problem in and of itself.[3] It was now evident, however, that the life circumstances of the Katkari throughout the district would get a lot worse if many others were forced to leave their homes. Enclosure and eviction seemed likely to intensify, especially in areas affected by Maharashtra's economic boom. The dilemma we faced was how to raise this issue in villages not threatened by immediate eviction, without imposing the topic or ignoring other matters of immediate concern. While in some communities people were panicked by the threat of eviction, in others they were oblivious to the sword hanging over their heads.

After much discussion by the research team and informal consultation with people in the Katkari community, our response was to launch a Freirian process of 'problem posing' involving sharing of information and dialogue (Freire 1970). That is, we asked Katkari from hamlets affected by enclosures to come with us to other hamlets and relate directly what was happening in their hamlet. News of enclosures and evictions had spread naturally among Katkari hamlets, giving Katkari in other hamlets reason to gather to hear the stories and discuss the relevance of these stories to their own situation. These informal discussions, sometimes with leaders in the hamlet and sometimes with anyone willing to gather spontaneously, eventually led to decisions by those involved to sit together

---

[3] Bokil (2006) and Heredia and Srivastava (1994) both mention the problem of an insecure gaothan in Katkari villages, but focus their attention on other issues.

and explore more carefully why the hamlet did not have a land title and what this meant in their lives. In follow-up meetings, the problem tree method was used to explore links between the lack of a title to the village site and specific situations and stories of direct and immediate concern in the hamlets. The exercise raised a strategic question: should the Katkari pay attention to the legal status of their hamlet?

Problem tree is a method of inquiry well known among development practitioners in India. It is a common tool in participatory rural appraisal (PRA) and an integral part of goal-oriented project planning (known by the German acronym ZOPP [Zielorientierte Projektplanung, Goal Oriented Project Planning]) championed by the German development agency, Gesellschaft für Internationale Zusammenarbeit (GIZ), the Japan International Cooperation Agency (JAICA) and many European development organizations. The method is typically used, as it was by us, to broaden thinking about a problem and see how it is linked to other issues in a systematic cause–effect manner. The tree metaphor and the drawing of the roots and branches of the tree help to elicit and visualize causes and effects without having to rely on literacy to communicate and compile information. In the meetings with the Katkari, participants decided to replace the metaphor of a tree trunk, roots and branches with the notion of the 'parents' and 'children' of the situation, a language they felt better reflected their relationship to the hamlet.

Figure 2.2 illustrates the reasoning that emerged in Siddheshwarwadi, a large hamlet in Sudhagad taluka. The participants, a group of eight men and four women, pointed out that the hamlet sits on parts of three larger properties owned by landholders from the non-tribal village of Siddheshwar. According to the group, these landholders knew they would have to give up land if the hamlet acquired legal title, a prospect that landholders resisted because government compensation for land is very low. Government inaction was another immediate reason why the hamlet did not have legal title, a situation sustained by landholders' close personal ties and the payment of bribes to government officials. Discussion also acknowledged the indifference among people in the hamlet and the fact that they had not actually demanded title. Participants explained this inaction as a lack of awareness regarding legal rights, poor organization in the hamlet and fear of the landholders. These reasons, they said, were the parents, grandparents and ancestors in explaining why the hamlet did not have a legal title of its own.

While the parents of the problem emerged quickly from the group and generated no surprise among them, the shift to the children of the

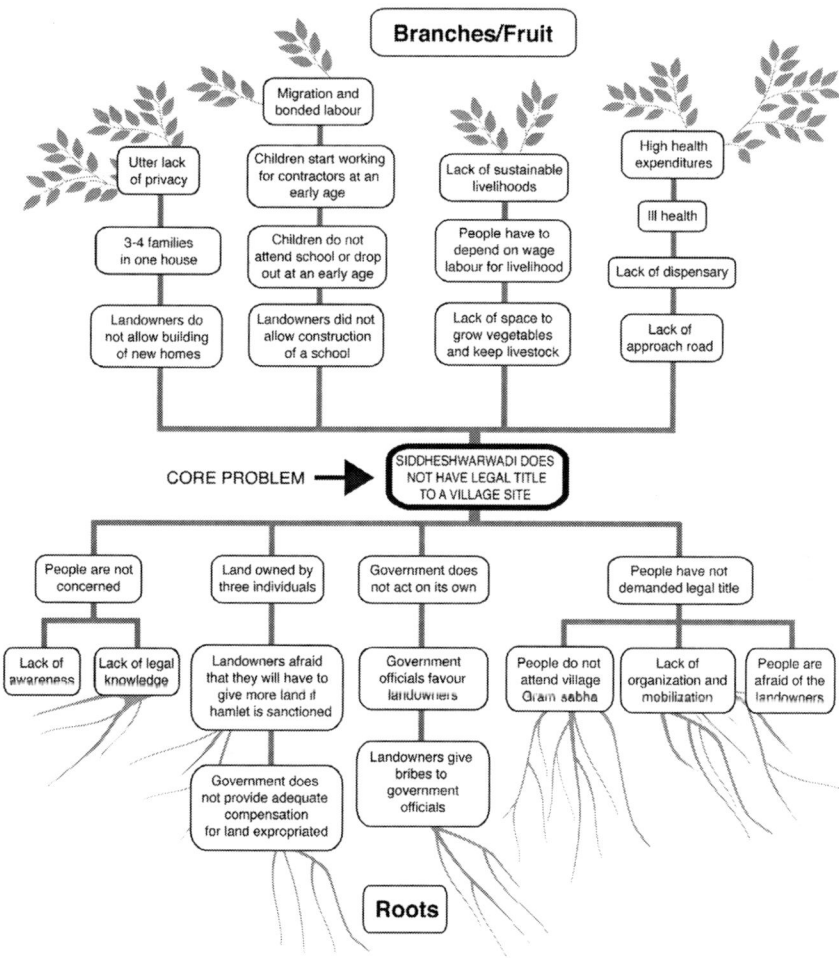

Figure 2.2: Reasons for and implications of not having legal title to a village site in Siddheshwarwadi

Source: Author's field notes, July 2005, Siddheshwarwadi.

problem brought a lot of energy into the discussion. A recent decision by one of the landholders to block the construction of a school in the hamlet was very telling for participants, once they framed it in relation to the core problem and its causes. Government officials had offered to build the school in the hamlet but the landholder had objected. Consequently, it was built in a much smaller, non-tribal village some distance away. Because the new school is far away, children of the Katkari do not attend regularly, or they drop out at an early age. Children not in school are usually taken to work on the brick kilns, where at least they can be cared for on a daily basis. Participants lamented this situation, which they felt ultimately brought their children into bonded labour at an early age. Other consequences of not having title to land for the hamlet were also identified, including the absence of basic amenities, a ban by the landholders on new house construction and insufficient space to grow vegetables and keep animals. Discussion linked each 'child' to a later generation until no more consequences could be identified and participants felt that the story was complete.

The problem tree assessments in Siddheshwarwadi and nine other Katkari hamlets made the specific problem of legal title visible to the Katkari, and to us, in a way it had not been visible before. It brought related ideas into a single conversation and a larger picture. While causes and effects were often similar from one hamlet to another, the final product, and the dialogue that occurred along the way, was not formulaic. The connection between ownership of the gaothan and other matters of immediate concern was drawn out in each case with local colour infusing what participants considered meaningful and useful to understanding why their hamlet did not have legal title. The level of detail in each assessment and the logical connections between elements also varied from one setting to another in response to local stories and the informal and personal interactions among participants. The process lent itself to these kinds of interactions.

In villages where enclosure and eviction were hard realities, the chance to tell their stories broadened people's understanding of the problem's scope and of the root causes they would need to address if they were to take control of the situation. Recurring themes were knowledge of legal rights and the importance of community organization as a first defence. In villages that had not previously thought seriously about legal title to the village site, reasons to do so were identified and sharpened. For some hamlets, constraints on schooling and the education of children became motivating ideas, while for others the barrier to new house construction thrown up by the landholders was most important.

In all cases, the collaborative analysis also showed that the problem was a very difficult one to resolve. It had several root causes well beyond the control of the Katkari, including inaction by government officials and inadequate compensation for landholders. While people could imagine taking steps to inform themselves about their rights, they also felt helpless in the face of the powerful links they saw between landholders and government officials. Some participants concluded that they simply could not dream of or hope for any improvement in their situation. Others, while desperate to act, were overwhelmed by the challenge of organizing the entire community around the issue.

The scope of the problem, and the daunting conclusions reached by the Katkari, are both a strength and a weakness of root cause and problem assessment tools such as the problem tree. The focus on root causes seeks to move thinking about a problem beyond the immediately obvious symptoms, with a view to identifying corrective actions. To provide a bridge from understanding of the problem to the corrective actions, the problem tree is often followed by the development of an objectives tree, or tree of means and ends. This method involves restating the core problem as though it had already been resolved, thereby converting it into a positive scenario.[4] The effects are similarly rephrased into *ends* that are realized when the positive scenario is in place and the *means* to achieve them. In the ZOPP methodology, means–ends thinking provides a basis for project and programme definition and strategic planning.

In a number of hamlets, participants used the tree of means and ends to build a collective vision that could both inspire and guide action based on people's own analysis of the problem. Figure 2.3 shows the tree of means and ends developed a few weeks after the activity depicted in Figure 2.2 by a larger group in Siddheshwarwadi, including most of the people involved in the problem tree exercise. The original problem, its causes and its effects were reviewed and then reworded as though they had been resolved positively. This gradually built a pathway to a future where, for instance, children would have an opportunity to complete school and various potential improvements to the village site and individual households would become available. The end that generated the most excitement in the group, however, was an idea not mirrored in the original problem tree. One of the participants, inspired by the positive image of the village emerging from the discussion, said that with a secure village site they could build a community stage for cultural events. The Katkari have a unique style of music and dance that they enjoy immensely and are very fond of celebrations of all kinds.[5] Other

---

[4] For detailed instructions on the Tree of Means and Ends method, see Tools and Software at: www.participatoryactionresearch.net

[5] Gaikwad (1995) reports that the Katkari's Khatmiri dance is no longer practised except in very remote villages. It has, however, experienced something of a renaissance in some communities in Sudhagad, as has the practice of storytelling accompanied by the vibrating sound of a unique instrument, the *pitali*: a wide brass plate that resonates with a droning sound made by running hands down a stick placed in the middle of the plate and fastened with a blob of beeswax.

participants enthusiastically agreed that having a stage on which to perform their music would bring immense benefits to community life and foster the unity among residents needed to pursue any number of other collective actions. This vision galvanized the discussion and launched people into thinking about ways to achieve their dreams. They concluded that a legal title for their hamlet was worth pursuing and that they could do things to begin to make it happen. The analysis became a motivating force in the community and was widely discussed beyond the small group of men and women directly involved.

Image 2.2: Dwarkanath Lakhma Ghogharkar (left) and another Katkari musician playing the pitali. The brass plate makes a droning sound as an accompaniment to story telling

Developing the tree of means and ends was a turning point in Siddheshwarwadi. The participants had never before considered what it meant to have a collective dream, distinct from individual desires and aspirations, or the literal notion of the dreams people have when they are asleep. The dreams that emerged and the path to these dreams helped many overcome the indifference and sense of helplessness they felt in response to the enormity of the problem. This energy, and the many smaller conversations it generated, also helped to develop a consensus within the community as a whole that gaining title to the village site was

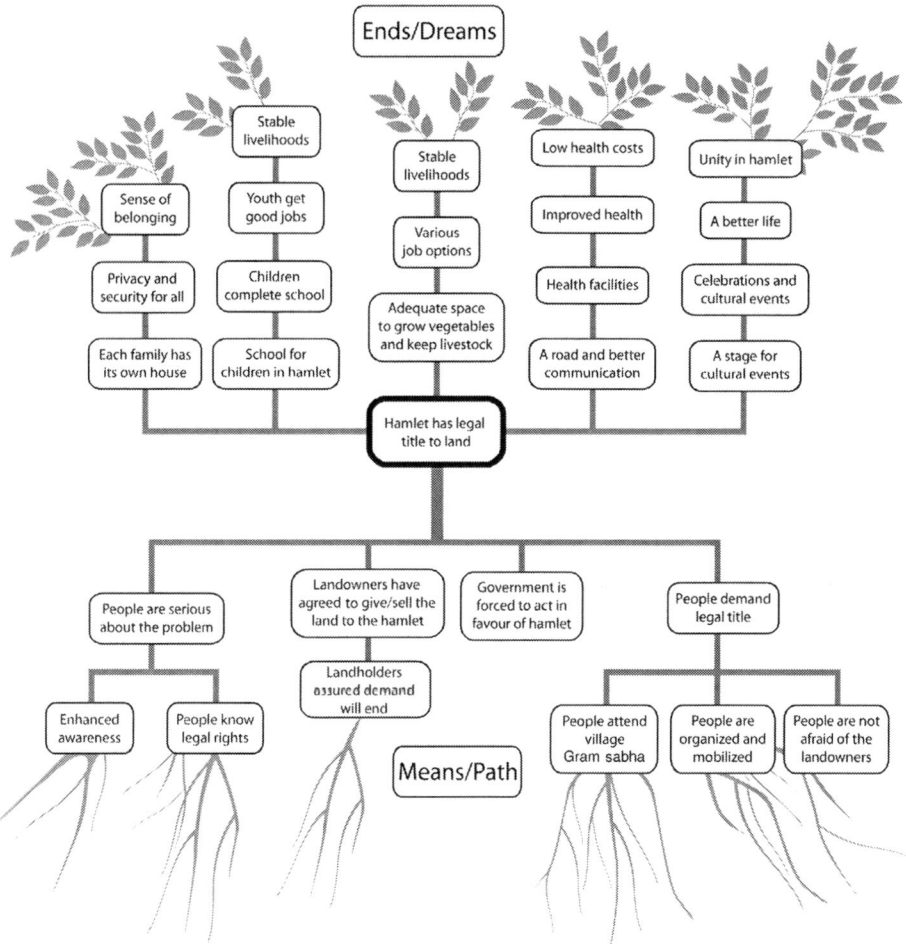

Figure 2.3: Dreams and a path to a legal title for Siddheshwarwadi

Source: Author's field notes, August, 2005, Siddheshwarwadi.

important and worth fighting for. As a symbol of their resolve, the community elders and other residents of Siddheshwarwadi later raised and ceremoniously anointed a stone pillar (*ves*) marking the entrance to their hamlet. Rituals of this kind had been used in the past to mark the boundaries of Katkari communities. They were hopeful that the gesture would not raise alarm among the landholders but rather would be seen positively by them, as a symbol of the boundary of their village site, beyond which the Katkari would not expand.

Image 2.3: Community elders of Siddheshwarwadi raised and ceremoniously anointed a stone pillar (*ves*) marking the entrance to their hamlet. This became a symbol of their resolve to stay

Genuine interest in securing a village site was kindled in other communities as well, both those where the threat of eviction was palpable, and those where the risk seemed more remote. The tools used to support this shift in thinking – the problem tree and, in some cases, the tree of means and ends – played a key role in creating a meaningful context for discussion and sharpened individual and collective understanding of the gaothan problem. It engaged both the Katkari and the research team in a collaborative process of posing a problem and formulating a motivating vision of the future. Strategic directions also emerged. In the days and weeks following the assessments, participants began to speak with greater confidence about the importance of legal title to the future of their hamlet and the need to make it happen through their own efforts. Assertive public gestures, such as the erection of a *ves* outside the village of Siddheshwarwadi and decisions in other hamlets to stay put despite harassment by landholders, emerged as bold steps and tangible expressions of this new resolve. Katkari began to talk about making demands collectively and directly to government officials and to members of the broader village community.

Validating the Problem

Small group discussions with the Katkari about the causes and effects of an insecure gaothan – and the means and ends to change the situation – transformed people's understanding of how the gaothan linked to other matters of concern to them and what might be possible if title to the village site were to change. The inquiry became a consensus-building and action-oriented process aimed at generating a causal explanation and a course of action that could motivate and guide people. An assessment of the same question was also undertaken separately by the research team using the validation method.[6] This prompted us to examine the impacts of an insecure gaothan with survey data from the study area. The two lines of inquiry fed into each other and helped to triangulate information by giving a more complete view of the situation.

To assess the effects of having and not having a legal gaothan, we tested the relationship between a lack of gaothan and various other important expressions of extreme poverty and social exclusion referred to by the Katkari during the problem tree analysis. Correlations with a p-value of 0.10 are used to illustrate the statistically significant relationships.[7]

First, people living in hamlets that do not own the village site are more likely to have lower educational levels and to experience greater barriers to educational opportunities compared to people living in villages with a secure gaothan. The survey showed that while only a few Katkari communities have a primary school, regardless of the legal status of the village site, villages without a gaothan are also significantly less likely to have a nursery (balwadi or anganwadi) in the village. The percentage of children in school between 6 and 14 years of age is also much lower when the village does not have a gaothan, as is attendance at secondary residential schools. These correlations are consistent with Katkari observations that landholders don't allow the construction of schools and nurseries in the village and that this has a direct effect on children attending school. Katkari explained as well that schools in non-tribal villages are not well attended by Katkari children because they feel the prejudice of other students. Male and female literacy rates, already the lowest for any population in the state of Maharashtra, are also significantly lower in villages that do not have a gaothan.

Second, hamlets without a secure gaothan are significantly less likely to have access to sources of clean drinking water. Drinking water wells, expensive to drill and maintain, are less common in villages without a gaothan, and the period of water scarcity in the village is also longer.

---

[6] Results not shown. For detailed instructions and adaptations of the validation method, see Tools and Software at: www.participatoryactionresearch.net.

[7] A p-value of 0.10 indicates that we can be 90 per cent certain the results are not due to chance. The survey methods are described in Chapter 1.

Slightly more than half of the villages without a gaothan experience extreme water scarcity for three months or more, compared to about 39 per cent of villages with a gaothan.

Third, people living in hamlets without a secure gaothan are significantly less likely to have secured the legal documents they need to exercise rights as Indian citizens. Voter identification cards, caste certificates, ration cards, registration as a family under the poverty line and registration under the Antyodaya Anna Yojana Programme (public distribution system providing access to subsidized food grains) are all much lower in hamlets without a gaothan. This relationship probably reflects the obstacles families face when trying to satisfy the residency requirements for these documents. Applications for documents such as the caste certificate require 15 or so other supporting documents and several visits to government offices in the corresponding taluka headquarters. Katkari hamlets without a secure gaothan also tend to be further from the taluka headquarters where caste certificates for tribal people are obtained.

Fourth, families living in insecure hamlets are significantly less likely to have a title and survey of their agricultural land assets. This makes them even more vulnerable to encroachment than Katkari in other communities. Land grabbing by non-tribals was experienced by 190 households in the data set, or 2.1 per cent of all Katkari families in the three talukas surveyed. Two-thirds of these cases occurred in hamlets that do not have a secure gaothan, suggesting that families in these communities have more difficulties protecting their lands from encroachment.

While these correlations demonstrate meaningful relationships among the variables, direct causal connections cannot be automatically inferred. Acquiring legal title to a village site will not necessarily lead to better access to water, higher educational achievement, secure identity papers or protection of land assets. It is evident from the survey data on Katkari living conditions presented earlier that all Katkari communities in the three talukas are extremely poor, regardless of the legal status of their village site. Horrific living conditions are the norm in Katkari hamlets throughout the state of Maharashtra. The findings do, however, support key conclusions of the problem tree analysis and provide additional evidence that the Katkari's difficult circumstances are worsened by the vulnerability arising from an insecure village site. They also point to several considerations not mentioned by the Katkari during the collaborative inquiries, that is, the vulnerability of Katkari land assets and the paucity of legal documents. As readers will see in the next section, these gaps shed light on Katkari attempts to engage with the gram panchayat, the local government body at the village and small town level.

Creating the Conditions for Success

In the weeks following Katkari discussions of the causes and effects of ownership of a village site, consensus emerged in all 10 hamlets involved that recognition of their place of residence was a matter of interest and importance. Our review of laws that apply to the creation of villages, shared with the Katkari during various meetings, suggested that the gram panchayat could initiate an application for a gaothan. While this information later proved to be incomplete, the research team thought that the gram panchayat could apply more pressure on the Revenue Department than a simple petition from individuals or groups. Our concern at the time, shared by the Katkari, was that without support from local authorities, Revenue Department officials would simply ignore them. Neglect by the government, not service, was the common experience of Katkari in all of the affected hamlets.

While the strategy for engagement was clear enough, developing and presenting a gaothan application for approval by the gram panchayat was a significant challenge for the Katkari. Katkari in most hamlets rarely participate in the periodic meetings of the gram sabha, which bring together all residents over the age of 18 from the non-tribal villages and associated hamlets. Few Katkari are elected to formal positions in the gram panchayat, such as the sarpanch. The survey of 313 Katkari hamlets in Karjat, Khalapur and Sudhagad found that most families (86 per cent) had never attended a gram sabha, and only 91 villages had some representation among the elected representatives that make up the gram panchayat in each village. No cases were reported of a Katkari occupying the paid position of gram sevak (panchayat secretary hired by the Revenue Department). To participate in the gram sabha, by presenting a topic for discussion and decision in this forum, would be a major step. People would need to stand up collectively and as individuals in a local situation fraught with sharp power imbalances and unknown risks. Given this uncertainty, discussed at length in small groups and informal meetings, the Katkari decided that before they could take any action they needed to know more about what to expect from the gram panchayat and other stakeholders, such as the landholders and various government officials.

This question prompted an assessment by the Katkari of the stakeholders that needed to be involved in applying for gaothan, and strategic thinking about the conditions needed for success. To facilitate the discussion we used the tool 'Stakeholder Analysis CLIP'.[8] We selected the tool because it offered a way to engage the Katkari in strategic thinking about the perennially difficult question of power. It builds on the notion of 'communities of interests' used in stakeholder theory to name individuals, groups or institutions who gain or lose from a situation (their interests). To this concept of gains and losses are added ideas from political economy and social anthropology. The sources of power that stakeholders can apply to a situation (coercive power, authority, wealth, information and communication as power) are assessed by the actors themselves. They also identify real or potential opponents and allies based on the history of conflict and collaboration among stakeholders – the past and present interactions of communities of interests reflecting both local and global factors of social change. The overall assessment is a social actor alternative to positivist methodologies that pay little attention to how people act on their own real-life conditions, the weight of internal differences within communities and the external factors embedded in community life. It also questions much of the standard wisdom of stratification theory and political economy based on handy class definitions that the researcher can apply to all situations. Instead, the tool focuses on specific social actors that should be involved in the inquiry process and what they can do to solve problems and achieve their goals using the resources and allies they already have or seek to obtain. Thinking about stakeholders in a particular situation involves people in discussions of locally meaningful expressions of the power, interests and legitimacy of the stakeholders involved, as well as the record and social history of trust, collaboration and conflict. As such, the tool offers a pragmatic and culturally sensitive approach to exploring current and possible scenarios, the key problems they raise and strategies to transform them in a particular context.

Figure 2.4 shows the assessment of local stakeholders carried out in Ambewadi, a hamlet that had recently been enclosed by a landholder

---

[8] CLIP is an acronym for Conflict and Collaboration (C), Legitimacy (L), Interests (I) and Power (P). See www.participatoryactionresearch.net for details on using the tool for stakeholder analysis.

who threatened the inhabitants with eviction. Katkari in this hamlet had decided to stay and to fight for recognition of their residence. Over the course of an evening, 12 Katkari (seven men and five women) gathered to discuss the situation and the prospect of presenting a gaothan application in the gram sabha. The picture that emerged from their

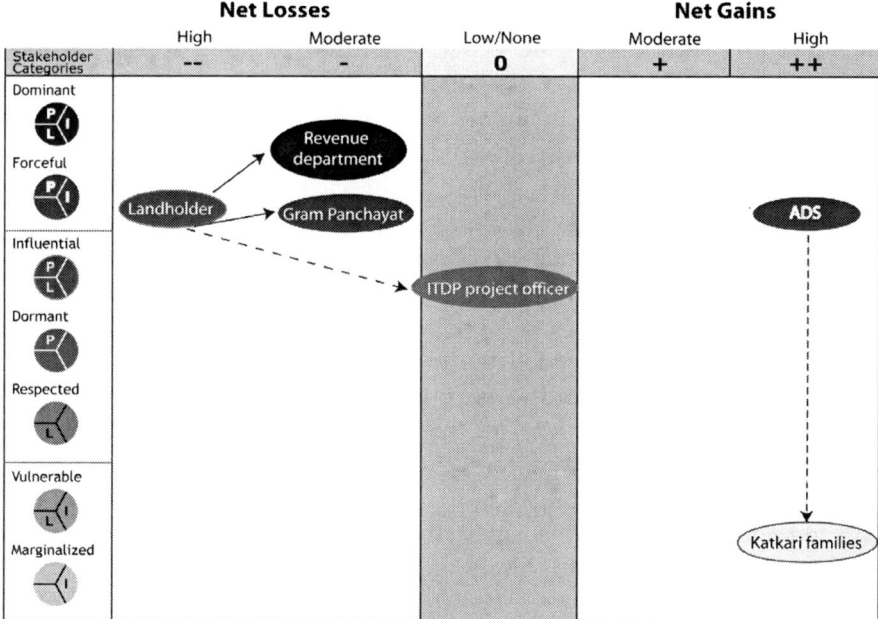

Figure 2.4: Stakeholder positions on a proposed Katkari gaothan application, Ambewadi, period 1

Source: Author's field notes, December 2005, Ambewadi.

Note: Posititions in the table reflect the presence or absence of power (P), interests (I) and legitimacy (L) held by each stakeholder. Of the six stakeholders identified (in the body of the figure), three would likely reject the application because their losses would be from medium to high (left side of the table, showing medium to high losses represented by '-' and '- -' headings, respectively). They include the landholder, the gram panchayat, and the Revenue Department. These same actors are relatively powerful in the situation (upper half of the figure in a row with P for power, reflecting stakeholder categories with medium to high levels of power). The landholder would likely make use of his past relations of collaboration with the other stakeholders (represented by solid or weaker dotted arrows) to reinforce his opposition to the application. In this scenario, the Katkari are isolated and vulnerable; while they have lots to gain ('+ +' rating), they have little power (lower stakeholder category). They also have only one ally (ADS) linked weakly (dotted arrow) to the community through a history of collaboration on land issues.

analysis was a stark reminder for them and for us of how isolated and vulnerable the Katkari were on this issue, and precisely what would need to change to improve their chances of success. Of the six stakeholders identified, three would likely reject the application, including the landholder, the gram panchayat, the Revenue Department (represented by the gram sevak) (upper left side of the figure).

The thinking by the Katkari that went into describing the stakeholder structure and what they could expect from the proposed application was richly detailed. Participants identified examples of the use of power in other situations familiar to them and rated the extent to which each stakeholder they identified could use their power to oppose or promote the application in the gram sabha. In the case of the landholder, they talked about his power to purchase support for his position (economic power) and to hire goons to harass the Katkari (coercive power). Consequently, they rated his power to oppose the application as high, an assessment that placed the landholder in the upper half of the figure. Participants also recognized that the landholder would lose a lot if he were forced to sell his land at government rates rather than to external land agents. This placed him on the far left side of the figure, showing high net losses ('- -'). Furthermore, the landholder had a legal land deed, a fact that gave him legitimacy in the eyes of other stakeholders. He had already shown his resolve to evict the Katkari by enclosing the hamlet with a fence and would likely make use of his past relations of collaboration with the other stakeholders (represented by arrows) to reinforce his opposition.

The political authority of the Revenue Department, the gram panchayat and the Integrated Tribal Development Project (ITDP) were recognized as other forms of power that could be applied to the situation. High ratings on power were given to both the Revenue Department and the gram panchayat in view of their roles in the gram sabha. According to the Katkari, both stakeholders would likely see more losses than gains from the proposed application. Recognition of Katkari rights to a gaothan would require the Revenue Department to order a survey of the hamlet and compensate the landholder financially. They would see the resolution as nothing but trouble, given the many other demands on their time and resources. The gram panchayat would see losses as well, due to opposition from the landholder and new demands on village resources if the hamlet were eventually incorporated into the village site. Participants concluded that, on balance, the gram panchayat had little to gain from supporting the application and that they had a legitimate right to object.

The ITDP officer was also recognized as a legitimate stakeholder, but one with less power and less to lose from the petition (represented by his middle position). He is responsible for addressing Adivasi concerns, but Ambewadi is outside of the Additional Tribal Sub-Plan for Karjat, and thus much less important to him than other Adivasi communities. The Katkari knew him to collaborate occasionally with local contractors when providing services to Adivasi communities, a relationship that participants felt might lead him to support the landholder's position.

According to participants, only ADS and the Katkari would gain from the proposed application. They felt that the Katkari had a lot to gain because it would help them resist eviction from the hamlet. The current location gave the Katkari community a base for seasonal migration to brick kilns and future access to job opportunities in the area. Moving to a new location would be difficult and costly, and would probably result in the hamlet breaking up, along with the loss of relationships formed among the various families during the 45 years since it was established. Their dependence on the current landholder had declined in recent years, so opposing him would come with fewer costs. While the Katkari would stand to gain by applying for a gaothan, the resources, influence, authority and other forms of power they could use to achieve their goal was rated by participants as low. They had no money, lacked knowledge regarding their rights and were isolated from local and broader government bodies and external organizations. This isolation meant that the rights of the Katkari hamlet would not be seen by others as legitimate. In the eyes of the landholder, the gram panchayat and maybe even government officials, the Katkari were vagabonds moving about in search of employment and without a history of prior participation in the institutions of village life. Participants lacked confidence, as well, that their community had the resolve to develop and present the application collectively and forcefully. Overall, they saw themselves as having neither the rights nor the resolve of a legitimate stakeholder.

The participants considered ADS to be a relatively powerful stakeholder in the situation because of its prior work with officials in the Revenue Department and its detailed knowledge of legal issues affecting tribal populations. They gave a medium rating to ADS on this factor. They also recognized that ADS had something to gain from the gaothan application because it would enhance the organization's ability to lobby on behalf of other Katkari communities and demonstrate the value of its work. Participants nevertheless wondered how long ADS would support them if things did not go well. The ADS staff present at the meeting expressed their commitment, but had to recognize that the bonds of trust and collaboration were still relatively weak. In Ambewadi, ADS had mostly worked on the land rights of individual families and was not known by all households in the hamlet. The relatively weak and one-way relationship between the Katkari and ADS (represented by a dotted arrow) was especially important to the Katkari participants considering the many collaborative ties they noted among other dominant and opposing stakeholders. These realities left the Katkari with few real or potential allies, and in conflict with the landholder, their former benefactor.

Assessments in other hamlets showed that the stakeholder structure, and the key problems it raised, were equally unfavourable. For example, in Nadode Katkarwadi, a hamlet in Khalapur taluka, a coalition of three powerful stakeholders – two landholders and a gram panchayat with whom the Katkari had never interacted – would likely oppose the proposed action. Other stakeholders were neutral at best. The Katkari families saw themselves as a marginalized entity with a weak relationship to others, including ADS, with whom they had only worked on police cases and individual land claims. While participants in the discussion expressed a strong desire to secure a place in the village gaothan, they felt that collectively there was not enough organization or commitment among the families in the hamlet to defend or promote their claim in the gram sabha against these more powerful, opposing stakeholders. Under these conditions, gaining approval for the proposed application would be an uphill task.

The unequal and opposing relationships among various key stakeholders involved in the situation was not that surprising to the Katkari or to us, given the extreme poverty of the community and its history of social exclusion. However, discussing these details in each hamlet grounded and stimulated thinking about ways to manage and transform specific social relations, including efforts to empower themselves through information, measures of cooperation and compromise with landholders to reduce conflict, and appeals before the gram panchayat and government officials to public values of justice and the common good. While tentative and uneven from hamlet to hamlet, discussion led to various strategies for empowerment, for persuasion and for establishing new relationships. For example, Katkari could compile proofs of residence such as house taxes, electricity bills and voter registrations to document and demonstrate to the government and to local officials that they were not simply homeless vagabonds without ties to the community. They could talk to members of the gram panchayat about their difficulties, and assure them that their intention was to press the Revenue Department for fair compensation for the landholders. This was important, participants felt, to avoid placing blame and responsibility on the landholders alone. They could also learn more about their rights and responsibilities as members of a village and begin to participate in the institutions of village life. These actions might demonstrate their resolve to stay and begin to build a positive relationship with local officials.

Participants in the various assessments decided during or after the meetings to create a hamlet-level gaothan action committee (GAC) as a focal point for plans to inform and mobilize villagers, collect documents, and lobby other stakeholders. The committee structure is commonly used in rural India for programmes of all kinds and was familiar to the Katkari. Committees were created in all 10 villages, ranging in size from four to six people. Older villagers suggested the names of people who were young, bold and had an understanding of local issues, could be activists in the committees, and could encourage other people to participate. Each committee included at least one or two literate Katkari able to communicate fluently in Marathi as well as in their own dialect, at least one woman, and two to three older men with a positive profile or leadership experience in the community.

In the weeks that followed, the committees began the tedious work of collecting proofs of residence door to door. They made copies of house tax receipts, residence certificates from the gram panchayat, caste certificates, ration cards, voter identification cards, electrical bill payment receipts, school certificates and proof of age documents. It was a difficult work because most houses are in such disrepair that people lose their documents to the weather or neglect. Often the documents are not understood or valued. Many households simply never had basic identity papers in the first place, a situation the survey data shows is very common in Katkari villages throughout the three talukas. Nevertheless, documents were collected and copied for as many households as possible, focusing on those documents that could stand as proofs of residence in the revenue village. The committees, guided by elders in the community, also drew maps showing the boundaries of the hamlet and noted when the community was first established. Timelines of the history of the hamlet created with the help of elderly residents helped in this regard. While travelling to workplaces or socializing in the evenings, people shared what they had learned with others, raising the general level of knowledge and understanding in the hamlets.

The research team contributed to this process by compiling all of the documentation into a portfolio on the hamlet and making copies to go back to individual households. We also collected the '7/12 extract' (a land deed) for the lands occupied by the hamlet from the regional taluka headquarters of the Revenue Department. This document showed the legal ownership and boundaries of land where the Katkari now lived. With the support of the committees, we offered information sessions on a variety of topics. Building on a long history of practical activism by ADS and SOBTI, these sessions dealt with how to get a ration card, how to submit an application for a crop survey, how to pay the land price for unregistered tenants, how to register the names of legal heirs, how to get a death certificate, and so on. These procedures were often of immediate and practical interest to people who in the past had been faced with the challenge of acquiring legal documents. The sessions also introduced information on land rights, the operations of the gram panchayat and how these related to infrastructure and welfare provisions that could bring some immediate relief to people. Many attended, often in the evening, including some non-tribal members of panchayats who were new to their positions or simply had not participated before in discussions of the roles and responsibilities of the gram panchayat system.

Frequent visits by the research team to the hamlets and neighbouring revenue villages opened relationships with some heads of the gram panchayat (sarpanch) and with the gram sevak. Informal, personal interactions with them focused on the legal and ethical issues at stake, including the longstanding contributions of Katkari labour to agriculture and industry in the area, their many years of residence in the villages and the existence of government provisions for extending a gaothan and compensating landholders. We emphasized the responsibilities of the Revenue Department and the ITDP to Adivasi and poor, landless families and the right of landholders to compensation. The practical and potential social costs of evicting large numbers of families from their homes were also mentioned. The goal of these discussions was not only to inform the stakeholders about the scope and impact of the problem but also to take stock of their position and possible response to Katkari petitions for support. Only a few attempts were made to discuss the matter directly with landholders, as these often led to defensive reactions and an opposition to gestures of compromise and openness to negotiation on the part of the Katkari. Our involvement was particularly troubling to the landholders and a source of additional tension that we tried to avoid by being discrete in our movements in the villages and avoiding direct contact with landholders.

The effects of these strategies were monitored by the Katkari themselves, and they adjusted their actions periodically in light of new information about the shifting scenario. For example, after four months of work, the gaothan action committee in Ambewadi decided to repeat their assessment of the stakeholder structure (Figure 2.5). It showed some important improvements. The regional head (*tehsildar*) of the Revenue Department in Karjat had asked his officials in a memo to provide all the help they could to securing gaothan on behalf of Katkari families. Various elected representatives of the gram panchayat, including the

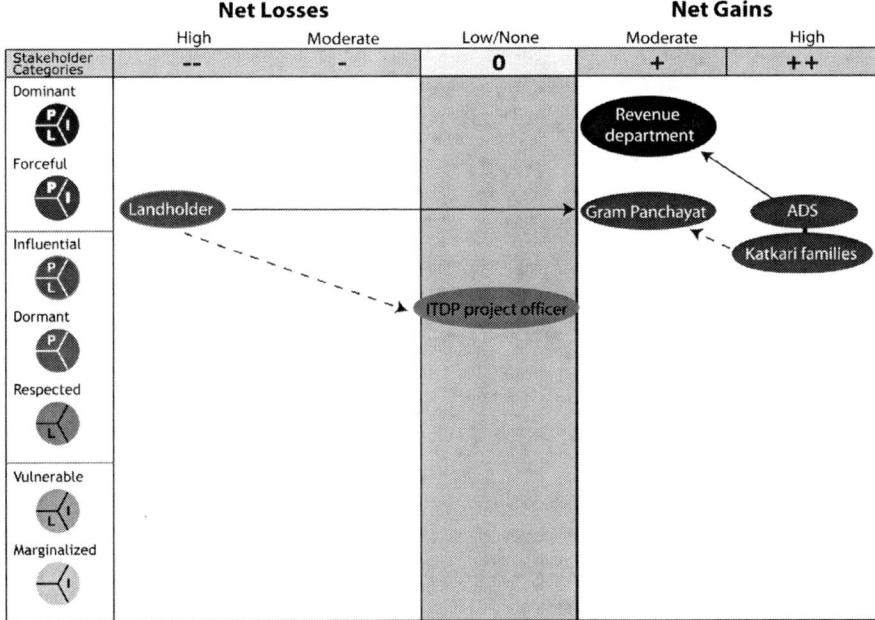

Figure 2.5: Stakeholder positions on a proposed Katkari gaothan application, Ambewadi, period 2

Source: Author's field notes, March 2006, Ambewadi.

Note: The figures shows that while the landholder remained opposed because of the losses he would suffer from a resolution in support of the Katkari (left side of the figure, showing high net losses represented by a '- -' heading), other stakeholders now recognized net gains from the claim (middle or right side of the figure, representing a neutral effect, '0', or medium positive gain, '+'). Importantly, both the Revenue Department and the gram panchayat now recognized the legitimacy of the Katkari claim and the merits of incorporating the hamlet into a village site, factors leading to a shift in their position. The Katkari had gained in power through their own efforts to inform themselves and organize at the hamlet level, and strengthened their relationship to ADS. Shifting alliances seemed to have isolated the landholder to some extent.

sarpanch, said they now understood the situation better and recognized the legitimacy of the Katkari claim. They assured the Katkari they would help to the extent possible and would call on the government to provide compensation to the landholder. Even the project officer for the ITDP, while rarely in the hamlet, did not want to be seen to be supporting the landholder against a tribal clientele. The landholder in Ambewadi, while still harassing the Katkari and threatening to evict them, was now alone, without assured support from other stakeholders.

Thinking about the new conditions led to difficult and risky decisions by the Katkari as to whether or not they should proceed with the presentation and request in the gram sabha. Participants in Ambewadi were encouraged by the statements of key stakeholders such as the Revenue Department and the sarpanch of the gram panchayat. They were also happy with their own efforts to inform themselves, their success at compiling relevant documents and the level of participation and agreement about what to do that had been created among Katkari in the hamlet. The new story they began to tell reflected greater confidence in themselves, expressions of support received from other stakeholders and a stronger and broader set of relationships to stakeholders. While initially they thought that they would be alone in their struggle with the landholder, and that they would lose, they concluded after the second assessment that the conditions were now much more favourable. As a result, the gaothan action committee decided they were ready to present an application before the gram panchayat and encouraged all Katkari families to attend the next village assembly.

New assessments in other hamlets also showed positive shifts in stakeholder structure, attributed by participants to the actions they and others had taken to organize themselves and persuade others regarding their claim. However, the timing of these shifts and impacts on subsequent actions varied. In Nadode Katkarwadi, for example, a second assessment after four months of concerted effort by the gaothan action committee identified a change in the position of only one stakeholder, the tehsildar in the Revenue Department. Several visits to his office by members of the committee and the research team seemed to make him more receptive to the issue. On the last visit he told his officials, including the gram sevak, to cooperate if the resolution was presented in the gram panchayat according to proper procedures. While we could not be sure of his commitment to follow through on the application, his outward position was more favourable. Still, participants deemed this as insufficient to change their minds about presenting at the gram sabha. They decided to wait and continue their work. Important shifts in the positions of other stakeholders in Nadode began to emerge only some six months after the initial strategy was launched. Some members of the gram panchayat, including the sarpanch, began to openly support the idea of integrating the hamlet into the village gaothan. The sarpanch argued that it would bring new resources into the community and be good for village development. The landholders, while still opposed, seemed to be more isolated. Furthermore, a division between them emerged, with one of the landholders saying he would not go against a majority verdict in the gram sabha, provided there was no encroachment on his neighbouring lands. Importantly, by the third stakeholder assessment, the gaothan action committee had finished collecting proofs of residence from households in the hamlet. Virtually all families in the hamlet now understood that legal title to the hamlet was a right they could demand, and many were highly motivated to present their claim. It seemed that the conditions were better than they had ever been, and that approval of an application for a gaothan would be passed at the gram sabha. All that remained was to wait for the appointed day.

Submitting Applications before the Gram Sabha

The gaothan action committees in Siddheshwarwadi, Wavloliwadi and Vakanwadi presented their applications in their respective gram sabhas, and all were approved without incident. The reasons for these decisions reflected considerations that had emerged during assessments by the Katkari of the stakeholder structure in the hamlets.

The balance of power in Siddheshwarwadi and Wavloliwadi, at least with respect to an application for a gaothan in the gram sabha, was very different from that in other study hamlets because the sarpanch of the gram panchayat representing both hamlets was a Katkari. Furthermore, the owner of the largest part of the Siddheshwarwadi site had indicated in advance that he did not want to oppose the Katkari, whom he relied on to tend his fields. Meanwhile, the landholder in Wavloliwadi was a social crusader running schools, colleges and other educational institutions for the poor. While this landholder did not want to turn the land over to the Katkari, he was not willing to go out of his way to openly oppose Katkari living on a small parcel, for fear that it might damage his reputation. The resolve of both landholders to exercise power in the context of the gaothan application was not high. The resolution to support an application passed in both hamlets.

Vakanwadi was a special case among the hamlets that had prepared applications for discussion in the gram sabha. This hamlet is located on forest land owned by the Forest Department, so there was no question of landholder opposition in a gram sabha. Forest Department officials have no role in a gram sabha and would eventually have other opportunities to oppose implementation of the resolution. The resolution passed, with no response or comment from the Forest Department.

Different decisions and outcomes emerged in seven other hamlets in Karjat and Khalapur talukas. The first gram sabha in these talukas took place in Nadode in Khalapur. The Katkari were so keen to present their case that many working at brick kilns some distance away requested permission from the brick operator to return to the hamlet a day before the gram sabha. They knew that the landholders were divided and that the sarpanch and gram sevak were openly supportive. This knowledge had been reflected in the assessment of the stakeholder structure undertaken by Katkari in the hamlet. Despite this optimism, the gaothan action committee decided to send only one person to the meeting, so as not to draw attention to a large crowd of Katkari. This would have been a very unusual sight in Nadode, and might have alarmed other villagers. The research team stayed away as well, to avoid being seen as interfering in a formal meeting of the village.

Things did not proceed as expected, however. A written request for recognition of the Katkari hamlet in the gaothan of Nadode was submitted, along with copies of supporting documents. These were discussed by the gram panchayat, which was expecting the request, and the gram sevak prepared an approval document. Minutes after the meeting was adjourned, the landholder rushed to the gathering with a number of supporters and violently threatened the Katkari representative of the committee. He also loudly admonished the gram sevak, a young woman, for passing a resolution affecting land he legally owned. The gram sevak was so frightened by the confrontation that she immediately tore the approval document to pieces in front of everyone. The Katkari man walked away, shaken but unharmed.

News of this confrontation spread quickly among the gram sevaks throughout the area, undercutting their support for such resolutions. They told us and the gaothan action committee members that they did not want to risk another confrontation and would need to see a statement of agreement from the landholder before they would place the application before the gram sabha. Support from other government officials also seemed in doubt.

In Nadodewadi, the Katkari were clearly frightened by the incident, and worried they might be physically or sexually abused by goons hired by the landholder. The risk of a similar occurrence was discussed by gaothan action committees in other hamlets that were ready to present applications. Of these, six decided to abandon their plans. They feared that open conflict with the landholders could make matters more difficult for them by accelerating the process of enclosure and eviction, or worse. The high hopes, based on months of preparation, were dashed.

The strong resistance by the landholder in Nadodewadi, and the decision on the part of the gaothan action committees in many study communities not to present applications in the gram sabha, put an immediate halt to the inquiry. The research team stopped going to the study villages to ensure that we were not putting any pressure on the Katkari to take further public action. The risks to the Katkari directly involved in the committees, their families and their neighbours were real and the team wanted to avoid making the situation any worse. We learned through indirect queries and in personal discussions with Katkari outside of their communities that many people in hamlets where the petitions did not proceed were demoralized. They had concluded that they could not advance their cause and would eventually be evicted. At the same time, they said that their view of the landholders had changed. While many had looked upon their landholder as a kind of benefactor, they now realized just how strongly the landholders opposed them.

While the events cast a sombre cloud over almost a year of determined effort and intense interaction, an unexpected turn of events in Nadodewadi shortly after the confrontation during the gram sabha brought everyone back from the edge of despair. A member of the research team stumbled across a land deed for one *guntha* of land (1,000 sq ft) while going through the documents of one of the Katkari families in the hamlet. The family members did not know what the document meant, but they had kept it for many years. Guided by this document, we initiated a search for similar documents in the tehsildar's office. The search revealed that 47 Katkari families in the hamlet had each been allocated one guntha of land on the site of the hamlet many years earlier. It came to light in a subsequent interview with an elderly Katkari resident that a survey of their hamlet had been done in the 1970s, and houses were built for them by the same landholder who had confronted them in the gram sabha. The elderly man remembered that the houses had a common wall and were of such poor construction that they needed to be repaired or replaced within the year. This information led us to an astounding discovery. The landholder had won a contract to build houses for the Katkari under the Indira Awas Yojana (a government housing programme). This programme was linked to the gaothan extension scheme of the time and was intended to provide housing for vulnerable populations. The substandard houses were built, but the Katkari were not told that the transfer of landownership was part of the arrangement. Titles to a ghartan (or house site) issued by the Revenue Department were either not delivered to them, or their meaning was not explained. Furthermore, because many of the houses were constructed with a common wall, the hamlet had occupied less than 25,000 square feet of the 47,000 square feet of land approved and paid for under the scheme. For 35 years the Katkari in this hamlet had lived confined to this smaller space under the yoke of this and other landholders, providing them with free labour and services on the assumption that some payment was needed to occupy their land. They did not know they were actually owners of the land! After learning of this situation and receiving copies of the individual land deeds collected from the tehsildar's office, the Katkari in Nadode Katkarwadi immediately surveyed and occupied the full extent of their hamlet. This success was beyond what anyone had anticipated or achieved in any of the other hamlets. While still not incorporated formally into the village site of Nadode, the hamlet was now secure and the Katkari residents no longer feared eviction.

Working with Complexity

The exercise of power by landholders to strike fear into the hearts of the Katkari and to undermine their resolve, witnessed after the gram sabha in Nadode, had a profound effect on the research team. It put into sharp relief the multiple vulnerabilities and difficulties faced by the Katkari.

In hindsight, some of the obstacles we faced could not have been predicted. For instance, government plans to extend the limits of Mumbai, announced a few months after the research began, dramatically pushed land prices up. The effects were particularly strong near major highways in both Karjat and Khalapur talukas. Landholders in these areas were enthused by the sudden increase in the value of land and went on high alert for any opportunities to gain from it, and for any threats to their ownership. By contrast, land prices in Sudhagad, further from Mumbai, did not experience these effects. The impact of these macro dynamics varied enormously at the micro level from place to place and depending on the idiosyncratic interests of particular landholders.

Twists and turns in the struggle for a secure hamlet were a fundamental challenge to the assumptions the research team had used to make sense of the situation and to plan detailed and targeted actions with the Katkari. While successful in one hamlet, the attempt at holistic and strategic thinking developed with the Katkari quickly fell apart in others once the depth of opposition was revealed. Further analysis showed that the unequal relations of power between landholders and the Katkari, anticipated from the beginning, went far beyond direct confrontation with landholders. They were expressed as well in the relationship of the Katkari to government officials, to the gram panchayat and to all potential employers of unskilled labour. A long history of severe exploitation and social exclusion had fragmented the community and deeply eroded its self-confidence. Many things would need to change on many fronts simultaneously in order to achieve the apparently straightforward goal of a secure village site. There would be no easy solution.

Given these many obstacles, the team decided to rethink its approach to working with the Katkari. As described earlier, after the Nadode incident we stopped going to the study villages to ensure that we were not putting any pressure on the Katkari to take further public action. Later, however, the various organized groups in the hamlets once again began to contact the team and ask for meetings. The threat of eviction was as tangible as ever. People said that they wanted to do something, but were not sure what. The research team was not sure either. We agreed, however, to investigate the reasons why people in some hamlets were not willing to take a public stand and to use this understanding to plan future actions.

The invitation to return to the hamlets prompted us to redo our initial assessment of the inquiry plan, and to revise downward our estimate of the chances of successfully securing village sites. When we reflected on what we had learned, we concluded that we now had more complete and reliable information and knowledge regarding the various conditions and factors affecting the action research plan. By trying to solve the problem, we increased our understanding of the main hurdles and the strongest barriers to achieving the goal. All in all, we knew that the chances of success were low, and we knew what we were up against. The action research endeavour, summarized by point 'B' in Figure 2.6, was now more correctly seen as a significant challenge, rather than a blueprint that could simply be planned and implemented.

The shift in thinking about the nature of the inquiry and the kind of planning it required, consolidated in the new assessment, was unsettling

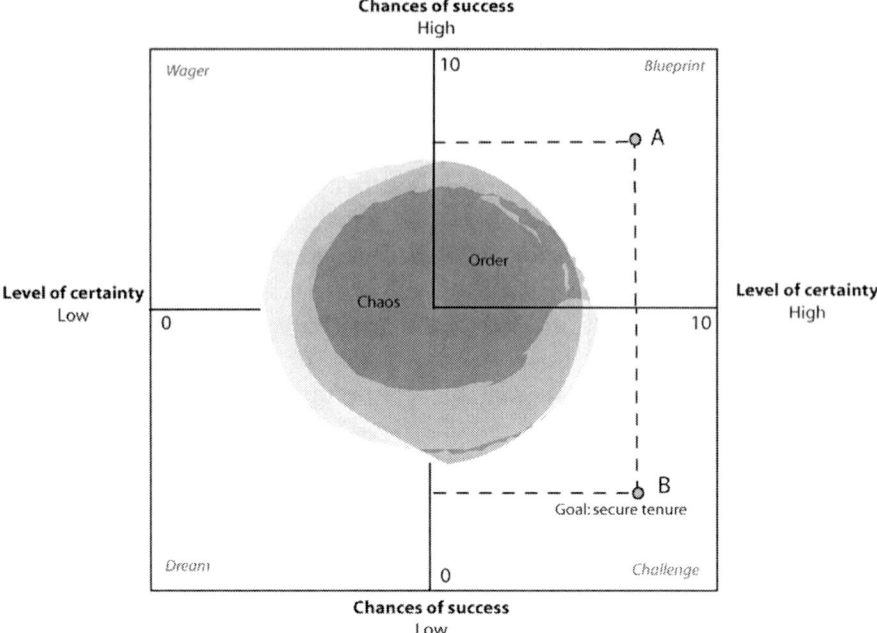

Figure 2.6: Assessment 'B', chances of success and level of certainty

Source: Author's field notes, April 2006, Pali, Maharashtra.
Note: Point 'B' shows the interaction of two estimates. On the vertical axis, the chances of successfully securing village sites received a low rating. On the horizontal axis, the level of certainty regarding knowledge of conditions and factors affecting the proposed action received a high rating. Where the two ratings intersect places the action research project in the lower right quadrant. This is the world of relative 'chaos', where plans can only be treated as working hypotheses subject to continuous adjustment 'in the middle' of multiple streams of action and reaction by different parties.

and a test of the team's own expectations, timelines and resolve. Suddenly, the inquiry was a very uncertain endeavour with no clear end in sight. While this was a cause for worry, it was also a useful conclusion as it pointed to a new kind of planning. Instead of a plan-and-implement approach to the inquiry, the team consciously adopted a *continuous action–reaction* model guided by *working hypotheses* regarding what needed to shift in the situation in order to increase the chances of success. This did not involve abandoning all efforts to plan. We still needed to be efficient in the use of limited time and other resources to pursue the goal of securing village sites. We just didn't plan everything out well in advance and in great detail, assuming that the outcomes and results of each action could be fully anticipated. Using the Process Mapping tool (Annex I), we paid more attention to how the outputs of one activity fed into the next activity as an input and adjusted plans accordingly. Plans became more flexible and iterative while maintaining a sense of purpose. Once we recognized and accepted how difficult the goal was, and that some obstacles would be hard to predict, the inquiry process could remain open to the lessons of failure, the reality of dead ends, and the possibility of new directions unplanned and unanticipated. The next chapter delves into the Katkari and research team explorations of these sources of complexity and the new directions that eventually emerged.

3

Understanding Complexity

The small victory for the 47 families with solid title to their land in
Nadodewadi rekindled the inquiry's sense of purpose and inspired
the Katkari to take up once again the goal of acquiring gaothan for their
hamlets. Over a period of several months, the various gaothan action
committees once again began to contact the research team and ask for
meetings. The threat of eviction was as tangible as ever. People said that
they wanted to do something, but were not sure what. The research
team was not sure either. We agreed, however, to explore the many
issues that people were raising about why people in some hamlets were
not willing to take a public stand on the gaothan issue, and to use this
understanding to plan future actions. Fear of the landholders was very
much at the forefront during these discussions and became a key question
the Katkari wanted to explore further.

This chapter discusses crucial results from the efforts to make sense of
the Katkari's fear of landholders immediately following the gram sabha
process. While for many Katkari, overcoming their fear initially seemed
like an impossible task, their own interpretations of the threats they faced
launched several new lines of action and inquiry. These unfolded in
unexpected ways and at different rates. We needed new participatory
inquiry and planning methods to take us beyond the simple chain of
cause and effect revealed through the problem tree. Tools were needed
to explore the interaction of various factors affecting not only the gaothan
problem but also the broader life dilemma of the Katkari. These brought
into focus persistent constraints on the Katkari's ability to exercise their
rights to land and livelihood, and the multi-faceted and multi-dimensional
nature of their struggle. The narrative of this book and the organization
of its remaining chapters reflects this new orientation, shifting from a
linear and chronological presentation of events to an account of key

directions and working hypotheses used to navigate through the complex social landscape.

The Forces at Play

Sarang Katkarwadi in Khalapur was one of the first hamlets where we and the Katkari revisited earlier assessments in light of stakeholder responses to the gram sabha process. The hamlet is located a few kilometres from a major highway between Mumbai and Pune and is very near the non-tribal village of Sarang, a prosperous agricultural community with access to a constant source of irrigation. Many Katkari in the hamlet work for periods of time as agricultural labourers on these farms and migrate to brick-making units at other times of the year. A few Katkari households work on a sand-dredging operation for a contractor in Sarang village. Because of its prime location, the land under the hamlet had been sold to a Mumbai-based land speculator some two years earlier. While the new owner had taken no action against the Katkari, or even met with them, people in the hamlet did not wish to do anything that would provoke him. This was the reason why they had not presented an application for a gaothan to the gram sabha. The Katkari found themselves in a situation of extreme uncertainty, with fear of eviction by the landholder on one side and a resolve to stay in the hamlet on the other. This prompted the gaothan action committee and a few others in the community to request a meeting in the hamlet with the research team to discuss the situation and to develop a new plan that would advance their goal, but not put them at risk of immediate retaliation from the landholder. The goal was not simply to understand the fear, but also to manage it and create some resolve to overcome it.

To support the discussion, the research team opted to use the force field method.[1] Our reasoning was that planning and decision making by the gaothan action committee would benefit from an appreciation not only of the factors driving fear of eviction by the landholder, but also of any factors that counteracted the fear and stopped the situation from getting worse. The force field method recognizes both driving and counteracting forces and supports a discussion about things people can do to strengthen or reduce the forces at play.

---

[1] For detailed instructions and adaptations of the force field method, see Tools and Software at www.participatoryactionresearch.net.

Discussion of the forces driving fear of the landholder was quite animated, leaving the participants feeling that their situation was very bleak. First in the list of driving forces was the fact that the landholder had a legal title to the land. Participants gave this a strong rating (4 out of 5) as a driver of their fear, because the landholder could also count on the police and other authorities for support. Second, the high price of land created pressure on the landholder to sell and to evict the Katkari at any cost. Participants gave this factor a weight of 3 out of 5. Other factors driving their fear also entered the discussion. There was no *gauki*[2] or other established local authority to rally people to defend the community against the landholder. While many in the hamlet had formed a general idea that they had a right to stay on the land, participants felt that most were still quite unsure of themselves and could be easily confused and intimidated by the landholder. Some participants also felt an obligation to the original owner of the land. These factors received moderate to low weights as drivers of their fear.

The greatest weight, 5 out of 5, was given to livelihood dependency. Participants said they were generally fearful of landholders because they depended on them entirely for their livelihoods. Even though the new landholder was not local and had not employed them, people feared that any defiance would inevitably undermine their livelihoods, either directly through his influence on other employers, or indirectly by creating a backlash against the Katkari.

Counteracting factors identified by the participants offered only very limited scope to manage the situation. Legal provisions proclaiming their housing rights and laws protecting tribal populations from severe forms of exploitation were noted but given low scores (2 and 1 out of 5, respectively). Participants felt that they had never really benefited from these kinds of measures in the past and had little reason to trust them now. The provisions by the government to compensate landholders in cases of land expropriation also received a low score from participants (1 out of 5), because they knew that the rates normally used by government agencies were much lower than market land prices and would be rejected out of hand by the landholders.

The most powerful counteracting factor identified by the participants was their physical possession of the land (*wahi wat*). This, they recognized,

---

[2] Gauki is a traditional village or hamlet level institution predating the Gram Panchayat.

provided them with some defence. So long as they remained in the hamlet, it would be difficult to evict them. The participants noted, however, that the vast majority of residents in their community migrated to distant brick kilns for extended periods of time, leaving the whole hamlet very vulnerable at that time. They decided to strengthen this defensive measure by building on the youth leadership in the community, another existing counteracting factor they felt they had some control over. The commitment of young leaders to remaining in the village, evidenced by their efforts to collect residence proofs, learn about their rights and participate in the gaothan action committee, gave people some confidence. The youth could continue to help organize the community, share their knowledge of legal rights with others in the community and call on people to return to the hamlet from the brick kilns at the first sign of any eviction threat.

The overall assessment made by participants, summarized in Figure 3.1, was that the driving forces were more numerous and outweighed the counteracting forces. Key driving forces, including livelihood dependency, high land prices and land title, were beyond their control. Participants could not think of any actions they could take to reduce the strength of these factors. This conclusion reflected the extreme vulnerability the participants felt. The Katkari were resisting eviction, but also feared open conflict with powerful actors that could make things worse for them not only by uprooting them from their homes but also by blocking their access to work. For the research team, it became clear that livelihood dependency was a significant reason why the Katkari in Sarang Katkarwadi remained fearful and reluctant to take any action that might make their situation worse. As discussed subsequently, this factor also emerged in other analyses as a persistent constraint on the ability of the Katkari to exercise their collective rights to a village site.

The Dynamics of Fear and Vulnerability

In Narsurwadi, 14 people (10 men and four women) gathered to formulate a new response to their earlier decision to drop their application for a gaothan. Most of the participants in the meeting had recently returned from working at brick kilns, and were now making ends meet by collecting and selling firewood or working as day labourers on local farms. Some had participated in the earlier problem tree assessment, and shared the main results of that exercise with the larger group. After a round of tea and snacks, people discussed various factors that they felt

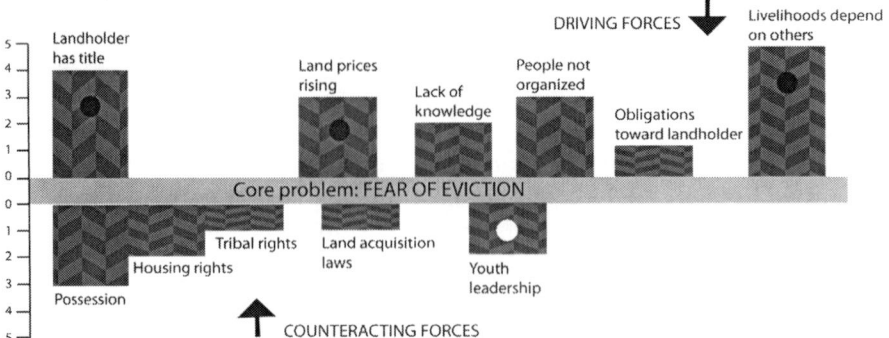

Figure 3.1: Forces that drive or counteract fear of eviction by landholders among Katkari in Sarang Katkarwadi

Source: Author's field notes, May 2006, Sarang Katkarwadi.

Note: The figure shows the forces that drive or counteract fear of eviction by landholders among Katkari in Sarang Katkarwadi, rated on a scale of 1 to 5. The driving forces are more numerous and outweigh the counteracting factors. Three of these, indicated with a black dot, are beyond their control. Possession of the land is the strongest counteracting force, although weakened by the seasonal migration of many of the residents. Youth leadership offers some scope for strengthening land possession further as a counteracting factor, and is an asset they control (white dot). It also provides hope that the community will be able to enhance knowledge of their rights and organize itself, thereby reducing the weight of these factors as drivers of their fear of landholders. Nevertheless, livelihood dependency threatens to tip the situation against them. It has no counteracting force working against it at present, and remains a significant reason why the Katkari in Sarang Katkarwadi remain fearful and reluctant to demand rights to a gaothan. Columns without dots represent factors over which control is neither strong nor weak.

were important to understanding the fear they continued to experience, and selected seven they felt were the most important. Some came from the results of the problem tree and others were added in light of the gram sabha experience. The group agreed that the purpose of the exercise was to see how the various factors underlying their fear interacted with each other and to decide which ones among many to focus on.

The research team opted to use the system dynamics method, an adaptation and development of input–output analysis used in economics and economic planning.[3] The method helps to identify entry points into a system based on an assessment of how elements in the system interact to create specific behaviours and situations. Our reasoning was that the

---

[3] For detailed instructions and adaptations of the system dynamics method, see Tools and Software at www.participatoryactionresearch.net.

complexity of Katkari thinking about their fear of the landholders would be better understood in the context of relationships among parts and the whole system, rather than through an assessment of factors in isolation. A systems perspective, rather than the simple linear causality of the problem tree method, might help make a complex situation clearer so that people could decide how to be strategic in their actions. At the same time, the research team wanted to explore the use of this more advanced tool in an attempt to scale up the level of detailed reasoning by participants and deepen the dialogue. We knew that the Katkari were highly motivated and we wanted to give them something new and engaging to think about and work with.

Image 3.1: Rajeev Khedkar facilitating a discussion in Karjat using the System Dynamics method. Wax figures made by the Katkari represented each factor in the analysis.

To begin, participants made rough drawings on paper to represent each selected factor. The core problem from the problem tree analysis (Katkari are at risk of eviction) was included in the analysis to see whether or not it interacted directly with the other factors as a cause or an effect. The factors were:

1. The hamlet residents are at a risk of eviction (represented by a drawing of several huts surrounded by a barbed wire fence).

2. Government agencies and political groups neglect the Katkari (represented by several figures squatting on the ground outside of a government office building, indicating that they are not given proper treatment and not visited in their own village).
3. People in the village are not organized (represented by two persons facing opposite directions).
4. People in the village fear the landowners (represented by one person touching the feet of another).
5. People in the village must migrate regularly and for long periods in search of employment (represented by a family walking with baskets on their heads).
6. Landholders are resolved to retain ownership of the village site (represented by a person standing firmly on the village land).
7. There is lack of civic amenities in the village (represented by several huts separated from each other, with no road, electricity, well or anything else in between).

The research team then facilitated a step-by-step discussion of each factor and the extent to which it contributed to or caused each other factor in the analysis. A scale of 0 to 10 was used to show the causal weight of each factor. One person had seeds of *gunj* (*Abrus precatorius*) with him from his nursery, so the group members decided to use the seeds to indicate the ratings. The question was posed one factor at a time and reasons for the ratings were discussed until participants reached agreement on the appropriate score. For example, participants argued that government neglect contributes strongly to the risk of eviction, a lack of civic amenities and dependence on migration. High scores (10, 9 and 8, respectively) were given to show the causal weight of government neglect on these three factors. They said that only governments could reduce the risk of eviction, provide civic amenities and create employment schemes as alternatives to migration. They also noted that without the active support of the authorities, they could not risk confronting the landholder. Participants noted that a history of government neglect of the Katkari also gave the landholder greater confidence that he could control the situation and hardened his resolve. Scores of 6 out of 10 were given to show the causal weight of government neglect on both these factors.

A large table was developed on the ground throughout the conversation, which continued for more than two hours until all factors were rated (Table 3.1). There was general agreement on scoring for most of the points and on the reasoning behind the scores. One point of

Table 3.1: The interaction of factors causing fear of the landholder, Narsurwadi

Factor	Risk of Eviction	Government Neglect	People are not Organized	Fear of Landholders	Migration	Landholder Resolve	Lack of Civic Amenities	Cause Index
Risk of eviction	X	4	4	8	4	3	9	32/60
Government neglect	10	X	4	6	8	6	9	43/60
People are not organized	8	7	X	4	5	3	7	34/60
Fear of landholders	8	3	3	X	3	2	3	22/60
Migration	9	8	9	6	X	2	8	42/60
Landholder resolve	9	2	2	8	1	X	6	28/60
Lack of civic amenities	1	2	2	1	3	1	X	10/60
Effect Index	**45**	**26**	**24**	**33**	**24**	**17**	**42**	**211/420(50%)**

Source: Author's field notes, May 2006, Narsurwadi.

longer debate was the effect of poor amenities on the insecurity of the gaothan. Two members of the group felt that this effect was high because it undermined people's connection to the village, but most others felt this was not significant. After discussing the link between these factors, the majority view that poor amenities contributed little to the risk of eviction was accepted, resulting in a score of 1 for this causal relationship.

At times, participants inverted the direction of the causal relationships (confusing the extent to which A contributes to B with the extent to which B contributes to A). This was frustrating for some, but also elicited additional points not initially expressed. The correct scores were brought together in the table by the research team through careful cross-checking with the participants.

Once the scoring was completed, and during another tea break, a member of the research team calculated the sums of the various rows and columns and created a summary figure of the results on a large sheet of paper. The result is shown in Figure 3.2. Each of the four quadrants of the figure represents the kind of factor that is obtained by calculating the extent to which it contributes to others and depends on them. Each factor is either mainly a cause of other factors (upper left corner of the diagram), an effect (bottom right corner), or both a cause and an effect (upper right corner). Alternatively, it can be a factor that is relatively independent of others (lower left corner).

The graph format was new to participants, but the meaning of the four quadrants was explained progressively as the discussion continued. The group began by looking at the three factors in the upper left quadrant of the figure, factors that are mainly causes of other factors in the system. They include neglect by government agencies and political groups, migratory livelihoods and lack of organization. After discussion, the group confirmed the summary observation that these factors are key causes of their fear, the risk of eviction and the sorry state of amenities in the village. They described the hierarchical relationship between the two sets of factors as one of parent and child. The figure showed as well that the core factor (risk of eviction) is both a cause and an effect of other factors in the system. The participants made sense of this result by pointing out that so long as the village site remained insecure, it would be easier for government officials to ignore them, local organization would remain difficult and release from the cycle of migration elusive. Fear of the landholder and the lack of amenities (bottom right side factors) are effects of these other factors.

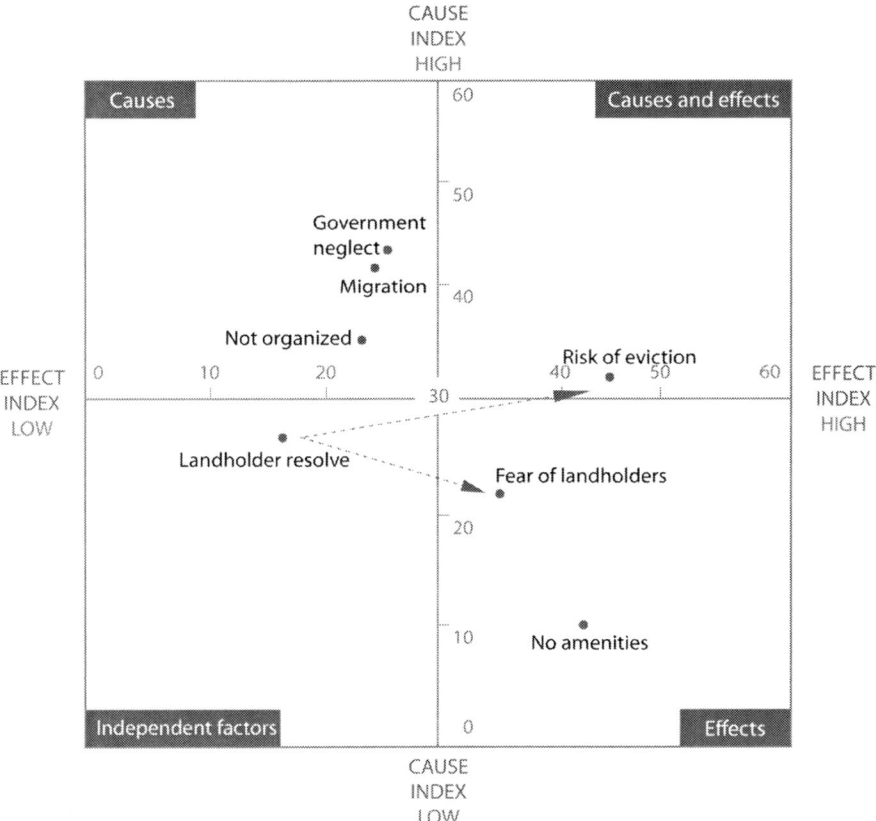

Figure 3.2: The interaction of factors contributing to the fear of landholders in Narsurwadi

Source: Author's field notes, May 2006, Narsurwadi.

Note: Three factors located in the upper left quadrant are key causes of the overall situation. They drive the fear of landholders, increase the risk of eviction and ultimately limit the scope for properly developing amenities in the village. The landholders' resolve to keep the land, while an important factor, is neither a cause nor an effect of the three key causes. It is independent of them. Landholder resolve does, however, interact directly with both the risk of eviction and the fear experienced by the Katkari (see the high causal scores in Table 3.1 and the arrows in the figure above showing the causal relationship). Actions based on the analysis focused on the three key causes in the upper left quadrant and efforts to overcome fear of landholders.

The location of landholder resolve in the lower left quadrant of the figure initially puzzled the participants and the research team. After reviewing the ratings in the table, however, the participants and the research team realized that the landholders' resolve contributes to some factors but not others. Landholder resolve to keep the land increases the risk of eviction, the Katkari's fear of the landholders and, to a lesser extent, the lack of amenities in the village. This resolve has little causal influence, however, on the other causes of their fear: government neglect, migration and a lack of organization. These factors exist independently of the landholder resolve. This contradiction of the main tendencies is indicated in Figure 3.2 by an arrow showing the relevant causal relationships. It served to remind everyone that the resolve of the landholder took some of its power from the broader context where government neglect, migration and a lack of organization in the hamlet played primary roles as persistent constraints on the life situation of the Katkari.

The factor that received the greatest attention during discussion and interpretation of the results was migration. Participants concluded from the summary figure that migration was a root cause of many of their problems, and consequently a key entry point for actions aimed at reducing their fear and improving the overall situation. They said that migration created an impression of impermanence and neglect, making the hamlet even more vulnerable to enclosure and eviction. Non-tribals, including government officials, see the Katkari as vagrants, not village residents. Migration therefore contributes to their neglect by government officials and political leaders and weakens village-level organization. Moreover, migratory labour at brick kilns and charcoal operations is very unstable and highly exploitative work, and only provides a partial livelihood. Workers remain dependent on the landholder and other local employers for bridging work between periods of migration. This vulnerability, they said, was a key reason why they were fearful of confronting the landholder directly over the village site. Breaking this historical client–patron relationship could make matters even worse for them, not only by uprooting them from their homes but also by pushing them even more forcefully into bonded work on brick kilns. Lack of gainful local employment, in turn, forces them to accept the inappropriate terms and conditions of the brick unit contractors, reinforcing the pattern of migration.

After three solid hours of work, and many lively debates about the relative weight of different factors, fatigue set in and the session came to a close. Participants agreed on the strategic entry point – breaking the bonds of migration – but left discussion about specific lines of action until later, when people were rested and had let the ideas settle. They left, however, with a greater understanding of how their fear of the landholder connected to other life circumstances and other groups. By placing their fear in this broader context, it seemed more manageable to many. People said they felt more relaxed. The earlier decision to drop their application for a gaothan was also seen differently. What emerged later was a new decision by the gaothan action committee to take the application for a gaothan that they had already developed for the gram panchayat directly to the tehsildar in their region. They felt this would allow the Katkari to continue the struggle in an organized way, focused on overcoming government neglect, while avoiding direct confrontation with the landholders.

System dynamics assessments in other villages brought up similar themes and relationships, namely, the strong impact of migration and the considerable weight of political marginalization and isolation from government administrative supports. Interpretation and decision making varied, however. In Nadodewadi, the village where an application to the gram sabha was presented, approved and then torn up the by gram sevak, participants identified the fear of physical violence and the fear of sexual abuse as contributing factors requiring immediate mitigating actions. As a result of their analysis, they decided to prepare themselves to collectively contact the police should they need protection. In Ambewadi, the analysis brought to the fore the persistent and profound impacts of migratory livelihoods, but also some different options. Unlike people in Narsurwadi who do not engage in any agriculture of their own, some Katkari households in Ambewadi grow crops on land leased from residents of the nearby non-tribal village of Potalpali. This possibility gave participants scope to discuss land-based alternative livelihoods and plan actions accordingly. The topic of alternative livelihoods as a response to migration became crucial during another assessment, reported in a later chapter. Their analysis also brought to light their fear that the landholder would become even more strict and exploitative if they were to try, and fail, to get official support for their position.

In Dhoklewadi, the analysis focused on an even broader set of factors. Residents in the hamlet said that they had woken up to the dangers of an insecure gaothan, and wanted to find a long-term solution to the situation of vulnerability they faced on many fronts. In response, the research team facilitated a discussion of a wide range of problems or difficulties raised by the participants, and of how these interacted with each other to create a situation of extreme vulnerability. To carry out the assessment, people gathered in the small hut of one of the residents, providing some relief from the intense summer heat. The eight persons, six men and two women, had a good rapport with the facilitators, and so it was easy to begin discussions. They raised and selected eight difficulties for detailed discussion:

1. Families migrate to brick kilns.
2. They are landless.
3. They regularly take advances from the contractor.
4. There is lack of other employment in and around Dhoklewadi.
5. There is a high level of alcoholism among families in Dhoklewadi.
6. Katkari families are exploited by the contractor.
7. Dhoklewadi village lacks civic amenities.
8. Children are deprived of schooling.

They then scored each factor one at a time, based on the extent to which it caused each other factor (Table 3.2). These scores were adjusted along the way in light of discussion and the reasons provided for the scores. The research team then calculated the sums of the various rows and columns and created a summary figure of the results on a chart for discussion (Figure 3.3). The women made black tea for all and bananas were shared before launching into a discussion of the figure. Various insightful moments and shifts in thinking that emerged during this process were used by the Katkari to guide subsequent actions.

Discussion of the results with participants started with the upper left quadrant, showing that migration to brick kilns and the lack of local employment drove the other difficulties experienced by people in the hamlet. People said that, as a consequence, children were deprived of education and they were unable to develop the hamlet as they would like (lower right quadrant). Exploitation by the contractors (lower right quadrant) is also an inevitable effect of their dependence on migration and the lack of alternative local employment in the first place. The high total row scores (see the cause index in Table 3.2) for migration and local employment point to the heavy weight these two factors exercise on the other difficulties faced by the Katkari.

The practice of taking an advance from the contractor and the high level of alcoholism among families in Dhoklewadi, both factors appearing in the upper right quadrant, are both causes and effects of the problems at hand. They are both a consequence of migration and lack of local employment, and contributing causes of exploitation, a lack of civic amenities and inadequate schooling. Participants said that once they migrated to the kilns and were bound to the contractor through an advance, exploitation through manipulation of their debt and wages was

Table 3.2: Ratings for the interaction of difficulties people face in Dhoklewadi that produce and reinforce livelihood vulnerability

Factor	Migration	Landlessness	Advance	Lack of Employment	Alcoholism	Exploitation	Lack of Amenities	Deprived of Schooling	Cause Index
Migration to brick kilns	X	6	8	6	7	9	8	10	54
Landlessness	6	X	4	2	4	5	4	4	29
Advance	10	2	X	4	9	10	5	8	48
Lack of local employment	7	2	7	X	6	7	6	8	43
Alcoholism	6	2	8	6	X	6	5	7	40
Exploitation	1	4	8	3	7	X	4	3	30
Lack of amenities	1	3	2	4	7	2	X	5	24
Deprived of schooling	1	1	1	1	4	7	4	X	19
Effect Index	**32**	**20**	**38**	**26**	**44**	**46**	**36**	**45**	**287/560 (51%)**

Source: Author's field notes, May 2006, Dhoklewadi.

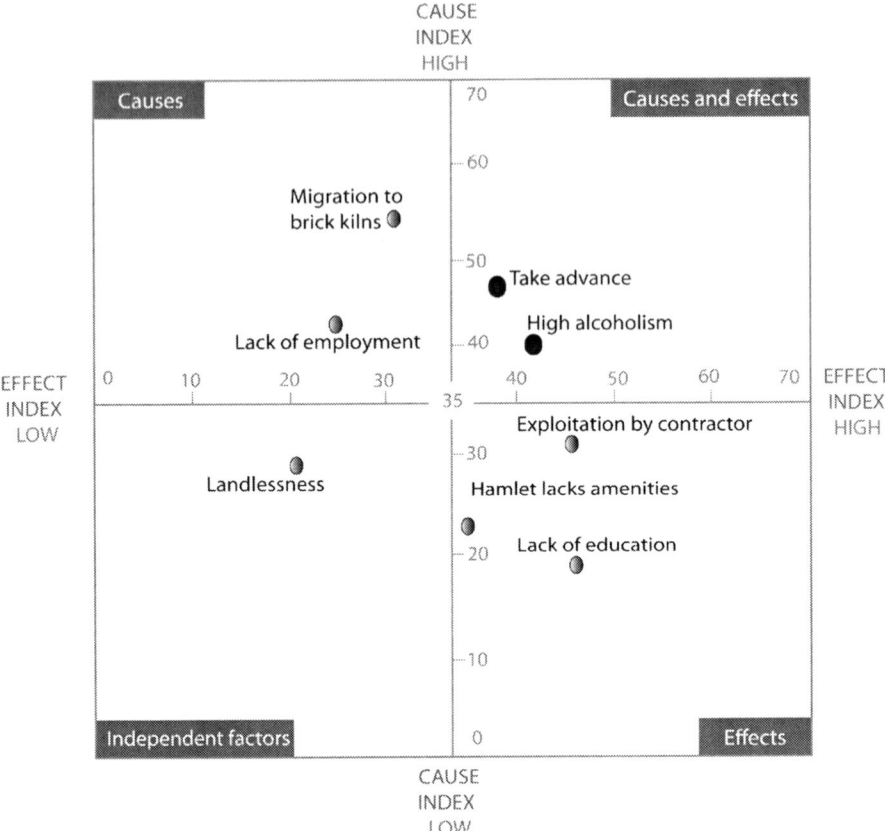

Figure 3.3: The interaction of factors that contribute to vulnerability in Dhoklewadi

Source: Author's field notes, May 2006, Dhoklewadi.

Note: Migration to brick kilns and the lack of alternative forms of local employment (upper left quadrant) drive many of the other difficulties faced by the Katkari. Because of these factors, people are exploited by the contractors, the hamlet lacks amenities and children are deprived of education (effects). Taking an advance plays into this situation; it binds them to the brick kilns, making it easier for contractors to exploit them. It also contributes to their alcoholism, which in turn reinforces their desire for and dependence on an advance and the money from migration. These two factors (taking an advance and high alcoholism) are strategic by virtue of their position as both causes and effects of the situation of vulnerability. Also, participants can imagine steps to act on them directly. Landlessness is a factor in their vulnerability, but generally independent of the other factors considered. Landlessness merits a unique assessment to bring out the various factors it interacts with, as it does not interact strongly with the factors considered by the Katkari in this exercise.

inevitable. These two difficulties (advance and alcoholism) also interact with each other – most of the advance is spent on drinking and gambling during festivals immediately prior to migration. Because they spend all their money on alcohol, they must borrow again. Participants realized that these two factors are tightly bound as both causes and effects of each other and direct contributors to the overall situation of vulnerability faced by the community.

Landlessness, a factor the research team had initially thought would be seen by the Katkari as a major cause of the other problems, ended up in the lower left quadrant as an independent factor. While it has weight in the situation (for example, a score of 6 out of 10 as a cause of migration: see Table 3.2), the matrix of ratings suggests that landlessness does not interact strongly with the other assessed factors producing livelihood vulnerability. Discussion revealed that in this hamlet, people did not look on land as an attractive source of livelihood. Most do not own land and farming has never been an important occupation for them. Furthermore, past attempts by some Katkari in the hamlet to acquire dalhi lands were always met with government indifference and even hostility, especially from Forest Department officials who threatened them for encroaching on forest lands. While participants recognized that landlessness contributed to their livelihood vulnerability, the discussion showed that it interacts mainly with other factors not considered in the analysis (attitudes towards agriculture, the poor quality of available land, experiences with government). This prompted a later and separate analysis to bring out the various factors landlessness did interact with, a theme addressed in a later chapter.

The thinking among participants in Dhoklewadi converged around several key conclusions and actions that they could take in both the short and longer terms. First, participants concluded that refusing an advance from the contractor was important to breaking the cycle of migration and exploitation. They felt that the practice of advances from contractors, which had been going on for a long time without any opposition, should and could be resisted collectively. They committed to immediately talking with others in the hamlet about the problems created by advances. Resisting this, however, would not be easy. One of the Katkari participants told a story about a festival that happened the previous year. He said that he had some money of his own saved at the time of the festival, but the sheth came to the hamlet when he was away and forcibly left behind Rs 4,000 with his wife. All of that money was later spent on alcohol, in addition to his original savings. Migration could not be avoided.

Second, participants agreed that working to reduce the level of alcoholism and gambling in the community was important and something they could act on independently. Discussion of the topic was impassioned, with people fully aware of the difficulties. Some pointed to the need to improve opportunities for meaningful education and literacy as a counteracting force against alcoholism. Others said that religious activities and inspiration had successfully weaned some youth away from the clutches of alcohol. They said that spirituality challenges alcoholism and gambling and that steps could be taken to nudge and guide the youth in the hamlet towards a spiritual path. This would be difficult, however, and would require sustained attention to the youth and a commitment to changing their own behaviour as well. For some in the group, a shift in thinking occurred regarding alcoholism, which they had previously viewed as simply a consequence or outcome of their situation and a source of happiness in the midst of their miseries, not a problem on its own, one with negative consequences. This was a motivating insight, prompting several people to say they intended to speak up against the routine and excessive consumption of alcohol in their own families and in the community at large. It was a difficult and emotionally charged issue deemed to require much more reflection and discussion within the community.

The discussion around education also generated a lively debate. During the scoring process, women in the group felt very strongly that by depriving their children of education they were also contributing to the children's future exploitation. As parents they would not have been cheated and exploited by the contractor if they had been literate. By depriving their children of schooling, they were perpetuating the cycle of exploitation. This argument was accepted by the entire group and resulted in a high score (7 out of 10) for this factor (see Table 3.2). It also reinforced their resolve to stop taking advances. Someone in the group commented that the advance locked them into a situation where they had to take their children out of school when they migrated to brick kilns. This interrupted the schooling of the children and made it more difficult for them to return to school later in the year.

Finally, participants agreed that they could not develop better lives unless they were able to develop alternative livelihoods. This was crucial to breaking the cycle of migration, indebtedness, exploitation, illiteracy and village poverty. Initially, they considered the goal to be beyond their means. As the discussion continued, however, participants gave examples of others in the hamlet who had started to rent land from non-tribal farmers for farming, making it possible for them to avoid migration.

Some in the community were raising local breeds of goats and doing fairly well at it. Discussion also opened up as to the potential of the dalhi lands they once had access to. Participants thus established a connection between landlessness and the lack of local employment, a connection that had not been there when they first scored the relationships between factors. This led them to rethink how landlessness contributed to their situation and to become more interested in accessing their dalhi lands as a potential asset they could use to develop alternative livelihoods. As discussed in a subsequent chapter, the Katkari in this and other communities later actively organized themselves in response to the Forest Rights Act and the opportunities the act presented to advance their claims to dalhi lands.

New Directions

Analysis with the Katkari about the dynamics of fear and vulnerability laid the groundwork for later developments in the inquiry. New directions emerged that focused on three persistent constraints: government neglect, breaking the bonds of migratory labour and gaps in both hamlet-level and collective organization.

Work on each of these constraints unfolded unevenly over a number of years, in response to small successes, setbacks and stakeholder interventions that could not be predicted in advance. The design of new inquiries often depended on the prior assessment of the performance of key factors (for example, assessing the actual organizational capacities emerging in Katkari communities before doing any strategic planning with them). Process and decisions regarding what to do next had to wait for the results of prior activities and responses from particular stakeholders (for example, securing caste certificates to support applications for government assistance, and then government replies to written applications for land). While the central purpose remained constant – securing shelter and tenure over village sites – the Katkari and the research team began to work on various fronts simultaneously and with varying levels of intensity over time and in difference spaces. For the research team, the challenge was in weaving the multi-hued threads together using a flexible but structured methodology. Change along the way, trial and error, and unexpected results became the rule.

The concluding chapter of this book contains a timeline showing the chronological sequence of events from the beginning of the inquiry to the present day. However, given the methodological and chronological discontinuities affecting the research process, a linear presentation in the forthcoming chapters would be confusing to readers, and would probably fail to capture the logic and coherence of each working hypothesis. A different kind of narrative is needed. Consequently, the remainder of this book follows each of the main working hypotheses and lines of action one by one, even though they unfolded concurrently over several years.

We will begin with the persistent statement by the Katkari that they are routinely and thoroughly neglected by government. The next chapter will explore this experience, and provide detailed evidence of government failure to implement its own policies.

4

Addressing Government Neglect

Until recently, the Katkari gaothan problem was largely invisible to activist and development organizations working in Maharashtra, including ourselves. In the absence of pressure from the Katkari themselves, government officials also neglected the issue. Interviews by the research team with the gram sevak and other local government officials indicated that when the inquiry started, they were largely unaware of the scope and impact of the gaothan problem on the Katkari. Nor had they thought about the emerging risk of widespread evictions in the rapidly changing economic context and real-estate frenzy. Officials were unacquainted with the history of the previous gaothan extension schemes, and unclear about the bureaucratic procedures and relevant laws, regulations and policies. Their failure to implement policies from the past was not evident to them. Nor was it of any real concern or priority. The Katkari had exerted no demands on officials, so the problem was out of sight and out of mind.

Following the challenges by landholders to the local gram sabha process, the research team and the Katkari resolved to engage with government actors at the taluka level and higher, not only to pressurize them to act but also to provide them with relevant information and analysis showing the scope of the problem, the legal basis for resolution and the moral and ethical obligation to act. This chapter reports on interactions among the research team, the Katkari and government officials on all of these fronts, aimed at helping officials see the light as well as feel the fire. As might be expected, we often met with bureaucratic indifference and inertia. In response, the research team and Katkari from hamlets already mobilized around the issue began to engage with a much larger number of Katkari communities, with a view to building a united front and mounting collective pressure on government agencies. The Right to Information Act was used to collect information on past policies and identify the firm measures of government institutions, laws and procedures that could address the bureaucratic and administrative gaps and conflicts in power. This eventually led to legal counter-measures under the Prevention of Atrocities Act, a key turning point in the Katkari struggle to exercise collective rights to a village site. This chapter examines these activities against the background of previous government responses and Katkari reflection on the reasons why their concerns had been so long neglected.

Previous Government Responses

The modern legal framework pertaining to the gaothan builds on provisions in the Constitution of India and various state-level laws that enable government officials to declare villages as independent legal entities. Clause (g) of Article 243 of the Constitution of India (Part IX: The Panchayats) states that a 'village' means 'a village specified by the Governor by public notification to be a village for the purposes of the Part and includes a group of villages so specified'. Villages and hamlets are grouped together under the village with the largest population, and this is designated as the revenue village for the purpose of coordinating the collection of taxes in all associated villages and hamlets.

The Bombay Village Panchayats Act, 1958, acknowledges this definition and goes on to say that 'where circumstances so require, provision is made to include or exclude any local area from area of a village or to alter the limits of a village or to take away that local area from the concerned village by notification issued' (Gupte 2006a, 10). Section 122 of the Maharashtra Land Revenue Code, 1966, adds to this provision by indicating that

> It shall be lawful for the Collector or for a Survey Officer acting under the general or special orders of the State Government to ascertain and determine what lands are included within the site of any village, town or city and to fix from time to time, to vary the limits of the site determined aforesaid, regard being had to all subsisting rights of landowners. (Gupte 2006b, 92)

The code also provides guidance on how to conduct a survey and how to levy (or exempt) taxes on lands in village sites.

The acquisition and transfer of lands for the purpose of establishing a gaothan is supported by the Land Acquisition Act, 1894, which allows the Government of India and state governments to acquire any land for a public purpose, so long as due process is followed and compensation is provided. This law, first enacted by the British government, was adopted after independence and continues to be used to acquire land from individual landholders for government schemes such as housing, health and educational programmes, as well as for rural planning and the establishment of industrial sites. As can be imagined, it is a controversial piece of legislation because it has been used to establish special economic zones of questionable public good, and because compensation to landholders is highly variable and loosely controlled. It is also a highly bureaucratic process subject to cumbersome and lengthy procedures (Tayal and Jacob 2005). It is clear, however, that the acquisition of land for the establishment or extension of a village site is fully within the purview and intent of the act.[1]

The government can also use other legislation to secure housing land for people living in rural areas. The Bombay Tenancy and Agricultural Lands Act, 1948, creates provisions aimed at regulating the rent paid to landholders and ensuring security of tenure for tenants. This act also severely limits the conditions under which tenants can be evicted from a house they have constructed, whether they actually pay land rent or not. Section 16 of the act states that 'if in any village, a tenant is in occupation of a dwelling house built at the expense of the tenant or his predecessor in title on a site belonging to his landlord, such tenant shall not be evicted from such dwelling house'.

The limitations on eviction from dwellings created by the Bombay Tenancy and Agricultural Lands Act, 1948, combined with the passage of time to create the conditions for landless tenants to apply for outright ownership of land they occupied under the federal Limitation Act, 1963. In short, the Limitation Act states that the active occupation of land (or encroachment on land) with the full knowledge of the legal owner for a continuous period of 12 years or more constitutes grounds for the

---

[1] While the act expressly includes all lands in India as lands subject to acquisition under it, in practice the Forest Conservation Act, 1980, has severely limited the ability of governments to acquire forest lands for the establishment of village sites and other non-agricultural uses. This situation is discussed later in Chapter 5.

acquisition of title by 'adverse possession'.[2] While subject to various interpretations in different jurisdictions in India, the act can and has been used to regularize encroachment on land for agriculture and for housing. Proof of residence (house tax receipts, electricity bills, ration cards, residency cards, etc.) and an agricultural labour certificate issued to landless and small farmers typically accompany successful applications. Today, the act is periodically used to acquire housing sites (ghartan) on behalf of landless tenants by fixing the land price and arranging for tenants to pay instalments to the government instead of the landholder. The process is very lengthy, however, and only applies to individual claims to a housing site, not to the collective claims of a village or hamlet. Individual claims in Maharashtra under this act have typically taken 10 to 15 years to complete. Use of the legislation is politically very sensitive, and is generally shunned by politicians and government officials alike because of strong resistance from legal landholders who ultimately forfeit their title with no compensation. A Supreme Court bench comprising Justices Dalveer Bhandari and H. S. Bedi recently requested the central government to take a fresh look at the act and suitably amend the land laws that recognize 'adverse possession' as a means to acquire title over land.[3]

These interrelated and mutually reinforcing laws comprise a legal framework that support the creation of a gaothan, and the extension of existing ones.[4] Four aspects of this framework need to be highlighted in the context of the Katkari experience. First, a village is designated as such by state government authorities, and in particular by officials of the

---

[2] Sridhara Babu, 'Adverse Possession as Explained by Supreme Court of India', Tumkur, India, 27 April 2010. http://sbn-caselaw.blogspot.com/2009/10/adverse-possession-as-explained-by.html (accessed on 11 February 2012). Interpretation of adverse possession has evolved over time and in different jurisdictions in India, but generally emphasizes the requirement that the land be occupied openly and continuously in a way that prevents possession by the legal owner.

[3] Supreme Court of India judgement dated 23/09/2008, CIVIL APPEAL NO. 1196 of 2007 Hemaji Waghaji Jat. Appellant Versus Bhikhabhai Khengarbhai Harijan & Others. Respondents JUDGMENT by Dalveer Bhandari, J. dated 23/09/2008.

[4] Bokil (2006) points out that the Bombay Prevention of Fragmentation and Consolidation of Holdings Act, 1947, also allows for the conversion of common land into a gaothan to meet the needs of a growing population. Various government orders cited by Bokil refer as well to provisions to use waste lands for housing sites granted to individual families belonging to backward communities and nomadic tribes.

Revenue Department, through public notification and survey. This is an administrative procedure under the control of the state government. Second, a village is not necessarily a single, contiguous space but may be a conglomeration or patchwork of villages and hamlets. Fragments of land comprising a hamlet distant from a village may be designated as part of the village, or notified as an independent village site. Third, the Land Acquisition Act, 1894, provides the most effective means to acquire land for a village site. While land reform legislation such as the Bombay Tenancy and Agricultural Lands Act, 1948, and provisions under the Limitation Act, 1963, can be used to acquire individual housing sites (ghartan), successful claims weaken the collective position of villages and hamlets in need of common areas such as schools, community centres and 'wada lands' for tethering cattle or storing fodder and manure. An example of this negative effect is described below. Finally, collectors can issue a notification to create or extend a gaothan and order a survey and compensation for landholders, if they are acting under general or specific orders of the state government. These orders have historically taken the form of gaothan extension schemes coupled with housing programmes set through state government policies.

Gaothan Extension Schemes

The problem of overcrowding in rural villages has been mentioned in every five-year plan by the Government of India and the Government of Maharashtra, from 1951 to the present. In 1961, the Government of Maharashtra introduced the first gaothan extension scheme with a 10-year horizon for addressing the problem.[5] A government resolution (GR) (No. LND/3960/ 20698-A dated 9 June 1961) was passed by the state legislature to address the problem of 'inadequate living space in villages'.

The objective of the 1961 scheme was to speed up the extension of village sites. It recognized that a secure space was a necessary condition for implementation of an effective housing and village development policy. The preamble to the scheme notes that:

> Inspite of repeated instructions from time to time regarding extensions to existing *Gaothan*s either by the addition of conveniently situated Government lands or by acquisition of suitable plots of land, the progress

---

[5] This section is based on a reading by the authors of government resolutions and circulars accessed through the Right to Information Act, dated between 1961 and 1988.

achieved in this respect is too slow to ensure a planned development of village *Gaothans* within a reasonable period of time. In the face of increasing pressure of population for additional living space and the enormity of the problem of congestion it has created, the measures taken so far have been found to be inadequate and people in most villages have neither room for themselves or for their cattle. In order therefore, to relieve congestion in *Gaothans* and to provide for people sufficient space for their houses and cattle, Government has decided to organise a campaign for acquisition of new *Gaothan* sites in such villages where this is necessary.

The GR goes on to list amenities to be provided for village sites including open wells/borewells, schools, playgrounds, *chavdi*/samaj mandir (community meeting halls), internal roads, open gutters, common toilets, open space for cattle to stand, bus stands, paddy threshing floors, community grazing land, a cemetery, open space for a village market, land for temples/places of worship and enough open space to take care of future housing needs of the village. It suggests that local gram panchayats pass resolutions expressing the need for an extension, and that information be collected regarding the needs of individual households. It also provides instructions and planning guidelines for local officials (collectors, tehsildars and others), and sets rules for the acquisition of lands to be included in a gaothan. These rules rely on the Land Acquisitions Act, 1894, which allows the Government of India and state governments to acquire any land for a public purpose, so long as due process is followed and compensation is provided. Various cost-sharing scenarios between the government and recipients of the land are allowed by the act, including the affected communities paying a portion of the cost.

The 1961 gaothan extension scheme and those that followed were typically coupled with a housing scheme to provide house sites (ghartan) to poor families and tribal communities in rural areas of the state. While the earlier schemes emphasized self-help and credit, later schemes, starting with the Indira Awas Yojana Housing Scheme, sponsored the construction of houses through private contractors and provision of free housing to selected groups. More often than not, this created enormous opportunities for corruption and the misuse of public funds intended for poor recipients. Heredia and Srivastava (1994, 116) report that housing schemes for Katkari in parts of Raigad district near Mumbai operated as a cash cow for local contractors and gram panchayats. They also typically resulted in substandard housing. As described below, the Katkari of Nadodewadi in Karjat were victimized by unscrupulous contractors-cum-landholders. Corruption and deliberate abuses of the legal provisions probably affected a great many Katkari as well as other tribal communities in the state.

Gaothan extension schemes were in place in Maharashtra from 1961 to 1991. During this period, various government resolutions, circulars and letters were issued to clarify or modify the procedures for implementing the schemes and to incorporate emerging priorities, including the special circumstances of nomadic tribes, backward classes and ex-criminal tribes. Government Resolution (GR) No. LND. 3962/107047-V, dated 2 January 1964, was the first to link the gaothan extension scheme to a separate scheme for the settlement of nomadic tribes, backward classes and ex-criminal tribes.

A year later, GR LND. 1065/1364-V, dated 5 April 1965, noted that:

> From the progress reports received by Government regarding the implementation of the above mentioned scheme it is observed that no good progress has been achieved so far. Since this is an important scheme which relates to the improvement of living conditions of the rural population, Government desires that special attention should be paid to its implementation. The scheme was also discussed in the regional conferences of the Collectors held at Bombay, Poona, Nagpur and Aurangabad, wherein the need for expeditious implementation of the scheme was explained to the Collectors, and the various points and difficulties raised by them were also solved.

To facilitate the prompt and proper implementation of the scheme, the 1965 GR provided supplementary instructions and clarifications on various points that are relevant to the Katkari situation. First, the GR noted that 'selection of site for extension of gaothans should not be restricted to the lands in the main villages only. But the lands in the hamlets and Wadis attached to the main villages should also be considered, if such lands are suitable.' The instruction was intended to ensure that the gaothan of tribal and marginalized groups on the outskirts of these villages also received attention, and that officials did not focus only on extensions to revenue villages where the better-off segments of the rural population were concentrated.

Second, the GR noted that in cases involving nomadic tribes, backward classes and ex-criminal tribes, the costs of acquiring private lands to be included in a gaothan were to be borne fully by the government and the levy of non-agricultural taxes on these lands was to be waived. The GR stated that these costs would be paid initially by the state government and reimbursed under the scheme by the central government following submission of detailed accounts.

While these steps were intended to better target the scheme, they may also have had a negative impact on implementation due to an increased workload for officials. Numerous GRs and circulars that followed refer to the complications of reporting to the central government on the acquisition of private lands and to the failures to do so. Some officials went to bizarre extremes to avoid having to acquire lands for the intended recipients. For example, a circular from the Commissioner's Office, Bombay, dated 1 December 1965, rejected a proposal for the acquisition of private land in Nasik district for a nomadic tribe because 'when persons were staying there for 70/75 years they cannot be treated as Nomadic [and therefore are not eligible for the scheme]'.

This problem was corrected in Circular No. LND/117597-Q, dated 9 September 1968, from the Revenue and Forest Department of the Government of Maharashtra. The circular states that:

> In a case recently brought to the notice of Government some of the people belonging to 'Nomadic Tribes' (Bhils) were reported to be unauthorisedly occupying a private land for the past 50 to 60 years. The questions which were referred to Government for orders were: (i) whether these persons should be treated as nomadic tribes inspite [sid] of the fact they settled in that land for the last 50 years, (ii) and whether the land unauthorisedly occupied by them needs to be acquired under the land Acquisition Act, even though these persons could be said to have become the owners of this land by adverse possession.
>
> Government has considered the above points and is pleased to direct that in the case of nomadics, residence at a fixed place is only one of the criteria and, therefore, a person belonging to the nomadic tribe does not cease to belong to that tribe, though he is staying in that place for several years. Apart from this, the persons belonging to the Bhil community are declared as 'Scheduled Tribes' and therefore, these persons can normally be settled under the sub-scheme 'settlement of nomadic tribes, backward classes and ex-criminal tribes' they being treated as belonging to Backward class communities.
>
> As regards the 2nd point, viz., whether Government should acquire the lands under Land Acquisition Act, occupied by these persons for a number of years, Govt. is pleased to direct that wherever such persons are occupying the private land openly for 50 to 60 years and are in

exclusive possession of that land, the right of the lawful owner to recover possession of the land encroached upon by these persons is extinguished under Section 27 of Limitation Act as the land is already in possession of such persons and as they have perfected their title against the original occupant there is no question of acquiring the said land under the Land Acquisition Act.

The strategy that emerged to minimize the need to pay the land acquisition costs and seek reimbursement for these from the central government, was to shift the focus of the scheme from complete reliance on the Land Acquisition Act, 1894, to the discretionary use of the Limitation Act, 1963. As noted earlier, the Limitation Act, 1963, states that the active occupation of land with full knowledge of the legal owner for a continuous period of 12 years or more constitutes grounds for the acquisition of title by 'adverse possession'. However, this shift probably also introduced a new implementation problem for government officials, namely, active resistance to the scheme by landholders who stood to gain nothing from the extension of a gaothan on their land. Implementation of the GR in these cases would inevitably have brought the officials concerned into direct conflict with landholders seeking to retain their lands or at least be compensated, adding another layer of complication to the implementation of the scheme for the benefit of tribal populations.

Government resolutions and circulars issued from 1961 to 1972 are replete with criticisms of failures to implement the gaothan scheme and of excessive delays in accounting to the central government for land acquisitions under the scheme.[6] The likely causes of these failures and delays were resistance by landholders, disinterest on the part of local Revenue Department officials tasked with the difficult and delicate work of acquiring land for the purpose, the absence of any sustained and organized political pressure to implement the schemes and the lack of detailed and coherent instructions for implementation. These constraints

---

[6] Resolution No. LND/3960/ 20698-A Revenue Department Bombay, 9th June, 1961; Resolution No. LNA (I) 3772. Commissioner's Office, Bombay, 1st December, 1965; Resolution No. LND.1070/16968-Q Revenue and Forests Department, 22nd September, 1970; Resolution No. LND.1070/187581-C Revenue and Forests Department, 27th February, 1971; No.GB/GTN/WS/VIII/2184. Collector's Office Kolaba Alibag, 19th September, 1972.

were compounded in situations involving tribal groups, for whom extra administrative work was needed to apply and account for central government financing of the scheme.

While implementation of the gaothan scheme proceeded slowly in different parts of the state, the Katkari seem to have suffered from systematic exclusion, an effect evident from Revenue Department correspondence of the time.. For example, Bharje village, a non-tribal revenue village in Sudhagad taluka, was permitted to extend its gaothan in 1973 .[7] The government acquired the land from a *khot* (landlord) under the Land Acquisition Act, 1894, and provided compensation. The legal land deed (7/12 extract) states that the land was transferred to the village. However, the gaothan was not extended to include various longstanding Katkari hamlets located around Bharje village. Officials did not actively investigate and survey the situation of landownership for these hamlets, even though the scheme was expressly intended to benefit the most vulnerable populations. The Katkari communities living around Bharje village remain vulnerable to eviction to this day.

In the Panvel division of Raigad district, instructions from the deputy collector issued in 1988 to the tehsildar of Sudhagad taluka directed the latter to allocate a gaothan to several Katkari hamlets in the area.[8] The tehsildar was told to make appropriate changes to the land deeds (7/12 extract) with the approval of the landholder, where possible, or otherwise to use the provisions of adverse possession to transfer the lands to the concerned Katkari communities. A deadline of 5 September 1988 was provided, but the instructions were simply ignored. The lands referred to in the instructions remain in private hands to this day, and the Katkari hamlets do not have a secure village site. In another case, a list of tribal villages in need of a gaothan in Sudhagad, Pen and Karjat talukas was circulated to tehsildars by the deputy collector; the list neglected to mention the Katkari even though they were more numerous than many of the other tribal communities that were listed.

The role of landholders in limiting Katkari access to a village site, despite administrative support through the gaothan extension schemes, came to light through the Previous Responses method used in Narsurwadi, a hamlet in Sudhagad taluka. The story of previous government responses

---

[7] 7/12 extract for Bharje Village, dated February 26, 1973 and authors field notes of interviews with residents. February, 2009.

[8] Correspondence from Mr. Pravin Pardesi, Assistant Collector, Panvel Division, Raigad District, May 12, 1988.

was reconstructed by Bapu Hilam, a Katkari elder who had spearheaded an initiative to secure a village site 30 years earlier. He recounted that a demand for legal title to a village site, occupied at the time by 10 families, was first made in 1955. The land, which was owned privately by a non-tribal farmer in a nearby town, had been settled by the Katkari several decades earlier, but not developed as villagers would have liked. The demand, formulated as a letter to Revenue Department officials, was an attempt to place the problem faced by the village fully in the government domain. Care was taken not to place responsibility on the landholder. It took some five years of persistent requests for a response to their demand, before the government ordered a survey of the land and created a survey number. Opposition by the landholder intensified after the survey and by 1965 the two parties were in open conflict. Hilam, a charismatic person with various connections to the social services agencies of the region, mobilized support from elected representatives who lobbied government officials on behalf of the village. After a 15-year struggle, the conflict was finally resolved in 1970 by allocating land for 10 housing sites (ghartan) and by compensating the landholder for the affected area. In 1975, land deeds were issued, making the Katkari legal owners of the land they had petitioned for 20 years earlier. This result, however, was far short of the original demand for a gaothan. The land allocations were barely enough for the 10 original houses in the village and provided no space for new houses or livestock, backyard gardens and public goods such as a school and community centre. Moreover, after granting the land to the Katkari, the government issued a letter to the applicants stating that the sanction of land for the house sites (ghartan) extinguished all other claims of the community. This meant that claims for a gaothan site were forfeit.

The experience in Narsurwadi reinforces the conclusions by the research team that legal petitions for ghartan are a poor substitute for gaothan petitions, and can create significant barriers to the more meaningful goal of securing a village site. Petitions for housing sites are possible and winnable, but the social dynamics they create can also be highly conflictual. For example, in 2001, Katkari villagers in three or four villages in Pen taluka were encouraged and aided by a non-governmental organization (NGO) to submit individual claims to housing sites under provisions for adverse possession and claims based on the Bombay Tenancy and Agricultural Lands Act, 1948. In all, some 100 individual cases were launched, leading eventually to subdivision through survey for several dozen successful applicants. In one hamlet, however, the confrontation with the landholder had a significant negative effect not only on the people launching the claims but also on other Katkari in the village. The landholder felt that he had not been bothering the Katkari who were living on his land and, out of anger over the legal action, blocked them from taking water at his well and from using the road he had created near the hamlet. While eventually five or so families in this large hamlet received deeds for housing sites, the whole community was negatively affected by the conflict. Non-cooperation between the landholder and the villagers continues to this day.

Administrative Gaps

It is clear from the cases reported in the previous section that local factors involving conflicts with landholders played an important role in the failure of the gaothan extension schemes of the 1960s–1990s to reach the Katkari, despite the high priority they should have received as a PTG from the government. Even the smallest gains in specific villages, such as securing a ghartan, required years, or decades, of persistent effort. Most Katkari communities could not mobilize the economic and political resources needed to sustain these demands in the face of much more powerful landholders. Nor could they wend their way through the myriad of bureaucratic entanglements and active forms of administrative resistance blocking access to a village site. What is most disturbing, however, is that they did not get support for this struggle from the government agency responsible for overseeing the welfare of scheduled tribes in the state.

In the state of Maharashtra, tribal affairs are administered by the Tribal Development Department through Integrated Tribal Development Projects (ITDP) operating in designated Tribal Sub-Plan areas (Scheduled Areas). As in much of India, the ITDP reflects the shift in government policy towards Adivasi populations from an emphasis on welfare to development initiatives, first taken under the Fifth Plan (1974–79) (Xaxa 2003). While the ITDP is a major government project intended to benefit the Adivasi, and a funnel for considerable financial and administrative resources, it failed to help Katkari communities secure village sites at the height of the gaothan extension schemes. The reason for this is that the implementation of the ITDP has still not taken into account the significant resettlement of the Katkari over the previous 60 years. While the ITDP is present in Thane district and in the remoter parts of Raigad district, it does not actively engage with Adivasi communities in parts of these districts where large numbers of Katkari have settled in non-tribal villages. For example, the geographic boundaries of the Additional Tribal Sub-

Plan (A-TSP) for Karjat taluka excludes almost all Katkari hamlets in Karjat, because the people live in non-tribal parts of the taluka. Similarly, there is a Mini-Modified Area Development Approach (Mini-MADA)[9] in Sudhagad, but only seven gram panchayats with a total of nine Katkari hamlets, out of 71 Katkari hamlets in the taluka, are included in the management area. A mini-MADA also exists in Khalapur taluka, but few Katkari communities are included in it because they reside outside of the Scheduled Areas.

This administrative gap along with bureaucratic inflexibility means that most Katkari hamlets do not have the same level of access to support available to Adivasi in designated areas. Programmes for community projects, cooperative society schemes and individual loans are available to serve the multiple needs of tribal groups within the management plan areas. Funds available through the programmes can be used to purchase bullocks, rent loudspeakers for events, provide legal fees to set up cooperative societies, as well as to build roads, create residential schools and community centres, disburse small business loans for stores, carpentry shops and kilns, purchase musical instruments, buy agricultural implements and diesel pumps and pipes for irrigation, provide loans to cover labour costs for converting lands, and to assist with tree planting and the purchase of poultry. While the utility of these programmes for the Adivasi in general (Vaid 1992) and the Katkari in particular (Bokil 2006) has been strongly criticized, they do account for almost all of the funding and administrative attention available to support Adivasi populations in the state. Members of scheduled tribes living outside of the management areas receive very little attention. Thus, while the Katkari are a 'particularly vulnerable tribal group', they do not in fact receive the attention they deserve or the responsiveness required under government policy.

It seems likely that these kinds of gaps account in part for poor implementation of the gaothan extension schemes among Katkari population resettled in non-tribal areas. Today, the gaothan problem is not severe for most Adivasi communities located fully within designated Tribal Sub-Plan areas. For example, a survey by the research team found that all but three out of 32 Thakur and Mahadev Koli communities in Karjat taluka have a secure gaothan, no matter what the size of the village. In two of the insecure communities the land is owned by Thakur

---

[9] The Mini-MADAs are created for gram panchayats with tribal concentrations of more than 5,000 people and less than 10,000. A concentration of more than 10,000 tribals and less than 50 per cent of the total population requires a MADA plan.

residents in the village, and there is no pressure on the population to leave. In the other insecure village the landholder has agreed to transfer the village site to the Thakur community, as part of a broader deal he made to remove unregistered tenants from his adjacent lands. While this does not mean that Thakur and Mahadev Koli communities are necessarily secure elsewhere in the state of Maharashtra, at least in Karjat taluka the problem is rare. By contrast, fully two-thirds of Katkari communities in Karjat taluka are without a gaothan. As documented earlier, the same high level of insecurity applies to Katkari in Khalapur and Sudhagad talukas.

Other factors that affect the status of particular Adivasi communities in the broader society are also certainly at play. Many members of the Thakur and Mahadev Koli own agricultural land, and are engaged in agriculture on lands surrounding their village site. They are not normally engaged in migratory livelihoods like brick making. Both communities are also well organized and politically strong. Governments cannot ignore them and landholders would not dare to evict them, even in cases where the village site is located on private land. These communities have relatively high literacy rates and tend to be well informed of their rights and legal protections. By contrast, the Katkari are mainly non-literate and largely unaware of their rights. They are not organized politically and have few means of making their claims collectively or forcefully. Furthermore, they have no allies to speak of. To non-tribals and government officials, they appear to be migrants and vagabonds rather than sedentary agriculturalists or established wage workers. They are considered socially inferior to virtually all other communities in the region, and are typically treated with active prejudice. As a result, the Katkari were largely excluded from the gaothan extension schemes of 1961–1991, and remain vulnerable to this day. It was not until early in the new millennium, with the rapid rise of a real-estate boom in Greater Mumbai, that the implications of this oversight landed on the backs of the Katkari, turning their general situation of extreme poverty into a crisis of considerable proportions.

Engaging the Revenue Department

Using the Right to Information Act, the research team reviewed documents that showed the government's failure to implement its own policies with respect to gaothan sites and to fulfil its duty and ethical responsibility to the Katkari. Information on the gaothan extension schemes obtained in this way proved useful to Katkari hamlets that brought forward successful applications in the gram sabha, and to communities that had failed to do so. Resolutions from the gram panchayat in support of a Katkari gaothan were approved in Siddheshwar for Siddheshwarwadi and Wavloliwadi, as well as in Adulshe, the revenue village connected to Vakanwadi. Gaothan action committees in each of these Katkari hamlets followed up this success by submitting a letter to the corresponding tehsildar in the Revenue Department, along with the resolution from the gram panchayat and supporting documents such as hand maps and proofs of residence that they had collected and prepared in the preceding months. The letter to the tehsildar from the gaothan action committee in Siddheshwarwadi is reproduced below.

Date: 11 July 2006

To: The Tehsildar
Tal. Sudhagad
District Raigad

Subject: Sanction of legal gaothan to a Katkari hamlet that has been in existence for several generations ...

Applicants: Gaothan Action Committee, Siddheshwarwadi, Post Siddheshwar, Taluka Sudhagad, District Raigad

Dear Sir,

We, the 116 Katkari families of Siddheshwarwadi village, kindly appeal to you that:
    We have been staying in Siddheshwarwadi village for several generations. The land belongs to three non-tribal individuals. We have to face several difficulties since our village does not have a gaothan and the land is privately owned. For instance, the land owner takes objection when we try to repair our old houses and does not give us permission to build new houses for the families of our married children. We cannot build a house under the Indira Awas Yojana without permission from the land owner. We can neither keep any livestock (cows or goats) and nor can we grow vegetables in a kitchen garden since we do not have any open space around our houses. We cannot even build a small cattle shed! Our village does not have a connecting road from the main road. Most importantly, there is no Anganwadi or Primary School in our village

due to the insecure gaothan. It is an irony that nearly 30 children from our village go to the Primary School in the nearby Pui village (about 1 Km away) while only 1-2 children from Pui village are enrolled in that school! How is it that a school has been set up in a village from where only 1-2 students go to school? And how is it that a village with 15 families has been given a Primary School while our village with 116 families does not have a school?

We have always been subsisting on the charity of the private landholder. We have to work for the landholder at any time he calls us and on wages that he offers. We have to often tolerate his ill behaviour and ill treatment.

We are the original inhabitants of this land. The government has notified our community as a 'Primitive Tribal Group'. Outsiders who have come and settled on this land much later have been given villages with all civic amenities and legal gaothans. We are giving the examples of Pui and Bharja villages. Pui village came into being on the present land about 50 years ago (1956). There are only 15 families in Pui. But still Pui village has been sanctioned a legal gaothan and has been given civic facilities like a tar road, well, hand pump, Primary School, etc.

The non-tribal villages thus have all civic amenities and security of tenure. How much more time should we live in an atmosphere of insecurity and rootlessness? Why the injustice and double standards? Is it because we are *Katkari?*

Tomorrow, if the landholder decides to sell the land and evict us from the village, where should we go? And what will happen to our deities? Our deities live with us in the village.[10] They take care of our families and children. Who will look after us if we move to a new place?

Our livelihoods too are insecure because of the insecurity of tenure. We have to work as bonded labour on brick and charcoal units in far away places. How long should we continue to suffer?

Our village is known by the name of the Revenue Village – Siddheshwar. Our village is thus an integral part of Siddheshwar village. We have attached a Resolution passed in the Siddheshwar Gram Panchayat for sanction of gaothan to Siddheshwarwadi. We request you to kindly consider extension of legal gaothan for our village.

---

[10] Sax (2010) explores how gods and other entities in the central Himalayas of north India inform village actions, taking on what he considers a form of agency. While we were unable to explore this idea with the Katkari, deities and the buried elders of the Katkari figured periodically in discussions and may have contributed to their resolve to stay in the hamlet.

Yours truly,
Members, Gaothan Hakk Kruti Samiti (Gaothan Action Committee)
1. Krishna Ganpat Waghmare
2. Baban Tulshiram Waghmare
3. Shripat Shravan Pawar
4. Nathuram Navsha Waghmare
5. Daji Chandar Pawar
6. Ms. Kusum Sakharam Pawar
7. Ms. Suvarna Bapu Pawar

This is a passionate statement of the constraints and abuses the hamlet has suffered for decades, and a reminder of the government's legal responsibilities. It is also an appeal to the ethical dimensions of the problem – the need for fair treatment of all communities and the redress of an injustice causing considerable suffering. This and the other submissions were major accomplishments for the communities involved, and a source of inspiration for hamlets that had not been successful in the gram sabha.

The sudden and favourable resolution of the conflict in Nadodewadi, with distribution of land titles to 47 families in the hamlet, motivated the gaothan action committees in other hamlets to engage directly with government officials in the Revenue Department. Over a period of several months, from late 2006 to early 2007, the various committees in all 10 study hamlets submitted their applications for a gaothan directly to the Revenue Department, with or without the endorsement of the gram panchayat. People in the hamlets said that by submitting their petition directly to the government, they didn't feel they were filing a legal case against a landholder, but rather demanding their rights from the government. As the committees had already compiled the necessary documents, applications for all of the remaining hamlets involved initially in the inquiry were easily prepared and submitted to the tehsildars at the taluka level in Karjat, Khalapur and Sudhagad and to the Raigad district collector at Alibaug. These actions were followed several months later by repeat visits from members of the gaothan action committees, making use of Democracy Day and other opportunities to directly address the officials. This was done discreetly, without drawing attention to their actions at the local level or making reference to specific landholders.

The research team reinforced the Katkari initiative by providing the collector and tehsildars with a list and map showing the location of 212 Katkari villages in the three talukas that did not have a sanctioned gaothan

(Figure 1.1). This information had been collected through the initial survey of Katkari villages in the three talukas and through the collection of the geographic coordinates of the hamlets using a hand-held geographic positioning device.[11] We also explained to officials how the situation had come about, noting that many Katkari communities were established decades ago when people migrated to the plains in search of employment, often with the active support of landholders who needed their labour. Details of previous responses to the gaothan problem, including copies of government resolutions on the gaothan extension schemes and procedures, were also shared with the officials, many of whom were not familiar with the schemes. This information demonstrated not only the scope of the problem but also provided specific evidence and policy references pointing to a solution that was possible and fully within the mandate of the Revenue Department.

These actions placed the issue of gaothan insecurity on the radar screen of government officials responsible for the three talukas, prompting them to inquire at higher levels. As discussed later, the process took almost a year to run its course and generated a mostly bureaucratic and completely unsatisfactory response.

Gaps and Conflicts

The initial efforts of the gaothan action committees and the research team to engage government officials, in particular the Revenue Department, were designed to both inform and pressure. This strategy emerged against the background of Katkari reflection on past experiences with government officials and their own analysis of the reasons for the neglect of their concerns.

One of the hamlets where the engagement strategy emerged was Wavloliwadi in Sudhagad taluka. People there expressed their ongoing concern about their insecurity and the distress they felt over the lack of interest shown by government officials and elected representatives in resolving the gaothan problem. They wanted to develop a strategy that might overcome the limitations of the past. The research team responded

---

[11] The research team would like to acknowledge the assistance of students in the Department of Geography at Carleton University who prepared the database and maps from coordinates provided to them, and to Amos Hayes of Carleton University for setting up an online map of Katkari hamlets: http://atlas.gcrc.carleton.ca/katkari/ (accessed on 12 February 2012).

to this demand by facilitating an assessment using the gaps and conflicts method.[12] This analytic tool provides a way to connect each cause of a problem to the kind of issue it represents, including the power of the various parties, their gains and losses (interests), the moral values they hold and the information and communication means at their disposal. It also distinguishes causes that are *gaps* (illustrating a lack of power, interests, values or information) from causes that are *conflicts* (involving a struggle over power, interests, values or information). The core problem, in this case ongoing government neglect of the gaothan issue, is mapped out by examining each cause through these lenses.

The analysis in Wavloliwadi helped participants separate the reasons for government neglect of the gaothan, and to bring each reason more sharply into focus (Table 4.1). Participants identified five reasons why government officials continued to neglect the gaothan problem and classified each in relation to various parameters introduced by the research team. The five reasons were:

1. Government officials and elected representatives gained from supporting the wealthy.
2. Katkari lacked resources to influence government officials.
3. Government officials believed the landholder was the rightful owner.
4. Katkari did not make demands on officials because they did not know what rights they had.
5. Elected representatives did not have an understanding of the scope and seriousness of the gaothan problem.

The structuring and ranking of the reasons for government neglect were strongly connected by participants to the economic wealth of the landholder, and more generally to the use of money and patronage to secure advantages from government officials. They argued that the officials favour the wealthy because they gain economically and politically from them. Officials will not do anything that might undermine these interests. Also, they have nothing to gain from a very poor community like the Katkari. Participants classified aspects of this situation as a conflict of interests. They recognized that officials ignored the gaothan issue so they may realize gains and avoid trouble from the landholder. These interests, and the lack of any economic or political gain from helping the Katkari, override the officials' obligation to act impartially.

---

[12] For detailed instructions and adaptations of the gaps and conflicts method, see Tools and Software at www.participatoryactionresearch.net.

Table 4.1: Mapping of the reasons why officials neglect Katkari demands for a gaothan, Wavloliwadi

Type of Issue	*Gaps*	*Conflicts*	*Ranking*
POWER	Katkari lack resources to influence officials.		2
INTERESTS		Officials gain from supporting the wealthy.	1
VALUES		Officials believe the landholder is the rightful owner.	4
INFORMATION/ COMMUNICATION	Katkari do not make demands on officials. Elected representatives do not understand the scope and impact of the problem.		3

Source: Author's field notes, February 2007, Vavloliwadi.

The Katkari also lack the power to influence government officials, a reason that participants classified as a power gap. Despite efforts by the gaothan action committee, organization in the hamlet is weak and the Katkari have no economic or political resources with which to press for their rights. Nor do they have the coercive power of landholders able to hire goons to intimidate and impose their will. Participants ranked this issue as second in weight among the issues contributing to government neglect of Katkari demands. Taken together, the top two reasons for neglect and related explanations reflect the emphasis participants placed on the economic forces at play defining their inferior position in society. This is consistent with Heredia's and Srivastava's observation (1994, 106, 113) that the Katkari are by their own account the poorest of communities and therefore have no scope to oppose or win against wealthier communities.

Information and communication gaps, both within the Katkari community and among elected officials, also contribute to neglect. Participants recognized their own failure to communicate or express their demands to both government officials and elected representatives and related this gap to their limited knowledge of the legal provisions pertaining to household land and village land. This makes it easier for government officials to ignore them. Elected representatives also lack legal knowledge and do not have any understanding of the enormity or seriousness of the problem. Consequently, they do not force government officials to act. Participants related these information and communication gaps back to the economic basis of neglect. Officials make no effort to understand the problem in a proper perspective because there is no economic gain for them. As a result, elected representatives and government officials do not act as they should. These issues were clumped together by participants as information and communication gaps and given a combined ranking of third among the issues at play.

Finally, participants felt that officials genuinely believed that the landholder was the rightful owner, and that the Katkari had no moral or legal claim to the land. After considerable discussion, participants classified this reason for neglect as a conflict or struggle over values – opposing values regarding the moral worth of the Katkari, which others use to judge the Katkari claims. They felt that government officials take a biased view against the Katkari on all matters because they consider the Katkari vagabonds and drunkards. Nonetheless, they gave these reasons the lowest rating because, in their view, the bias against them is more on account of the political and economic benefits officials gain than any sense of right or wrong.

Concluding discussions of the results of the analysis focused on the one area where participants felt they had some control and ability to act independently: the information and communication gap.

Scaling Up the Gaothan Demand

Assessments in Katkari communities regarding the reasons for government neglect of their concerns helped inform decisions by gaothan action committees and the research team on what to do next. The committees resolved to make their demands known using whatever resources were available to them. This initially took the form of applying directly to tehsildars in the corresponding talukas. The research team, with support from the committees, also resolved to work on the power gap by connecting Katkari communities in similar situations to each other, thereby enhancing the collective power of the Katkari to inform and communicate the scope and impact of the gaothan problem. How to scale up the gaothan demand became the focus for new actions emerging from the analysis and from the certainty that the government response would not be prompt.

The research team began to interact with an increasing number of Katkari communities in the three talukas. This was a conscious communication and information-sharing strategy while waiting for formal government responses. It was also a reaction to new and urgent developments. New incidents of enclosure and threats of eviction in Khalapur taluka came to the attention of the research team in 2007 and 2008, incidents driven by fresh economic development projects and spiking land prices. The sanction of special economic zones, government announcements regarding a new international airport near Panvel, the widening of the Mumbai–Pune Highway and other developments were converting the industrial corridor in Khalapur into a 'hot spot' of heightened eviction risk. Hamlets were suddenly enclosed with barbed wire and threatened with eviction, often following the sale of land to speculators.

News of these incidents spread very quickly among Katkari communities throughout the region. Suddenly, every community without a gaothan felt insecure. This swept aside the indifference the research team had initially encountered in Katkari hamlets where enclosure and eviction were not imminent. Many Katkari hamlets contacted members of the research team to request information about housing rights and help with organizing resistance. We responded to this demand by organizing 'cluster-level' meetings every two months or so. This meant bringing together Katkari from six to eight neighbouring hamlets to discuss the gaothan issue and any new developments. In these meetings, Katkari from hamlets involved in the initial study shared their experiences and strategies with others. Members of the research team provided facts about the legal issues involved, and explained the rights of communities with longstanding possession of village and housing lands. Our goal was to share the information we had collected through the inquiry thus far, confident that it would be useful to other hamlets confronted and enclosed by landholders. Much to our surprise, the informal meetings with Katkari in their hamlets were very easy to organize and discussions were very focused. People quickly grasped the situation and decided on immediate actions within their control, including the formation of gaothan action committees and the mobilization of people to obtain the basic documents needed to prove residence and support their claims.

Over a period of 18 months, from early 2008 to late 2009, the 'cluster-level' meetings engaged people from more than 100 Katkari hamlets. Awareness of the gaothan issue became widespread in virtually all of the 313 Katkari communities in the three talukas, broadcast through word of mouth by Katkari participating in the cluster-level meetings. Many communities chose to form gaothan action committees to work on

securing a village site. With help from the research team and Katkari in
the committees, families in these hamlets obtained basic documents such
as house tax receipts, ration cards, caste certificates and death certificates.
More than 70 formal applications for a gaothan were prepared and
submitted to the corresponding tehsildar by the committees. Information
on government schemes was shared during the various information
sessions, and, when requested, the research team helped to prepare and
submit applications for these schemes. Many committees also got into
the practice of independently following up on the submitted applications
directly in government offices, making use of Democracy Day and other
trips to government offices to inquire after their gaothan claims and
proposals.

By scaling up awareness about the gaothan problem in Katkari
communities throughout the region, the cluster-level meetings, in turn,
brought periodic and persistent pressure to bear on the Revenue
Department. After more than a year, however, the collectors in each
area came back with the same response, stating that the gaothan extension
schemes were no longer in force and that they therefore did not have
the authority and resources to acquire land for a gaothan extension. They
said that it was impossible for them to act because they first needed new
instructions from the government and financial allocations to acquire land.
They agreed to accept the applications from the Katkari hamlets, and to
keep these on file until new directions were given to them regarding a
renewed extension scheme.

The response from the collectors was disheartening. On the one hand,
it reflected a gap in the powers of the Revenue Department: control
over the resources needed to act on the problem is held by political
leaders, not the bureaucracy per se. On the other hand, it also reflected
the conflict of interests and conflict over values pointed to by the Katkari
assessment of government neglect. It echoed as well the long history of
gaothan extension schemes revealed in documents collected through
the Right to Information Act. Even when the resources were available
under previous gaothan extension schemes, the Katkari were largely
bypassed by these schemes. Why would it be any different now? The
official response left the Katkari as vulnerable as ever, and took the
situation to a new level. Not only did the Katkari need to prove the
validity of their claims to a village site, they also had to mobilize the
political support needed to reactivate the gaothan extension scheme and
sustain political pressure on the responsible officials. This was a formidable
task indeed.

Katkari in some communities responded to this bureaucratic limbo with direct action. First in Ambewadi (April 2007), then in Nadodewadi (September 2007) and finally in Asra Katkarwadi (February 2008), Katkari families removed the fencing around their hamlets. The fences were a direct threat to them, and Katkari felt that if the fences were left untouched, families would inevitably face eviction before any action could be taken by the Revenue Department. In these cases, the landholders were not members of the revenue village or living nearby, so people felt less intimidated compared to Katkari in villages such as Malegavwadi, where the religious trust was located next door. Other hamlets, such as Koshane Katkarwadi, also began to take a more militant stance to protect themselves from eviction, encouraged by the actions taken by community members in other hamlets. It was in Chinchavli Gohe Katkarwadi, however, that the tables suddenly turned in favour of the Katkari, opening up an entirely new strategy that would stop active evictions throughout the region. This was a turning point for the inquiry, launching a new set of inquiries and related lines of action aimed at addressing persistent government neglect.

The Seeds of Legal Action

Chinchavli Gohe Katkarwadi is a Katkari community located close to the Mumbai–Pune Express Highway in Khalapur taluka. Katkari had lived there since the 1980s, growing to a hamlet of 32 families. In 2008 the landholder, a non-tribal farmer from the neighbouring Chinchavli Gohe village, who for years had made steady use of Katkari labour on his farm, sold the property to a land speculator based in Mumbai. This severed the relationship of the Katkari to their original employer, although by this time many Katkari families in the hamlet were also migrating annually to brick kilns.

The new landholder's first act was to force three Katkari families with houses separate from the main section of the hamlet to remove their homes and rebuild closer to the other houses. The goal was to reduce the total occupied area. Once this was done, the landholder enclosed the community tightly with a barbed wire fence. He then told the Katkari that they should leave altogether because he was about to sell the land to a nearby plastics manufacturing company that would be building a factory on the land. He also said that they should not extend their houses or encroach on the fencing.

The actions of the land speculator panicked the people in Chinchavli Gohe Katkarwadi and prompted them to request a meeting with the research team to discuss the problem and what could be done about it. Some 11 men and three women gathered outside the home of one of the residents for an entire afternoon. As the threat of eviction was already evident to those involved, the research team opted to use the force field method rather than the problem tree method to conduct the initial assessment. Force field offered an opportunity to move immediately from the identification of factors contributing to the problem to an assessment of ways to act on those factors by strengthening or reducing the forces at play. Participants listed the factors that were contributing to the escalating threat of eviction, and rated them on a scale of 1 (weaker) to 5 (stronger) to show their relative weight in the situation.

Participants in the assessment said that the landholder had title to the land and therefore could count on the support of authorities, and possibly goons, to dispose of his land when and as he wished. They also noted that a large company located close to the village wanted to buy the land. They gave these two factors a lot of weight as driving the threat of eviction (5 and 4, respectively). Another stronger factor (level 4) contributing to the threat of eviction that participants identified was their own lack of detailed knowledge about their rights. While they had some sense that they were entitled to live there, most people in the hamlet were quite unsure of themselves. This, they said, made it easier for the landowner to confuse them and pressure them into leaving. Furthermore, they recognized that they had not registered their houses with the gram panchayat of the neighbouring revenue village even though they had lived there for decades. This made it difficult to provide authorities with proof of residence, a factor they gave a rating of 3. They also lamented that there was no gauki or other traditional authority in their hamlet that could organize collective resistance to eviction. Nor did they have contact with government officials of the ITDP or Revenue Department, and therefore could not expect any help from them. They gave both these factors a score of 2, noting that the lack of support from traditional and official sources would leave them on their own, and therefore make them more vulnerable to eviction. Relatively speaking, however, these two factors were considered of less weight compared to the others.

Discussion of counteracting forces focused initially on the Katkari's ongoing physical possession of the land. At first they gave this factor a rating of 4, but then reduced it to 3 when someone pointed out that the landholder had already managed to move three houses from their original locations. Possession was clearly not sufficient to stop a motivated landholder with legal title. They recognized that people in the village were now fully aware of the dangers of an insecure gaothan and highly motivated to do something about it. They were not convinced, however, that this resolve would carry much weight if they were to face an aggressive campaign to dislodge them. They gave this factor the relatively low rating of 2 as a counteracting force. The emergence of youth leadership in the village was identified as a hopeful sign because it partly counteracted the lack of organization in the village and the limited knowledge of rights held by most residents. Nevertheless, they gave this factor a score of only 2, as the youth were often engaged in industrial work and some saw the company as a potential employer. Finally, the research team pointed out that there were legal options available to them, including the possibility of filing a police case against the landholder under the Prevention of Atrocities Act. Participants gave this factor a score of 2, noting that the police were often antagonistic to their situation and might choose to beat them instead of helping them.

The group concluded, during discussions of the consolidated picture of the forces at play (Figure 4.1), that counteracting forces were quite weak compared to the driving forces, and that it would be an uphill task to safeguard the rights of the Katkari families in Chinchavli Gohe Katkarwadi. Nevertheless, the analysis gave the group confidence that they were right to oppose eviction, and that they would be better off if they were to work together as a village instead of facing the landholder as individual families. They also asked the research team to continue to meet with them and provide information they could use to strengthen their position. The seed for positive action was sown, reflecting a clearer understanding of the forces creating the problem and the opportunities they could use to address the issue.

During the months that followed the first meeting with Katkari in Chinchavli Gohe Katkarwadi, members of the research team met periodically with the newly formed gaothan action committee to discuss any changes in the situation and actions they had decided to take. Primary among these was that Katkari houses were to be registered in the gram panchayat, an action organized by youth in the village and completed in a short period of time (see Figure 4.1). The youth also started to collect copies of legal documents such as caste certificates and ration cards needed to advance their claims. The confidence of Katkari families

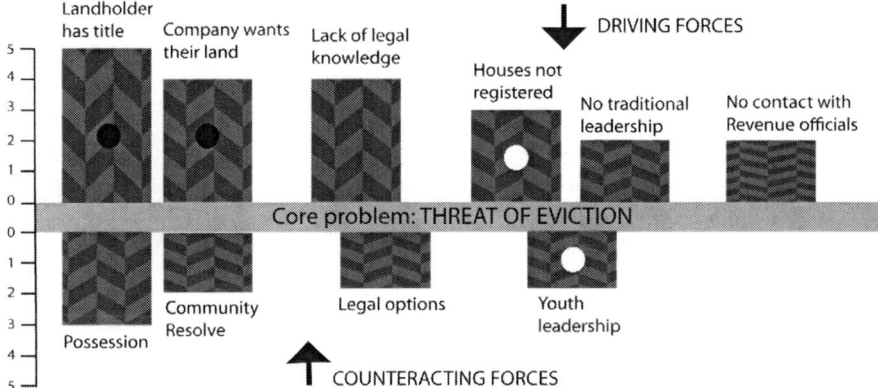

Figure 4.1: Force field of factors contributing to and counteracting the threat of eviction in Chinchavli Gohe Katkarwadi

Source: Author's field notes, January 2009, Chinchavali Gohe Katkarwadi.

Note: The figure shows the relative weight of factors on a scale of 0 to 5, factors over which the Katkari had no control (black dots), and factors they decided to work on, at least to start with (white dots). Columns without color dots are factors over which control is neither strong nor weak.

in the hamlet was much enhanced by these initial accomplishments, prompting them to submit a petition to the tehsildar for legal gaothan land.

After careful consideration, they also decided to follow up on the option of filing a police case against the landholder for forcing them to shift three houses and for erecting a barbed wire fence around the remaining village. This idea, first presented to them by the research team as an option, had initially been rejected based on fear of the landholder and the police. The change that led to filing charges was inspired by news about direct action taken in other hamlets where fencing had been torn down. People in Chinchavli Gohe Katkarwadi felt that eviction was imminent and decided they needed to act to protect themselves.

Pursuing Legal Countermeasures

The research team had always been aware of the possibility of bringing the Scheduled Castes and Scheduled Tribes (Prevention of Atrocities) Act, 1989, to bear on the situation as a defence against the threat of eviction. It was risky, however, for the Katkari. The risk was that they might experience a backlash from groups angered over the use of the act in this way. Backlashes of this nature had occurred in other parts of India, and were a risk in Maharashtra as well. Furthermore, the act was not normally applied in Maharashtra to deal with encroachment on land even though this was possible under the act. How officials in Khalapur would respond to a case involving land not formally owned by the Katkari was very uncertain, and therefore was a legal option that had to be treated with great caution.

The Prevention of Atrocities Act (PoA) was enacted by the Parliament of India in 1989 to reinforce articles of the Constitution of India protecting members of scheduled castes and scheduled tribes from extreme forms of humiliation, exploitation and dispossession rooted in the historical practice of untouchability and caste hierarchy. The act defines as atrocities a specific set of offences involving the use of force, intimidation, public humiliation, obstruction and other acts aimed at asserting caste-based dominance or dispossessing members of scheduled castes and scheduled tribes of their liberty or the material basis of their livelihood and well-being. Naval (2004, 76) characterizes these offences as 'hate crime or bias crime because the offender intentionally selects the person against whom the crime is committed or selects the property, which is damaged or is otherwise affected by the crime, on the basis of his caste'.

The legislation emerged in response to persistent atrocities against scheduled castes and scheduled tribes, and recognized that 'existing laws like the Protection of Civil Rights Act, 1955 and the normal provisions of the Indian Penal Code have been found inadequate to check these crimes' (Naval 2004, 75). Systematic and systemic prejudice against people born into the caste of Dalits, practised for centuries, continues unabated to the present day, expressed in a multiplicity of atrocities including rape, trafficking of children for the purpose of prostitution, mass murder, beatings and numerous acts of humiliation and harassment. The National Campaign on Dalit Human Rights reports that, on average, 27 atrocities against Dalits are committed in India every day. Examples validated by various sources include the massacre of 28 Dalits in Chunder (Guntoor district of Andhra Pradesh), the beheading of four Dalits working at a brick kiln in Indraruk village in rural Kanpur and the rape of a scheduled caste woman by a legislator in Bihar (ibid., 26). Kapoor (2007) reports on 1,266 human rights violations against Dalit women in a single taluka in Orissa between 1999 and 2003, most of which involved the kidnapping of girls and rape. Jayakumar (2006) also reports an increase in the incidence of atrocities affecting scheduled castes. Naval (2004, 27), a credible authority on the subject, notes that formal cases such as these 'are a drop in the ocean reminding us about the gravity of the problem'.

Atrocities of this kind are deeply rooted in the socio-economic conditions of scheduled castes and scheduled tribes. While untouchability is the human face of the atrocities, according to Naval (2004, 25), most 'are the direct outcome of agrarian tensions, ineffective implementation of the PoA Act, the Minimum Wages Act, rural indebtedness, the practice of bonded labour and half-hearted implementation of various development measures like allotment of surplus Ceiling land to SCs'. He also argues that the incidence of these crimes has increased steadily in the last decade as dominant castes have started to take retaliatory measures against scheduled castes and scheduled tribes who assert their constitutional rights to reserved electoral positions and government jobs.

Some 10,823 cases of crimes against scheduled castes and schedules tribes were filed in Maharashtra between 1987 and 1996, mostly in rural areas (Koli 2008). Koli, himself a police inspector, states that these cases mostly involved physical violence and acts of humiliation against individuals, most of whom were members of scheduled castes such as the Mahar. The crimes ranged from murder, rape and robbery to kidnapping and arson. No mention is made at all in his detailed report to crimes related to land issues. Based on discussions with police in Raigad district from 1999, when ADS first became involved in work on Adivasi land rights, we concluded that most officers were not well versed in the workings of the PoA Act and generally believed that the PoA was relevant only in cases of physical violence and humiliation. They also raised concerns about potential abuses of the act and suggested that a severe backlash might result from trivial or unjustified uses of what is a very punitive legal measure. There seemed to be little interest in using the act to deal with cases of encroachment on land.

The practice regarding use of the PoA in situations involving encroachment on land in Maharashtra began to change in 2003 when one of the research team (Bansi Ghedve) was advocating for the ceiling lands of Katkari families in Karjat taluka. Ceiling lands are areas acquired under the Maharashtra Agricultural Land (Ceiling on Holdings) Act, 1961, from individuals with holdings greater than the legislated legal limit. Redistribution of these 'surplus' lands among landless Katkari families had occurred on paper (deeds had been issued), but the new Katkari owners did not know the exact location of their lands and so had never occupied them. This uncertainty had been going on in the taluka for almost 35 years, during which time the original owners often used the lands.

Bansi helped the concerned Katkari families draft a letter to the tehsildar and surveyor concerning this oversight and requesting a survey. After many delays and attempts to shift responsibility for the survey from one party to another, a query into the case by a member of the legislative assembly prompted the appointment of an additional deputy collector to probe into the issue and to find a solution. He was authorized to undertake a survey of all the ceiling lands in the taluka that had been allocated to the Katkari, and to ensure that the lands were properly subdivided and physical possession granted to the rightful landholders. The process took two years to complete, but in the end some 72 families were able to get about 370 acres of ceiling lands. Our review of the documentation suggests that this resolved all pending cases of Katkari ceiling lands in the taluka.

While this process unfolded, two situations of encroachment on ceiling land were identified and linked to the PoA Act. In one case, a male business owner in Mumbai had purchased land from an agent to build a farm house retreat, without knowing that it was on ceiling land. In another case, a film studio had purchased a very large plot of land and built several large buildings before finding out that part of it was ceiling land. The additional deputy collector issued notices to the parties involved of potential charges of encroachment under the PoA Act, and called on them to explain themselves before a tehsildar acting as a judge on behalf of the government.

When the film studio's case was heard, lawyers for the studio argued that the encroachment was the government's fault because it had not indicated where the Katkari land was located in the first place. They said that the ceiling lands of the Katkari were only part of a much larger parcel of land they had purchased, and that they had unknowingly and unintentionally encroached on the land due to the government's incomplete work. The presiding tehsildar accepted this argument and decided not to proceed with atrocity charges against the studio or the Mumbai business owner, who used the same argument. As part of the settlement, the tehsildar ordered the Survey Department to allocate an undeveloped and alternative plot to the Katkari from within the larger plot. By mutual agreement, the studio and the Mumbai business owners kept their bungalows and wells and the Katkari gained possession of their complete allotment of ceiling lands. While the alternative land was less suitable for agriculture and farther from a river than their initial property had been, for the Katkari this was a big victory. They now had physical possession of land granted to them some 35 years earlier!

Another case of encroachment on tribal land occurred in Karjat taluka a few years later. This both clarified and added weight to the argument that encroachment on tribal land was an atrocity case and should be seen as such by Revenue Department officials and the police. The situation began when a young business owner (male) from Mumbai arranged to purchase 45 acres of land from unregistered tenants near Jambhulwadi in Karjat taluka. While the tenants, most of whom were Thakur, had occupied and used the land for agriculture, it had remained unregistered because of the considerable difficulties the Adivasi face when trying to get clear title to land. When approached by the business owner, the tenants decided to accept sums of Rs 5,000 to Rs 10,000 each, and extinguish their claims to the land. Soon after the purchase, the new owner fenced the land. He included in his parcel, however, an acre or so of land owned outright by an elderly Thakur man, who happened to be the father-in-law of a member of the research team. The Thakur man had received title and possession of slightly more than 4 acres of ceiling land in 1976 and had been working several paddy fields and upland areas for decades.

When the Thakur farmer asked the business owner to move the fence, he was severely beaten. The assault was attributed to family members of some of the Thakur tenants that the business owner had paid and whose land claims had been extinguished. This prompted the man's family to file a case of physical assault against them at the local police station. The case was accepted by the police, but they took no action to investigate the abuse or the encroachment that had prompted it. After a few months, the man's family tried to file a case of land encroachment under the PoA Act, noting that two of the specific offences identified in the act deal with encroachment on land.[13] Unaware of the details of the act, the police refused to file a first information report (FIR), saying that the case was a land issue and therefore subject to civil court, not the Criminal Code covered by the PoA Act.

While most such cases would have ended in a failure to file the FIR – an important first step in any legal process in India – the elderly

---

[13] The pertinent offences described in the act are: '(iv) wrongfully occupies or cultivates any land owned by, or allotted to, or notified by any competent authority to be allotted to, a member of a Scheduled Caste or a Scheduled Tribe or gets the land allotted to him transferred; (v) wrongfully dispossesses a member of a Scheduled Caste or a Scheduled Tribe from his land or premises or interferes with the enjoyment of his rights over any land, premises or water.'

Thakur man decided to pursue it further. He took the case to the deputy superintendent of police (DSP), drawing attention to the relevant features of the PoA Act and insisting that the report be filed. The DSP agreed and instructed local police to accept the case. In the meantime, the business owner had also been busy, using his contacts in Mumbai to ask the Home Ministry responsible for the police to reject the case. He argued that such a case brought severe penalties far beyond what was warranted. As a result of his efforts, the ministry advised the DSP to not file the case in haste but rather to investigate carefully first.

This chain of events led to the commissioning of an 'urgent government survey', paid for by the business owner. While attempts were made to bribe the government surveyor to find in favour of the businessman, in the end the government survey determined that more than an acre of land had indeed been encroached upon. This result prompted the police to agree that it was an acceptable case under the PoA Act. They still delayed filing the case, however, opting instead to arrange for an affidavit signed by the business owner saying that his original surveyor had made a mistake and that he had encroached unintentionally. Given the very severe nature of penalties under the PoA, the businessman was now desperately trying to step back from the situation altogether. He removed the fence and the police set the case aside. However, some months later, the police did file the case and put the business owner and his wife in jail for some days. This about-face seems to be due to the business owner's unwise decision not to honour bribes that he had offered the police to set the case aside. Eventually, the case was reviewed by a judge who ruled that the encroachment had been in error due to an improper survey and that the problem had been corrected in any case. The case was closed and no further action was taken by either party.

These cases of encroachment on land, while all settled in favour of the Adivasi involved, reflect common complaints that the PoA Act suffers from many failures in enforcement. While a potentially powerful counter to caste-based atrocities, nearly one-quarter of government officials charged with enforcing the act are unaware of its existence (Human Rights Features 2003). Unwillingness on the part of the police to file an FIR is a particularly troublesome stumbling block. And even when the police are aware of the scope of the act, 'upper caste policemen are reluctant to file cases against fellow caste-members because of the severity of the penalties imposed by the Act; most offenses are non-bailable and carry minimum punishments of five years imprisonment' (ibid.). Furthermore, very few states in India have actually created the separate special courts mandated under the act to speed up the legal process and ensure the timely hearing of cases. Swagat and Nirupama (2008, 169) note that most states 'have added the responsibility of trying the cases under this legislation on an already existing Court of Session'. This means that cases do not receive the special attention called for by the legislation. Follow-through is also weak: out of 147,000 PoA cases pending in the courts in 1998, only 31,011 were brought to trial and only 5.4 per cent of these resulted in a conviction. Of the total cases filed in 2002, only 22 per cent were brought to trial and of these only 2 per cent ended in conviction. This compares to conviction rates in cases tried under the Indian Penal Code of 39 per cent in 1999 and 42 per cent in 2000. Koli (2008) argues that the reason many cases end in acquittal is because there are so many gaps in the filing of the FIR. He notes that 'the Police Officers do not undertake expeditious and flawless investigation. Nor do they have an interest to do so' (ibid., 49).

The research team's experience of filing a police case under the PoA Act was put to good use when the village of Chinchavli Gohe Katkarwadi decided to protect itself from eviction. They filed a police case against the landholder for forcing them to shift three houses and for erecting a barbed wire fence around the remaining village, making reference to the appropriate clauses of the Scheduled Caste and Scheduled Tribe (Prevention of Atrocities) Act, 1989. In response to the written complaint, the DSP at the station referred the matter to the tehsildar, asking him to sort out the problem. The tehsildar, in turn, asked the talathi[14] and the circle inspector to determine the details of the case. Once this was done, the DSP and the tehsildar summoned the landholder and warned him not to fence the village or to evict the Katkari families. They told him that a case would be filed against him under the PoA if he did not take corrective action. The landowner was clearly frightened by this threat and immediately agreed to leave the hamlet alone. Katkari families in turn dismantled the entire fence and marked out a gaothan area larger than that indicated by their original housing sites. They then established vegetable gardens on the surplus land and even submitted applications for a crop survey of the cultivated land, While they have still not received title to the village site, harassment by the landholder stopped immediately.

---

[14] The *talathi* is the village accountant representing the Revenue Department. The *talathi* is responsible for maintaining crop and land records (the record of rights) of the village, the collection of tax revenue, etc. The *talathi* is generally in charge of a group of villages called a *saza*.

The Chinchavli Gohe Katkarwadi action, even without an official court case and associated prosecutions and defences, was a significant victory for the Katkari. It was the first time in Raigad district that a situation of enclosure and threatened eviction was explicitly connected to the PoA Act, not only in the minds of the advocates but also from the point of view of the Revenue Department and the police. Furthermore, it involved land held legally by a non-tribal person, but occupied for decades by a tribal community. This extended the concept of encroachment to situations where the legal status of the land was in contention. The incident received considerable attention in the local press, and sent a chill through the local real-estate industry. Suddenly, real-estate agents and landholders alike realized that eviction of scheduled castes and scheduled tribes occupying land they did not own but had occupied for many years could bring with it the risk, and the considerable penalties, of being convicted under the PoA Act. By 2010 they became more cautious as they realized that it would not be easy to remove Katkari and other tribal groups from land they occupy with resolve. This was enough to stop overt and blatant acts of provocation made against the Katkari and probably other communities as well, at least in the three talukas where the inquiry was active and publicity the greatest. While the multiple problems resulting from an insecure gaothan were not resolved, a significant respite had been achieved, at least for a while.

The tenor of the situation also changed for the Katkari. While previously they had reacted with fear and near panic when confronted by landholders seeking to evict them, now many communities were resolved to stay. Even in Malegavwadi, the hamlet that had prompted the study in the first place, the exodus provoked by the ashram ended after only five households had left the hamlet. The ashram administrators, resigned to the situation, converted their barbed wire fence into a permanent, high stone wall, shutting the Katkari out of sight of their clients. The Katkari, for their part, showed through their actions that they would not shift at any cost. In at least one situation we are aware of, a Katkari community directly and independently filed a complaint about a longstanding enclosure, in which they also made reference to the PoA Act and asked the police why charges had not been laid.[15]

---

[15] At the time of publication, this complaint had not yet resulted in an FIR by the police. However, an investigation has been launched by the tehsildar and the community remains in the hamlet.

Significantly, local police now seem to accept that land encroachment and forced evictions of Katkari are admissible under the PoA and that complaints need to be taken seriously.

To this day, the lull spawned by these actions, while going a long way towards creating some security against immediate eviction, has not resolved the core problem. The Katkari in hundreds of small hamlets throughout the three talukas remain without a secure gaothan that they can develop and call their own. Who knows how long it will take for unrelenting landholders and land speculators to find other ways to achieve their ends? To permanently resolve the gaothan problem, the Katkari must engage with politicians who can reactivate the gaothan extension scheme and apply sustained pressure on government officials to implement it properly. Otherwise, the issue will remain in limbo and village development will be subject to the whims of the landholders. The final chapter of this book examines efforts to revitalize Katkari collective organizations needed to build social and political cohesion and to create conditions for long-term and sustained improvements to their lives. First, however, we address efforts to break the bonds of migratory labour, a deep-seated and persistent constraint on the ability of the Katkari to exercise their rights to land.

5

Breaking the Bonds of Migratory Labour

Fishermen have been spotted near the stream. The *daku* fish tells his wife: 'Do not worry. I will be all right. Do not wipe your *kunku* till they rub *haldi* (turmeric, usually applied with salt to fish before cooking) in my eyes. I can come back even after they put me in the pot.'

– A Katkari tale about the *daku* fish

Interpretation: The fish known as *daku masa* does not die easily. It can survive out of water for a long time. The daku masa is telling his wife not to assume he is dead even if he is gone for a long time. He tells his wife not to wipe off her 'kunku' – the spot a married woman applies to her forehead when she weds but rubs off when her husband dies. He promises to come back.

The bonds of migratory livelihoods weigh heavily on Katkari efforts to improve their lives. They are like chains keeping the Katkari tied to highly exploitative work during part of the year and dependent on local patrons to bridge meagre earnings during the rest of the year. They are also a significant barrier to Katkari engagement in the political and social life of the broader community and an enduring source of vulnerability to eviction. They isolate the vast majority of the Katkari from mainstream employment and sources of power and integrate only the youngest and the strongest into the lowest rungs of the industrial labour pool. Breaking these bonds is a vital challenge with significant implications for virtually all aspects of their lives.

Jan Breman, a leading authority on India's unfree workforce, argues that direct intervention to end bonded labour has little or no chance of success. Measures such as the Bonded Labour System (Abolition) Act of 1976 and other laws and programmes to ban bonded labour have consistently failed due to 'official indifference and downright sabotage of efforts to put a stop to the social deprivation and subordination generated by this labour modality' (Breman 2010, 351). This lack of will reflects an official commitment to cheap labour policies above all other considerations and employers' determination to maintain a system that saves labour costs and provides them with a pliable workforce. Breman is also critical of civic society efforts to free workers directly through 'rescue and release' operations. These inevitably yield short-term success only. Poverty, he argues, drives workers back into bonded labour arrangements not long after they have been released. Only through indirect actions aimed at alleviating the root causes of bonded labour – extreme poverty and pauperization – can any real progress be expected. 'The lack of any alternative to meet their acute subsistence needs, leaves many landless with no choice but to sell their labour power in advance: for a shorter or longer term, to farmers or other employers, in or out of the village' (Breman 1996, 217). Generating employment for the most intensely deprived rural land-poor and landless through public works and other schemes such as the National Rural Employment Guarantee Act, 2006, and the Social Security Bill, 2008, offers some scope for safeguarding basic needs. Breman's appeal is to a course of indirect action aimed at establishing 'a floor of basic social rights to ensure that indigence does not reach a level below which it is no longer possible to lead a dignified human existence' (Breman 2010, 357).

Affirming the right to a dignified existence is a useful demand in the political environment of a democracy such as India and can be seen as a strategic leverage point in the Katkari struggle for village sites. Certainly, they are among the citizens of Maharashtra who are exposed to poverty in its most extreme form and are thus most vulnerable to becoming stuck in a state of debt bondage. Katkari analysis of their life experience shows little confidence, however, in solutions from the outside that do not directly engage them in defining and defending their interests. This chapter delves into the underlying conceptual model or worldview the Katkari use to guide their thinking about their livelihood options and choices. As part of this inquiry, the Katkari developed connections between and among efforts to revive and develop village-based livelihoods, unresolved rights to agricultural land and emerging opportunities in the mainstream economy. The analysis shed light on the main features of two contrasting livelihood models – migratory and village-based – and helped to explain Katkari reluctance to turn away from migratory livelihoods. Novel ways to reduce the sharp contrast between the two models also emerged and provided the Katkari and the research team with practical ideas for supporting a livelihood transition. These inquiry results later informed work on accessing land assets through the Forest Rights Act, as well as many other small initiatives to acquire livelihood assets and to exercise rights within the village and regional economy. The analysis reveals the severe limits on what the Katkari can achieve on their own, and the need for direct government assistance. But it also underlines the concrete gains to be had from concerted attention to the Katkari's own efforts to articulate their perspectives and engage in self-directed problem solving.

Shifting Worldviews

The research team used the Domain Analysis method[1] to elicit the Katkari view of livelihoods using their own words and concepts. It is one of a number of social adaptations of personal construct psychology created by Chevalier and Buckles (2012), drawing on a well-known theory in psychology and the cognitive sciences developed in the 1950s by George Kelly. The key assumption behind the theory is that people understand a domain or field of action by dividing it into parts and creating a description of the whole based on comparisons (or degrees of similarity and difference) between the parts. Applying the method results in a model of reality that shows how a particular group creates and organizes elements (in this case, livelihoods) and their contrasting characteristics (in this case, livelihood characteristics). In keeping with its clinical origins, the method is designed to support breakthrough thinking about ways to resolve tensions within a domain, using the words and worldview of the people involved.

Domain Analysis assessments were undertaken in two Katkari communities – Kumbarshet and Kamtekarwadi. The same steps were followed, starting with making a list of livelihoods of interest and selecting objects to represent each livelihood – a piece of charcoal to represent work at charcoal units, some millet seeds to represent upland agriculture, rice and a coin for paddy agriculture on rented lands, a small bundle of sticks for firewood collection, etc. People made drawings sometimes, and, in some exercises, sculpted objects from beeswax provided by the research team. They also gave reasons for including that livelihood in the list. In one hamlet, migratory labour on charcoal units was included because

---

[1] For detailed instructions and adaptations of the Domain Analysis method, see Tools and Software at www.participatoryactionresearch.net.

about half of the families in the hamlet work in this way. Local wage work was selected for a similar reason; the neighbouring non-tribal village hires many Katkari as agricultural workers on a seasonal basis. Some Katkari, including several in the group of participants, had managed to shift into farming on their own, prompting the group to include paddy agriculture in the list because it offered some clear advantages to these households (food security and income). They also included upland agriculture, knowing that some of the households in the hamlet have rights to dalhi lands on hillsides at a distance from the village, suitable for upland crops like millets and pulses. Few actually farmed their dalhi plots on a regular basis, but could do so if various constraints were overcome. The two forms of agriculture (paddy and upland) were included in the analysis as separate livelihood activities because of their different features and because people who engaged in one kind of agriculture usually did not engage in the other. People felt that fishing was important to all Katkari, so they included it as well. A woman in one of the groups said that collecting and selling firewood should be included since the commercial town of Pali is close by and provides a good market for firewood. This was an important livelihood for women in this hamlet, along with raising goats.

Image 5.1: Rajeev Khedkar facilitates a livelihood assessment in Kumbarshet, Sudhagad taluka, using the Domain Analysis method adapted from personal construct psychology

The research team proposed one significant livelihood characteristic – *work away* and *village-based work* – to participants in all three communities, because of the Katkari interest in developing alternatives to migratory work. This was used as a dependent variable to help guide and enrich the discussion. Participants rated each of the livelihoods on a continuum from one pole to the other for this main characteristic. They did this by placing the object that represented that livelihood somewhere between two cards denoting the contrast between work away and village-based work. The location of each livelihood on the continuum was then converted by the research team into a rating on a scale of 1 to 7, depending on how close it was to one or the other end of the contrast. Work at brick kilns, for example, received a 1 to show it was work away from the hamlet, while rearing goats received a 7 to show it was village-based. Wage work received a score of 4, reflecting the group's view that the livelihood was neither entirely away nor entirely hamlet-based. Stones were used to show the rating given for each livelihood. The research team then reorganized the symbols for each livelihood in order from one end of the continuum to the other. This resulted in a table on the floor the research team used to support a cumulative and collaborative interpretation of the results as the exercise proceeded (Table 5.1).

Other livelihood characteristics were elicited from the participants by comparing random sets of three objects (triads) representing different livelihoods. From the triads, participants identified two livelihoods that were similar in some way and different from the third livelihood in the triad. This led to a discussion of what the two had in common (similarities) and what was different about the third livelihood in the triad (differences). For example, participants in one exercise randomly compared goat rearing, firewood collection and work at charcoal units. They said that goat rearing and upland agriculture both *combine well* with other livelihoods.

'Goat rearing makes use of fallow agricultural fields, and fertilizes the soil with urine and manure.'
    'If you raise goats and offer meat others will come to work for you on your paddy field on a priority basis.'
    'If we do upland agriculture we can also find time to go fishing. The grains and fish make a complete meal.'

By contrast, work at charcoal units is *isolating*. People explained that while doing it, they could not do anything else for an extended period of time.

Table 5.1: Rating matrix for livelihood activities of the Katkari, reordered on the characteristic 'work away/village-based work'

Contrasting Characteristics	Brick/Charcoal	Wage Work	Firewood	Fishing	Upland	Paddy	Goats
1 = Work away 7 = Village-based	1	4	6	6	6	7	7
1 = Isolating 7 = Combines well	1	3	3	5	6	6	7
1 = No savings needed 7 = Requires investment	1	1	2	3	5	6	7
1 = Sporadic 7 = Steady	6	3	2	1	3	3	5
1 = In-kind benefits 7 = Cash benefits	6	7	1	5	2	3	5
1 = Individual work 7 = Group work	7	4	1	2	4	4	1
1 = Daily income 7 = Lump-sum income	4	2	1	2	6	6	4
1 = Maintain independence 7 = Obligation to take advance	7	4	1	1	1	4	1

Source: Author's field notes, March 2009, Kumbarshet and Kamtekarwadi.

The Katkari participants in both villages generated new contrasting characteristics from each new triad of livelihoods selected at random. Livelihoods that provided *steady employment* were distinguished from those that were *sporadic*. For example, work at a charcoal unit can last for six or seven months and agricultural wage work can continue for several months at a time. By contrast, fishing is very sporadic; it depends a lot on the season and seasonal variations and on when the need or desire to fish arises.

When assessing similarities and differences between livelihoods, participants noted that charcoal and brick making created an *obligation to take an advance*, a practice also associated sometimes with paddy agriculture. By contrast, livelihoods such as collecting firewood allowed people to remain *independent*. Participants felt this was an important contrast because of the long-term indebtedness that often resulted from taking an advance from contractors and moneylenders.

Another characteristic elicited through the triad methods was the contrast between livelihood activities that provided a *substantial lump-sum income* and those that provided only a small *daily cash income*. A large advance will be received by committing to work for the season at a charcoal or brick unit and the harvest of a paddy field can be sold all at once or in parts. This creates opportunities for investment, or for wild

Image 5.2: Katkari women rest on their way to Pali, Sudhagad with firewood for sale

expenditures such as heavy drinking during festivals and extravagant weddings. By contrast, firewood is sold in very small quantities on a daily basis, as are fish products. Both generate small amounts of cash for daily or weekly needs only.

The kind of return realized (*cash benefits vs in-kind benefits*) was also an important contrast to participants, emerging from comparisons of wage work with various forms of agriculture. *Group work* in charcoal and brick kilns and on the farms of others emerged as a contrast with *individual work* such as firewood collection and goat rearing. Finally, the money required to access the livelihood activity was flagged and rated, with contrasts emerging between livelihoods that *require a money investment* and those that can be easily accessed without any savings (*no savings required*). For example, to grow paddy the Katkari must not only rent land but also buy seed and fertilizers, pay for ploughing and pay the wages of other hired hands, all before any crop is harvested. They must also buy rice, both for the family and for the workers they hire. Money is also needed to establish a goat herd. By contrast, there is no need to spend money when collecting firewood; people simply go directly to the forest and carry the firewood to the market. No money is required to go to work on charcoal units, brick units or sugarcane plantations either, as the contractors collect and transport people from the village to the place where they stay for months at a time and provide for daily subsistence needs during the season. Fishing occupies a middle ground on this characteristic, as some money is needed to buy fishing supplies.

The gradual development of the table and its organization around the key contrast between *work away* and *village-based work* supported several important observations by participants in both assessments. They identified patterns along the way by looking for rows and columns with a similar number of stones. What emerged were associations between the first bipolar construct (*work away* and *village-based work*) and all other contrasts in the analysis. During the exercise, participants could see that livelihoods away from the hamlet (left side of the table) tended not to require any cash savings, but they also tended to isolate people from other kinds of work for long periods of time. This made it difficult to combine different kinds of livelihoods. By contrast, livelihoods involving work close to the hamlet (right side of the table) tended to combine well with other livelihood activities but required more money to access. The simplicity and rightness of the associations surprised the group, and launched a lively discussion. As the sun was setting, several people left to get lamps from their homes so that the meeting could continue. By the end of the sessions people felt clearer about why it was so difficult to make a transition from migratory to more sedentary, permanent livelihoods. The analysis also enhanced their confidence in new ideas about what kind of assets and livelihood strategies would help to support a transition, as described in what follows.

Following the initial analysis, the research team examined the data using specialized software.[2] The results confirmed and quantified the row and column similarities observed by the participants and provided additional insight into the structural features of the Katkari livelihood worldview. The data were compiled from two exercises using the same list of livelihoods and overlapping constructs. When combining the two tables, the research team carefully examined and compared the ratings, constructs and explanations provided by the Katkari, and used our best judgement to reconstruct a single table for analysis. Figure 5.1 and Figure 5.2 show cluster and principal component analysis[3] (respectively) of the combined data recorded in Table 5.1.

The results show that the Katkari livelihood system is polarized, with migratory work on brick/charcoal units and agricultural wage work at one end of an axis, and village-based livelihoods like goat rearing, agriculture, fishing and firewood collection on the other. Interpretation of this result by the research team, verified in discussions with Katkari

---

[2] Analysis of the conceptual grid prepared by the Katkari was done using RepGrid, a software developed for this purpose. Joint analysis of the statistical results was not attempted with the Katkari because this was not needed and because they were unfamiliar with the technology. Simple row and column comparisons by the Katkari did, however, converge around the main patterns. The more advanced and nuanced conclusions were shared afterwards with Katkari groups and helped to inform their decisions about the livelihood strategies they might want to pursue.

[3] The statistical technique called principal component analysis simplifies a data set by reducing the multi-dimensional relationships among observed variables to a cross-shaped, two-dimensional representation. The shorter the distance between livelihoods (dots) and characteristics (crosses) shown in the figure, the closer their relationship to each other. In the figure, the scores assigned to livelihoods and characteristics (the observed variables) are mapped in relation to two fictive variables. The horizontal line (first component) represents a fictive variable that accounts for 60.1 per cent of the total variance in the data (pattern of relationships among dots and crosses). The vertical line (second component) represents a fictive variable that accounts for another 27.5 per cent of the total variance. Together, the two principal components account for 87.5 per cent of the total variance, a very high level of explanation and statistical coherence.

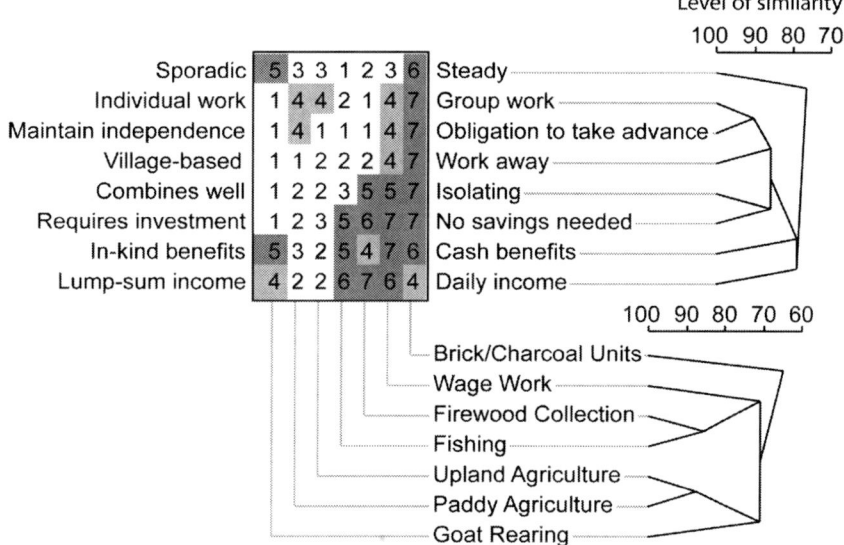

Figure 5.1: Cluster analysis of Katkari views on livelihoods

Source: Author's field notes, March 2009, Kumbarshet and Kamtekarwadi.
Note: The lower part of the figure shows that paddy and upland agriculture share many characteristics (87 per cent level) as do fishing and firewood collection (85 per cent level). Levels of similarity among the various characteristics of the livelihoods (upper part of the figure) show that group work also tends to involve an obligation to take an advance. These characteristics are, moreover, closely associated with work away, which is isolating but which does not require any savings. The opposite associations also hold. Individual, village-based work that can be managed independently combines well with other livelihoods and requires an investment to start. These tendencies are consistent with the general observation shown in Figure 5.2 that the Katkari livelihood system is polarized.

participants, suggests that the Katkari view their livelihoods in a pragmatic way. They recognize that all of the livelihood activities they are familiar with and are able to engage in, including migration to charcoal operations and brick kilns, are important to their survival. While they would like to break free from migratory labour, which is isolating and brings with it an obligation to take an advance, many are reluctant to do so. The activity provides steady employment over a long period of time and both a lump-sum and small weekly allowance are not available to them otherwise. The lump-sum advance from charcoal and brick units is

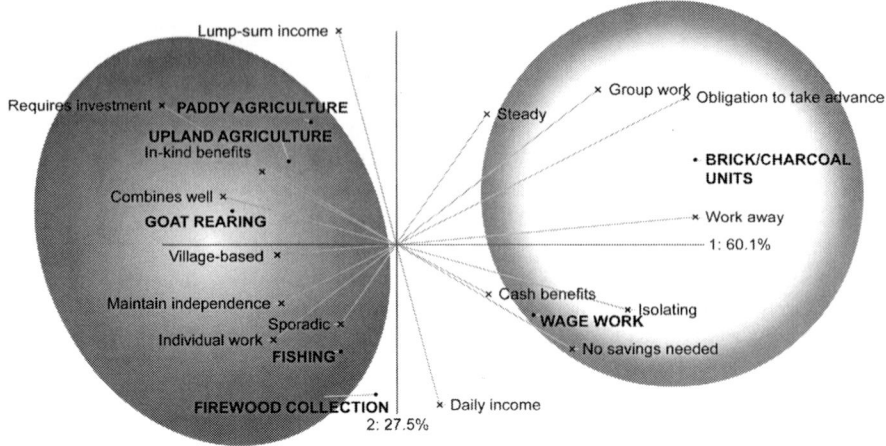

Figure 5.2: Principal component analysis of Katkari views of livelihoods showing two contrasting livelihood models

Source: Author's field notes, March 2009, Kumbarshet and Kamtekarwadi

Note: On the one hand, migration by groups of Katkari to brick and charcoal units provides steady work, generates a lump-sum income and involves them in an obligation to take an advance. While isolating the Katkari from other livelihoods, it brings cash benefits and requires no savings to begin. Wage work, which has many of the same characteristics, fills gaps in this strategy mostly by providing a daily income during the off season. On the other hand, paddy agriculture, upland agriculture and goat rearing require an initial investment. They are village-based livelihoods that combine well with other livelihoods and produce in-kind benefits as well as a lump-sum income. Fishing and firewood collection complement these by offering more sporadic employment people can engage in as individuals and thus maintain their independence. The two principal components (vertical and horizontal axes) account for a combined total of 87.5 per cent of the variance in the system.

appealing and explains why many continue to take it despite the obligations it creates. Within this model, wage labour plays a supplementary role during the off season.

By contrast, village-based livelihoods involve activities that combine well with other livelihoods, and usually generate some in-kind benefits in the form of food grains and goat milk and meat. They also tend to be individual as opposed to group-based. Independence can be maintained in this model, although an investment is required to start. The model shares one cross-cutting characteristic with migration: paddy agriculture, upland agriculture and goat rearing also generate a single lump-sum income, making them attractive in this respect. Shifting entirely out of the migration model to this alternative model is difficult, however, because of the investment requirement. Within this model, firewood collection and fishing provide sporadic work that generates a small daily income. In this respect, the two activities serve the same function as agricultural wage work in the migration model.

Learning opportunities emerging from this analysis focused on ways to reduce the sharp contrasts between the livelihood models available to the Katkari. Various ideas emerged by asking the Katkari to think of novel ways to combine the desired livelihood characteristics. For example, could they find a way to reduce the cost of engaging in livelihoods such as agriculture that generated substantial lump-sum incomes, without creating an obligation to take an advance? One idea that emerged was to share the rental of bullocks for ploughing, thereby reducing the money required. Pooling labour for other tasks (simulating group work) could also reduce the need for money and the need to take a loan. By reducing spending on gambling and alcohol, a common habit among both men and women in Katkari communities, households could make better use of the little cash they earned. This would make it possible to invest in livelihoods like goat rearing. The possibility of a common savings fund to set money aside for investment in agriculture was also discussed as a way to break into considering an alternative livelihood model.

These novel combinations of livelihood characteristics (village-based group work; investment without the obligation to take an advance; combining cash with in-kind benefits) provided the Katkari and the research team with a new lens to reflect on ways to break the bonds of migratory livelihoods. It moved thinking by the group beyond the polarized local conceptual categories into a new space of innovation and experimentation. In the social domain, this parallels the psychological process of breakthrough thinking central to Kelly's personal construct psychology. For example, the analysis drew attention to the potential role of land as a livelihood asset and as a bridge to other livelihood options. It became apparent to participants in the discussions that families engaged in any kind of agriculture were able to manage their livelihoods by drawing on supplementary activities such as goat rearing, fishing and forest collection to fill gaps. These activities combine well, and make it possible for families to support themselves throughout the entire year with both in-kind and cash benefits. This insight became a motivating factor for some Katkari participants with respect to ceiling lands and dalhi lands that they had access to, but did not cultivate actively. In various communities, participants decided that it would be worth exploring ways to make these lands more productive, without creating an obligation to take an advance. This, they felt, could give them some scope for shifting out of the exploitative brick and charcoal units and for combining agriculture with known and relatively attractive supplementary livelihoods. Later, with assistance from the research team, 10 families in one hamlet got grants from the Integrated Tribal Development Project (ITDP) to hire bullocks and pay for ploughing and manuring land for farming. Others also sought support to cultivate ceiling lands or to purchase goats. These actions, while limited in scope and plagued by management frailties, were conscious steps taken by Katkari families to improve their livelihoods based on a new livelihood worldview.

The results of livelihood assessments were informative for the research team as well, because the analysis helped to explain Katkari responses to many previous years of relatively unsuccessful attempts to support them in finding new livelihoods. For example, the failure of a teashop run by Katkari youth could now be seen as a flawed project, in part because it did not take into account how much it tied people down on a daily basis. Running a teashop was continuous, individual work that was impossible to combine with other activities and did not generate any scope for a lump-sum payment, key elements in the Katkari livelihood worldview. Other experiences with livelihood projects and programmes for the Katkari, such as furniture making and the production of pickles and preserves, were also reassessed by the research team in light of new thinking about Katkari perspectives on their livelihoods. More generally, the analysis reminded people that making the transition from one livelihood model to another depended on the right combination of activities by different members of households. This prompted the inquiry to shift attention from the description of livelihood activities and characteristics as perceived by people across gender and generational divisions, to evaluative statements about priorities and preferences reflecting different circumstances. Breaking the bonds of migratory labour would engage men, women and youth differently.

Gender Perspectives on Livelihood Options

Disagreements in views among participants in the Domain Analysis sessions were worked out through a process of group elicitation and negotiated ratings. While this was good enough for the purpose of generating a descriptive analysis of livelihoods, we needed another approach to explore disagreements in livelihood priorities between men and women and between older and younger members of families. During various meetings, women and young men said that while they agreed with the livelihood descriptions emerging from the assessments, some livelihoods were more appealing to them than others. These evaluative statements were explored later, through a simple ranking process using the disagreements and misunderstandings method.[4] Men and women gathered separately with a common list of livelihood options and ranked the options from the highest to the lowest priority. The rankings were then compared and any disagreements discussed and explained by the people involved. Several sessions of this type were convened by the research team, leading to local adjustments in applications made to the ITDP for livelihood schemes in different villages. The new assessments built on the general insight from the Domain Analysis that livelihood strategies could be combined in novel ways.

In one village, Talaiwadi in Sudhagad taluka, participants listed and prioritized eight livelihood options: goat rearing, fuel wood gathering, upland agriculture, non-timber forest products, *hamali* (loading and unloading trucks), agricultural wage work and work on charcoal units and brick kilns. In this hamlet of 63 families, about half actually migrate seasonally to distant charcoal units in Gujarat, Karnataka and other parts of Maharashtra, while another 15 or so families migrate to relatively closer brick units. Both groups engage in a variety of other activities at other times of the year. Older men tend to do seasonal work on farms in the area, while youth in the hamlet work periodically at loading and unloading goods and materials (hamali) at sites in towns. Fuel wood collection and sale is a steady source of income for most of the women in the hamlet, which is located close to a forested area and market.

Ranking of the relative importance of various livelihoods separately by men and women shows some common priorities but also a number of significant disagreements (Table 5.2). The biggest disagreements were encountered around the relative priority of migration to charcoal units and hamali, ranked as a high priority by the men and a low priority by the women. For the men, migration to charcoal units is a priority because it allows them to make more money than any other livelihood. Some noted that they had been able to save money and build good houses from the wages earned by migrating to charcoal units. For women, the

---

[4] For detailed instructions and adaptations of the disagreements and misunderstandings method, see Tools and Software at www.participatoryactionresearch.net.

benefits of the cash income are offset by the difficulties encountered in migrating every year to distant places in Gujarat, Karnataka and other parts of Maharashtra where the units are located. Everything is different they said – the people, the weather, the food and even the language – making it very difficult for them to manage the needs of the family:

> While men like to go out and stay in different places, our family life is disturbed when we have to migrate to the distant charcoal units. Furthermore, there is no guarantee that the money earned will be saved rather than spent by the men on alcohol and other vices.

Hamali, while a high priority for young men in the hamlet, presents a similar problem from the point of view of the women – 'it spoils our young men entirely because they spend it all on gambling, drinking, smoking, and so on. They develop very bad habits and do not fit in with the village life of the Katkari community.' The young men countered this view by asking, 'What is wrong if we spend some money on alcohol and tobacco? Women also drink!'

Table 5.2: Disagreements and agreements among men and women regarding livelihood priorities, Talaiwadi, Sudhagad

Livelihood Activity	Ranking by Men	Ranking by Women	Difference
Goat rearing	5	2	3
Charcoal units	1	6	5
Fuel wood	4	1	3
Upland agriculture	7	4	3
Hamali	3	8	5
Wage work	6	5	1
NTFPs	8	7	1
Bricks kilns	2	3	1
Level of disagreement			22/32 (69%)

Source: Author's field notes, February 2010, Talaiwadi.

Men and women also expressed disagreements with respect to fuel wood collection, goat rearing and upland agriculture. For women, fuel wood collection and sale is the most important livelihood because it enables them to earn money almost every day. While it is a long and arduous walk from the forest to the town, women sell the fuel wood immediately and so the money comes to them. This is used to buy food, medicines and other essential items. Women also ranked goat rearing highly because it can be done while staying in the village. They do not have to migrate, unlike when they work on charcoal units. The reasoning of the men went in the opposite direction and produced a much lower rank score: we get very little money from fuel wood collection compared to the daily effort we have to make, and goat rearing forces us to stay in the village all the time rather than leave for other work.

Views on upland agriculture also differed between the two groups. Women appreciated the three to four month's supply of food grains from upland agriculture, while the men emphasized the risks and uncertainty of the harvest due to rainfall, disease and damage from wild animals. Both groups lamented the harassment they faced from Forest Department officials when they grew crops on forest land, but ultimately the men placed this activity near the bottom and the women in the middle among priority livelihood activities.

Both groups had similar priority ratings for the other livelihoods discussed. Migration to brick kilns was placed among the top three by both men and women. They agreed that the work was important because it provided an income over a longer period compared to any other livelihood activity except migration to charcoal units. Women were more enthusiastic about going to the brick kilns because the sites were quite close to their hamlet, making it possible for them to return home once a week. They also said that the contractors were mild compared to brick contractors they had worked for in Pen or Panvel and compared to the owners of the charcoal units. A growing demand for bricks in the area had doubled the price of bricks between 2008 and 2010. Earlier, only large units employing 20 to 40 families met the demand for bricks, often located very close to the cities and far from Katkari hamlets. This dramatic increase in the price of bricks, fed by rapid urbanization and improvements to houses even in villages and smaller towns, had stimulated numerous very small brick operations, often close to Katkari communities. Nevertheless, work in the harsh sun is difficult and children do not go to school while they work with their parents. For the women, the impact on schooling for their children prompted them to rank this livelihood third, while for the men it was second, after charcoal making.

Views on wage work and the collection of non-timber forest products were also similar, appearing low in the list of priorities for both groups. Wage work is not available regularly and there is no guarantee of employment from one season to the next. While most families in the hamlet collect medicinal plants and other non-timber forest products for sale during seasons when other work is not available, the level of effort is high and traders pay very little. Women pointed out that people who dedicate a lot of time to collecting non-timber forest products could not raise goats. Goat rearing is a daily task and cannot be interrupted by extended periods of time in the forest.

The Katkari and the research team made various uses of this and other assessments of livelihood activities in subsequent actions. For example, participants in Talaiwadi decided to explore the possibility of setting up their own brick kiln, in response to rising brick prices and the demand for bricks in nearby towns. As discussed later, the economic boom in the area is creating opportunities to establish small enterprises, although few Katkari can actually become proprietors. The older men and women in the group also agreed on the potential of goat rearing to provide them with significant new income opportunities. They decided to apply for a grant from the IDTP to acquire goats and establish herds of their own. They also encouraged the young men to invest the money they earned during hamali work in goat herds to be managed by their mothers and sisters, until such time as they married and could manage the herds from within their own families.

These and other livelihood options were discussed in an ongoing way at various times and in various places over a period of several years, from 2008 to the present. In general, they focused on mobilizing resources from government schemes, exercising rights to dalhi and ceiling lands that could be transformed into productive assets, and making collective use of the skills and sources of power at their disposal to create new types of income and sustenance. A common theme, emerging from and reinforced by the group livelihood assessments, was to pursue livelihood options that reinforced or combined well with other livelihood activities. This, people felt, would eventually help them transition from dependence on bonded migratory labour to more independent modes of work. The shift would be very difficult and slow, however, with many unable to leave one mode of livelihood for another.

Negotiating a Fishing Contract

Meetings around livelihoods were of great interest to Katkari in many communities, leading to a wide variety of village-specific actions. In Siddheshwarwadi in Sudhagad taluka, people wanted to focus on making a successful bid on a fishing contract. The main non-tribal village, Siddheshwar, has within its gaothan a pond of about 2 acres in an area adjoining an ancient Shiv temple. The pond is now under the jurisdiction of the gram panchayat, which every year auctions the right to manage the pond for fishing. Competition for the rights varies from year to year, depending on the interests of different parties and weather conditions. In some years, non-tribals from Siddheshwar have bid on and secured the contract, while in other years it has been won by people from outside the village.

The Katkari had never before bid on the fishing rights, even though they are expert fishers and fish is a highly prized food in their culture. Katkari families are known to walk several kilometres just to catch a fish for a meal! Many Katkari in Siddheshwarwadi hamlet had for years pined for the right to catch fish in the Siddheshwar village pond located just below their hamlet. In 2008, a group of five Katkari families in the hamlet approached a member of the research team for help in developing a successful bid. They said that they were very interested in fishing the pond and could mobilize part but not all of the bid money. They also said that they were unclear about the process and wondered if they would be allowed to participate. This interest prompted a meeting to discuss the bidding process, and to assess the forces at play among the various stakeholders involved in the past. The goals were to identify possible sources of support and resistance to a bid from the Katkari. Stakeholder analysis CLIP, a method already familiar to those involved in the gaothan study, was used to support strategic thinking about actions to improve their chances of success in the bidding process.

Figure 5.3 shows the Katkari assessment of the stakeholders involved. Of the eight stakeholders identified (body of the figure), participants said that three would likely act against a Katkari bid for the contract, including outside contractors, local contractors and a key political leader in the area (left side of the table, showing medium to high losses represented by '-' and '- -' headings, respectively). The outside contractors had always won the auction, with the support of the political leader and local contractors who would normally assist in the management of the pond. The outside contractors were likely to make use of their past relations of collaboration with the political leaders (represented by arrows) to strengthen their bid and attempt to block the Katkari bid. In this scenario, the Katkari bidding families would be relatively vulnerable. While they had lots to gain ('+ +' rating), they had little power (lower stakeholder categories). Participants also recognized that while both the bidding families and other Katkari in the hamlet were highly marginalized stakeholders, they had relatively powerful allies that could help them influence the process. The sarpanch of the gram panchayat was a Katkari man from Siddheshwarwadi and could be expected to create space for the Katkari bid to be heard and considered.[5] He had a good relationship with the current gram sevak, the secretary of the gram panchayat responsible for administering the bidding process. SOBTI, through a member of the research team, was also well known in the larger village as a reliable and credible organization with a history of supporting Katkari livelihood initiatives in this and other villages. Participants concluded, however, that these advantages were insufficient to win the bid if the political leader sided with outside or local contractors. They also felt that other stakeholders would question their legitimacy as a contracting party by saying that they could not manage the fishing operation effectively and fulfil the contract responsibly. Other Katkari families stood to gain to some degree, as a successful bid would open the way to others in subsequent years, but they too were marginal in the stakeholder structure.

Discussion of ways to improve their position, and create the conditions for a successful bid, focused on the importance of consolidating support from the sarpanch, seeking support from the political leader and using their indirect relationship with the gram sevak to provide assurances regarding the legitimacy and seriousness of the Katkari bid. They thought they could use these alliances to establish a link through the gram sevak, a relatively neutral party in the situation, to the political leader.

This strategy, and the thinking involved, created cohesion within the group and strengthened their resolve to fight for the contract. They followed up first by meeting with the sarpanch to express their interest in and commitment to bidding during the auction. He agreed to tell members of the gram panchayat, including the gram sevak, that the Katkari would be bidding on the contract. They then requested a meeting with the local political leader and sent several representatives from the group with good standing in the community. During this meeting, they expressed their commitment to bidding, knowledge of where to get fingerlings to seed the pond, and plans to involve the entire Katkari

---

[5] Dwarkanath Lakhma Ghogharkar, a Katkari from Siddheshwarwadi, held the position of sarpanch for the main non-tribal villages of Siddheshwar and Wavloli for two-and-a-half years, between 2004 and 2006. The position was reserved during this term for a member of a tribal community, which he then won against other candidates through election. Further evidence of his leadership qualities is provided in Chapter 6 in a discussion of the Katkari Forum for Justice, which he helped to establish.

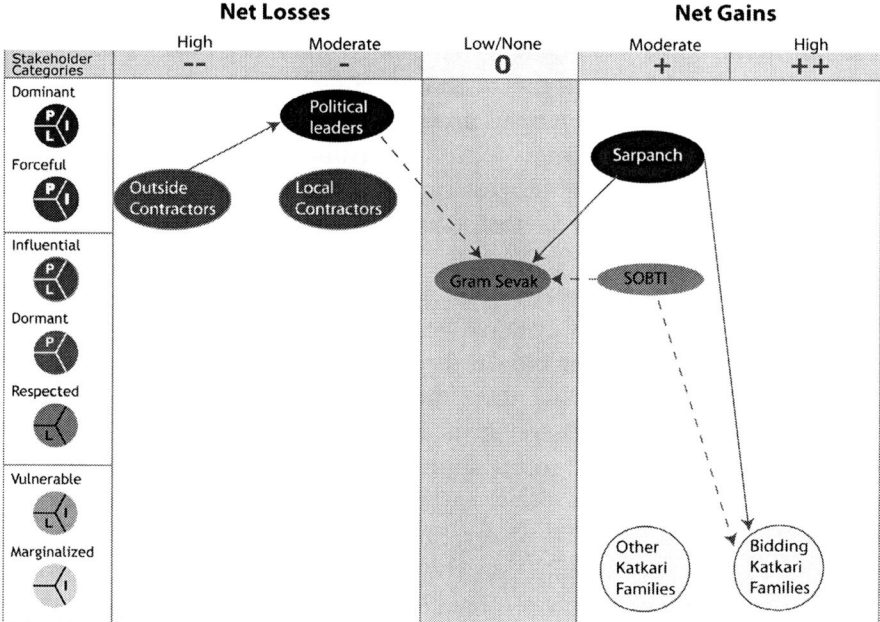

Figure 5.3: Stakeholder positions on a proposed Katkari bid for a fishing contract in Siddheshwar

Source: Author's field notes, November 2008, Siddheshwar.

Note: Of the eight stakeholders identified (body of the figure), three would likely reject the bid because their losses would be from medium to high (left side of the table, showing medium to high losses represented by '-' and '- -' headings, respectively). These same actors are relatively powerful in the situation (upper half of the table, reflecting stakeholder categories with medium to high levels of power). The outside contractors would likely make use of their past relations of collaboration with the political leaders (represented by arrows) to strengthen their bid. In this scenario, the Katkari bidding families are relatively vulnerable. They do, however, have two allies they can draw on to engage with the political leaders (sarpanch and SOBTI), working through the relatively neutral gram sevak.

community in harvesting the fish. The leader seemed impressed with the tenacity of the group, and took their gesture of appealing to him directly as a sign of respect for his position in the larger community. Considering the large size of the Katkari community in this and neighbouring villages, he may also have seen some political and electoral advantage from supporting an initiative likely to be seen favourably by the entire Katkari community. After hearing of the Katkari intentions, he decided not to invite outside contractors to bid. He said that there were already a number of local contractors planning to bid, and with the Katkari involved as well, there were enough bidders to hold the auction fairly. This transformed the scenario since, suddenly, the outside contractors, normally a powerful group, were no longer a threat. Finally, a member of SOBTI met with the gram sevak responsible for administering the bidding process and assured him that SOBTI would guarantee the bid money in case of any default by the bidding Katkari families.

When the auction actually took place, local contractors started the bid for the contract. The political leader then put in a bid of his own, even though he had never bid on the contract in the past. This signalled to the local contractors that they should be careful not to bid against him. He then signalled discreetly to the Katkari group that they should bid higher. The Katkari group submitted a bid for Rs 3,700 and the contract was awarded to them as the highest bid. While the Katkari families had only Rs 1,700 at the time of the auction, the gram sevak issued a receipt for Rs 3,700 on the understanding that SOBTI would provide the balance. This was repaid to SOBTI by the Katkari afterwards from the sale of the fish.

The Katkari group was, of course, delighted by their success and encouraged to do a good job. Fingerlings were purchased to stock the pond and the fish were fed and tended for several months. A particularly heavy rainfall caused some flooding of the pond and the loss of some fish, but at the end of the season a profit of Rs 5,000 was realized after paying all expenses. In addition, the families involved ate fish on a regular basis and, near the end of the season, opened the pond to everyone in the hamlet. During a community fishing day, every Katkari family collected about two kilos of fish for their own consumption, much to their pleasure. In short, the venture was successful. Moreover, it showed the families involved and the entire community that if they worked together and used the sources of influence available to them, they could engage with the broader village community and economy as actors in their own right. This gave the community a great deal of confidence, and encouraged others to consider small enterprises of their own. Shortly afterwards, one man set up a successful tree nursery to sell plants in neighbouring towns, while several others in the hamlet established very small brick operations of their own. As discussed subsequently, these and other kinds of initiatives broadened the economic base of the Katkari community in ways consistent with their worldview and taking into account the diverse priorities within their communities.

Acquiring Forest Lands

Engaging with the Katkari to assess their livelihoods prompted a shift in their perspective on the role of land assets in the struggle to break the bonds of migratory work. People established connections between efforts to combine upland agriculture with other village-based livelihoods and to their unresolved rights to agricultural land. This reinforced interest in acquiring the dalhi lands many had formal claims to but had not been able to use for decades due to harassment by the Forest Department and a lack of capital for land improvements. Fortunately, a shift in government policy on forest lands suddenly opened a door into upland agriculture that had previously been closed to the Katkari, just when their interest in this possibility had been rekindled.

The history and issues around forest management and ownership in India are vast and complex and have been studied in detail by various Indian scholars and activists (Baviskar 1995; Dalvi and Bokil 2000; Guha 1994; Kothari et al. 1996). The administrative roots of the problem began in 1867 under British rule when forests in many parts of India, including the Western Ghats, were expropriated and reclassified as forest land owned by the Forest Department. The British organized workers to fell the forests and transport timber, fuel wood and charcoal to industries and ships on the coast. Many of the forest workers in the Western Ghats were Katkari, recognized for their knowledge of the forest, exceptional strength and expertise at making charcoal. Sections of the forest lands, once deforested, were allocated to these workers on long-term lease so they could grow upland subsistence crops and establish their own communities, thereby maintaining workers *in situ* for when they were needed. Registered users paid an annual tax as well. Lands leased collectively by an entire community or group of families, the most common approach, were called dalhi lands, while lands held through an individual lease were called *eksali* lands.

Today, dalhi and eksali lands are formally owned by the Forest Department of the Government of India. This occurred in a smooth transfer of ownership after independence from Great Britain. Nevertheless, government resolutions issued by the state government in 1969 and 1970 called for the transfer of property rights over dalhi and eksali plots to the leaseholders. Implementation of this progressive decision was interrupted, however, during the period of internal emergency. It was then rendered more complicated by the subsequent involvement of the central government through the Forest Conservation Act of 1980 and the central government's implication in forest administration (Dalvi and Bokil 2000, 2845). While some lands were transferred in the 1970s, the national-level Forest Conservation Act undermined implementation of the state-level policy. It consolidated within the Forest Department of the central government decisions over the conversion of forest land for non-forest purposes, including agriculture. Amendments to the act in 1988 then banned the transfer of forest land to anyone other than a government agency, effectively putting an end to the transfer of dalhi lands initiated by the state government. Despite several decades of protest over this injustice, including significant mobilization of affected peoples, some 10,000 tribal households in Raigad and Thane districts alone, including many Katkari leaseholders, remained vulnerable to eviction by the Forest Department for 'forest encroachment' some 35 years after legislation was put in place to regularize their rights (ibid., 2846).

The rights of tribal people to forest lands have only recently moved forward as a result of the Scheduled Tribes and Other Traditional Forest Dwellers (Recognition of Forest Rights) Act, known as the Forest Rights Act. It was initiated by the Tribal Affairs Ministry of the Government of India as a way to follow through on earlier resolutions and to address the contradictions and barriers still facing tribal populations throughout the country.

Implementation of the act involves an application from claimants supported by two types of proof: residence in villages associated with the claimed land and cultivation of the land as of 13 December 2005, the date the act came into effect. The procedures also require the involvement of multiple actors including the Revenue Department, the Forest Department, the gram panchayat of corresponding villages, a forest rights committee constituted at the local level and claimants. These are intended to provide various checks and balances during implementation. In principle, organizing and coordinating all of these activities and parties is the responsibility of the Revenue Department. In fact, these officials have relied heavily on the unpaid contributions of many small non-governmental organizations working with tribal populations. Furthermore, implementation of the act did not begin in earnest until 2008, at least in Maharashtra.

The ADS and SOBTI, organizations directed by members of our research team, were among about 20 organizations in Raigad district who responded to the opportunities created by the Forest Rights Act, working with Katkari but also Thakur and Mahadev Koli communities in Karjat, Khalapur and Sudhagad talukas. Prior to engaging in this process, however, the research team discussed the history of dalhi lands informally with people eligible to make claims. What emerged from the discussions was that many had lost interest or any hope of using the dalhi land they had a right to. Assessments were planned that would shed light on the reasons for this and explore how this might impact the claims process.

The research team sometimes used the problem tree method and sometimes open discussion to raise the issues, depending on the time available and the extent to which groups were already committed to making claims. Even using this relatively simple tool, it took three months of village meetings and cluster-level meetings to engage people in careful discussions of the pros and cons of the dalhi lands, and to begin to formulate lines of action. The earlier livelihood assessments had raised the interest of many Katkari in the potential role of dalhi lands, but the scale of this new challenge was quite different. Thousands of individual families were in principle eligible to make a claim by virtue of their family links to registered dalhi plots.

The core problem that launched group discussions was why people in a hamlet were not actively cultivating their dalhi lands. Reasons were listed along with a chain of reasons underlying each initial response. For example, participants in assessments noted that their dalhi land was not easily cultivated because it was rocky and had been fallow for many years. After deeper probing into this cause, it became clear that while older members of the community recognized the value of millet crops grown in the past, the younger generation had not paid much attention to the land and left it fallow because they did not consider millets to be an important crop. Paddy was, in their minds, the only true type of agriculture and these lands were not suitable for paddy.

Harassment by the Forest Department was noted as another reason why people had stopped cultivating dalhi lands. Before the act was passed, Forest Department officials had actively harassed leaseholders on forest land over a period of 15 to 20 years. This involved a fierce campaign of burning millet crops and destroying nurseries. As a result, the Katkari, and other tribal communities as well, had to a large extent stopped cultivating the land.

The absence of bullocks and agricultural tools was also cited as a reason why dalhi land was not cultivated. Many participants traced this to poor incomes and poor access to government investment schemes. Land titles, it was noted, are needed to access government funds for agriculture, so this was also a deeper cause of the absence of bullocks and tools. Finally, people said that migration to brick kilns often overlapped with the beginning of the agricultural season when they would need to prepare and plant fields. Once in the cycle of migration, it became hard to engage in agriculture.[6]

The effects or consequences of not making use of their dalhi lands also emerged from the analysis. Participants recognized the merits of millets normally grown on dalhi lands, including the grain's highly nutritious qualities and the bridge it can provide during periods of food insecurity. The relative success of the Thakur as millet farmers was evident to all and helped to establish among the group that the activity was both viable and worthwhile. Participants also recognized that if they did not cultivate the land now, they might lose it altogether; under the Forest Act, claims not made immediately would be extinguished forever. Landownership in and of itself was also seen to be of value as it could enable access to government schemes and provide an asset of their own.

This line of reasoning was similar in many Katkari communities. The assessments brought into focus the various ways in which circumstances had now changed as a result of the Forest Rights Act. For example, active harassment of cultivators by the Forest Department had stopped immediately when the act was introduced. This gave people greater confidence and reduced their fear. The discussions also brought out more fully the potential value to them of upland millet cultivation, a practice that was part of their traditional livelihood but had fallen into disfavour.

The process of engagement with the Katkari around the dalhi land issue was greatly aided by the capacities developed in hamlets that had formed gaothan rights committees. Many of these committees reorganized themselves as the forest rights committees called for under the act and began to discuss the issue with other members of the community. They also began to mobilize people. First, they cleared as much of their dalhi land as possible and planted millets and pulses. This was needed to demonstrate use of the land. Second, they started the difficult task of collecting and submitting basic legal documents as part of their applications to the government. The process also involved interacting with government officials to facilitate the validation of hand maps and surveys of individual and collective plots.

---

[6] Gaikwad (1995) notes that the grazing of cattle by the upper castes makes it impossible to cultivate dalhi lands, a reason why the dalhi land issue holds little attraction for Katkari youth.

Despite a high level of motivation among the Katkari, the applications for land under the Forest Rights Act also raised a number of difficult dilemmas. It became apparent early on that establishing prior Katkari cultivation of the dalhi plots was hard to do in cases where cultivation had stopped years earlier. Upland cultivation of millets and pulses, while a legitimate and productive use of marginal land, leaves few traces of cultivation compared to paddy agriculture. Bunds and other structures required for paddy are permanent, while evidence of millet and pulse cultivation fades from the land in a year or two. In one village, for example, 40 families used to grow millets on their dalhi lands, but only 10 were able to generate proof of cultivation since 13 December 2005, the date the act came into effect. As a result of this difficulty, many individual claims were initially rejected by the Forest Department.

While administratively complex and time-consuming, over a period of 18 months, starting in 2008 and ending in 2009, over 1,000 individual claims were developed and submitted by Katkari forest rights committees to the appropriate authorities. Many were eventually approved. In addition to individual claims to dalhi land, 52 collective claims were submitted for Katkari hamlets located on forest lands owned by the Forest Department. Also rejected initially by the government, the collective claims were eventually accepted and converted into individual housing plots. While full-fledged gaothan rights were not sanctioned, the individual housing plots provided a secure home for Katkari in these hamlets and a base from which they could pursue more independent livelihoods.

Emerging Wage Labour Strategies

During the course of work with the Katkari on breaking the bonds of migratory labour, thinking by the research team and the Katkari about the role of wage labour in future livelihoods evolved considerably. The acquisition and development of dalhi lands, while an asset available to Katkari communities located close to their ancestral lands in the higher hills, was not a feasible livelihood for Katkari communities on the plains. In addition, many young men stated emphatically that they would prefer to work for others than for themselves, if that work were on better terms.

In some areas, opportunities for better-paid wage work were indeed emerging. The very developments that drove the risk of enclosure and eviction were also creating various new economic opportunities. Demand for young, male wage workers in particular was on the rise throughout the area. In Khalapur, the expanding industrial base requires a steady supply of workers to load and unload goods of various kinds, as does the zone from Nagothane to Copali via Pali (in Sudhagad taluka) where the emergence of a tube and steel industry and many food-processing units has increased demand for this kind of labour. The Katkari have many attributes for fulfilling this labour requirement, including an ability to work very hard under very difficult conditions. Wage work in these settings is a viable alternative to migration and to land-based employment and one with longer-term benefits for a large number of Katkari with few opportunities to acquire land.

The importance of emerging wage labour strategies, and their potential to help in breaking the cycle of bonded labour, first became evident to the research team in 2007, following efforts to scale up the gaothan initiative to communities beyond the initial study group. At this time, a relationship was developed between the research team and a group of young men in Mil Katkarwadi. This was a cluster of three small Katkari hamlets located 1 km from Khopoli town, a growing industrial centre on the Mumbai–Pune Highway. Work by the research team in this hamlet began with an exploration of the various reasons for their livelihood vulnerability. It eventually led to a concerted effort by the young Katkari men to help their community and other neighbouring Katkari communities acquire the caste certificates needed to affirm their identity as Adivasi, and thereby access various government supports.

Mil Katkarwadi sits on a small plot of forest land and has existed for more than 100 years. Since land owned by the Forest Department cannot be sold, there is little risk of private evictions, although householders living there say they have been periodically harassed by officials of the Forest Department, and prevented from developing amenities in their community. Currently, 80 families live in Mil Katkarwadi, but only eight families own cultivable land which they received under the ceiling land legislation. All other families are landless, despite longstanding residence in the area. Many people in Mil Katkarwadi (35 families) do manual work in and around Khopoli. Typically, they gather daily at a roadside labour stand (*majur adda*) where employers arrive to look for workers, contracted on a daily or task-specific basis. The work is poorly paid, demanding and often dangerous due to the industrial setting and poor safety measures offered by employers. Accidents at work sites are common. Even at the labour stand, people waiting for work have been killed by passing vehicles. Much of the work is offered for short periods of time, with no guarantee of ongoing employment. In some cases workers are given an advance from which interest and other charges are later deducted. While only eight families in the Katkari hamlet were migrating to brick kilns when the assessment was done, people in the hamlet said that it was an emerging trend due to the instability and poor pay of the work around Khopoli.

Our initial contact with this hamlet was through a group of six youth who regularly gathered at the labour stand. A member of the research team sat with them there and asked about their situation, including the status of the village site. After several casual meetings, the youth expressed an interest in discussing their livelihood situation in detail and agreed to convene a meeting in their village. Response to the invitation was strong, with 20 men and seven women attending. Of these, 15 worked as porters and contract workers in Khopoli town, eight worked as daily wage labourers and four were agricultural labourers. They expressed a common concern that many people in the hamlet had no option but to engage in poorly paid and very insecure day and contract wage work. The research team opted to use the problem tree method to explore this problem, beginning with an open discussion of the circumstances of their current work. The stories and chains of causes and effects are summarized in Figure 5.4 and below:

- People said that they had no land, leaving them with no choice but to engage in wage work. Participants connected this gap to neglect by the government during previous decades when tenancy or ceiling land legislation brought some benefits to landless populations. They never benefited, and consequently never practised settled agriculture as a source of livelihood.
- Wage work of any kind in and around Hoopla is scarce for people who have no vocational skills, such as themselves. A lack of literacy and education resulting from their conditions of extreme poverty is at the root of this impediment.
- Non-tribal people in the area are reluctant to give work to the Katkari because the Katkari are unable to convince employers to hire them. They cannot convince and negotiate effective working arrangements because people in the hamlet are not organized. Lack of organization in the community was seen as an important cause as well as an effect of being heavily engaged in poorly paid and insecure wage work.
- A steady decline in the availability of firewood and other forest products in recent years has prompted a shift away from this traditional livelihood to a greater reliance on wage employment.

Participants linked this to illegal felling of trees for timber (not for firewood) causing forest decline, a practice they said was sanctioned by corrupt Forest Department officials.

- Participants said that they were unable to access government employment and subsidy schemes, leaving them dependent on poorly paid and insecure day and contract wage work. They said that they were aware of schemes such as the public distribution shops and employment schemes for Adivasi, but did not have the basic legal documents (caste certificates, residence certificates) they needed to access these services. Obtaining legal documents from the government seemed to the participants to be a very difficult task, as it required literacy and lengthy procedures at distant government offices.

The consequences or effects of this current reliance on poorly paid and highly insecure wage work were also elicited from the group:

- An increasing number of Katkari migrate to outside areas. This leads to two distinct but related consequences: children receive no education, condemning them to an ongoing cycle of poverty and migration inevitably leads to exploitation by contractors and a cycle of bonded labour.
- Dependence on insecure and poorly paid manual work reinforces the low social status of the Katkari and seems to justify further discrimination and exploitation by other communities.
- Because the pay from wage work is low and the work itself intermittent, the Katkari are not able to save money to construct adequate houses or develop basic amenities in the hamlet. This leaves them unprotected from cold and rain and undermines their health.
- Wage work is controlled by many different employers. This fragmentation weakens organization among the Katkari, making it impossible for them to exert pressure collectively. The result is that it is easy for employers and government to ignore their demands.

The process of eliciting the various chains of causes and effects supported an animated discussion about the most important factors and those that might be priorities for action. People referred repeatedly to the pervasive lack of legal documents, including caste certificates, birth certificates and residence certificates. They drew out the connection between this gap and access to government schemes related to employment, village amenities, house construction and gaothan and dalhi land rights. Participants concluded that this was a core livelihood problem

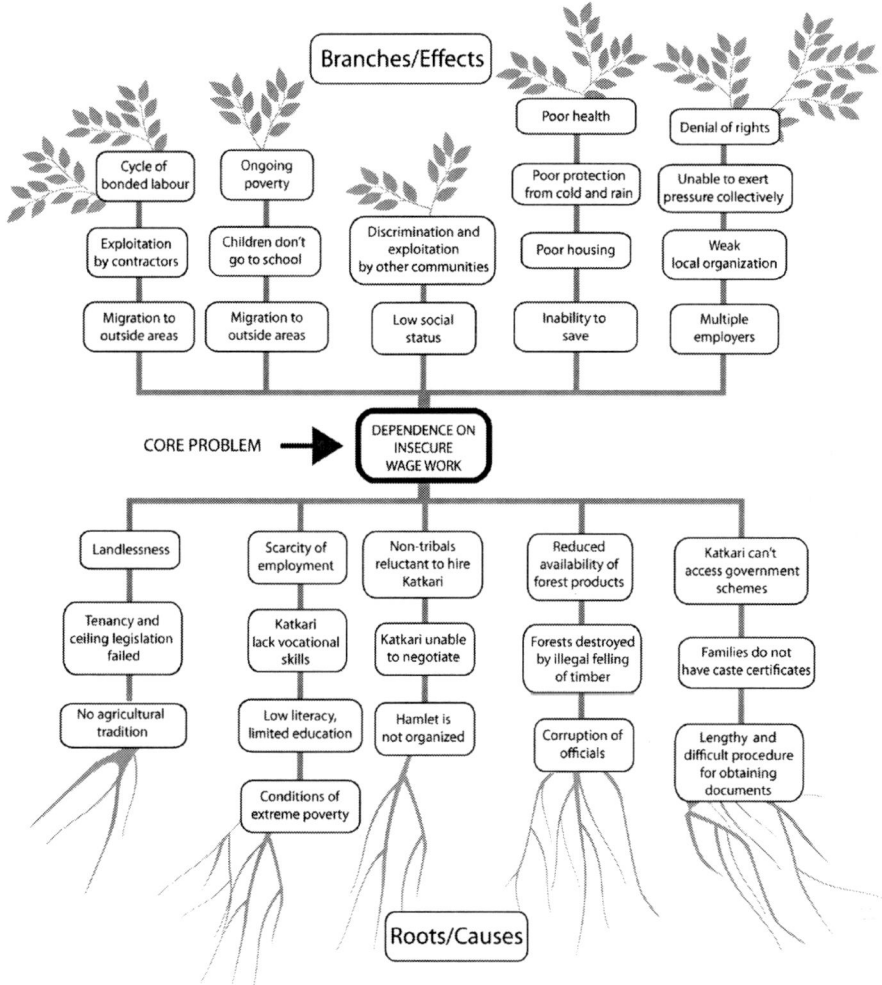

Figure 5.4: Causes and effects of dependence on insecure wage work among Katkari families in Mil Katkarwadi

Source: Author's field notes, December 2007 Mil Katkarwadi.

and a priority for action through their own efforts. A number of the youth involved resolved to learn more about the procedures for acquiring documents and asked the research team for training and assistance. They also decided to survey what legal documents were held by each family in the hamlet and to assist them in submitting individual and family applications.

As discussed in the next chapter, the work of these male youths from Mil Katkarwadi contributed significantly to broader efforts by the Katkari to affirm their identity and rights as Adivasi. Their work also brought about a dramatic shift in labour conditions for hamali workers in Khopoli. Over a period of several months in 2009, the group created and registered a local labour union with 30 members, all Katkari. Once established, they presented themselves to the industries in Khopoli in need of hamali workers and demanded that they receive the work on a priority basis. Labour laws in India support unionized workers in this sector and quite quickly the local industries in Khopoli responded by collaborating with the union. They started paying legal day wages and providing steady work to union members. Ongoing interaction with the community by the research team suggests that migration to brick kilns, a trend that had been growing in Mil Katkarwadi, slowed immediately. Some two years on, the union remains strong and active, having opened an office along the road to replace the original gathering place. Katkari union members from various nearby communities come to look for work and stay the night in the office if need be. The union also applied for funds from the ITDP that eventually resulted in a grant to pay the life and accident insurance premium for 500 registered families in various hamlets. While tentative, and a gain limited to the Khopoli area, it is indicative of an interest among male youth in emerging wage labour opportunities in the mainstream economy and of capacities to self-organize. Efforts to strengthen collective organization and abilities to exercise rights as Adivasi and Indian citizens are discussed in the following chapter.

6

Strengthening Katkari Collective Organization

To move beyond the limbo created by government neglect, the Katkari must engage with politicians who can reactivate the gaothan extension scheme. They must also apply sustained pressure on government officials to implement the scheme properly. Otherwise, the gaothan will remain out of reach and subject to the whims and personal interests of landholders. For many reasons, such actions are a major undertaking. Katkari communities today are highly fragmented, both socially and politically. Some form of new Katkari collective agency is needed to move beyond the ad hoc and patchy assistance provided by the research team and other activist organizations working with them.

This chapter reflects on efforts by the Katkari and the research team to strengthen Katkari collective organization (committees, youth groups, labour unions, associations) and capacities to bring specific interests and demands into the public sphere. We begin with a brief outline of the reasons why traditional leadership and organization in Katkari communities remains weak and of the systematic exclusion of Katkari from the mainstream political structures of representation normally available to people in rural communities. This is followed by an account of several Katkari initiatives to organize collectively, as supported and reinforced by the inquiry into the gaothan problem. The story provides insight into the opportunities being created by Katkari leadership and also highlights the ongoing constraints that undermine the Katkari's ability to make practical use of their numbers and potential political influence. These efforts can be seen as part of what Fuchs and Linkenbach (2004) have called 'tribal resistance' to attacks on the political bases of tribal existence.

Traditional Organization and Political Representation

The lack of organization among the Katkari was a recurring theme raised by the Katkari through their analysis of the causes of the gaothan problem. This situation can be attributed in part to the active dismantling of the gauki, an earlier Adivasi institution in many parts of India. Under the gauki system, male elders of the community represented the community in dealings with local governments, resolved local disputes and organized collective work needed by the community as a whole. The leadership of the gauki, and in particular the headman (*naik* or *knot*), allowed for negotiations with politicians on behalf of the community and delivered votes in state and national elections accordingly. Weling (1934) describes the gauki and headman social organization of the Katkari during the 1930s. He notes, however, that it was not as strong among the Katkari compared to other Adivasi groups in the area, such as the Thakur. While older Katkari remember that there once was a gauki in their old villages, they say that it did not survive the shift to new settlements on the plains.

The gauki, where it existed, has now been almost entirely displaced by the development of the village gram panchayat system. Today, the gram panchayat is the only institution formally recognized as a local government. When the gram panchayat was introduced in the 1960s, people were told that it would meet all local needs, including mobilizing government funds for local development. Expectations were high and traditional organizations such as the gauki collapsed. In many communities, a vacuum in tribal politics was created because the new gram panchayats were typically located in non-tribal villages and dominated by non-tribal representatives. This was the case even in the hilly tracts of Raigad and Thane districts where Adivasi are concentrated.

The political disenfranchisement of the Adivasi created by the gram panchayat system was partly corrected through the provisions of the Panchayats (Extension to the Scheduled Areas) Act of 1996. The act establishes the reservation of seats in proportion to the population of scheduled castes and tribes in the gram panchayat. It also allows the gram sabha (general assembly) flexibility to manage its affairs in accordance with tribal traditions and customs. These provisions have not benefited the Katkari, however, due in part to the administrative gap noted in Chapter 4 – the vast majority of the Katkari now live outside of designated Scheduled Areas. The provisions of the act are not applied to the non-tribal areas where they currently live. This gap is further compounded by the fact that most Katkari have not acquired caste certificates identifying them as members of a scheduled tribe. Without this designation, the Katkari cannot make use of other constitutional guarantees to disadvantaged sections of the people, such as the reservation of seats in the panchayat, the legislative assembly of the state and the parliament.

The impact of these various historical and administrative developments is evident. Despite many decades of living among non-tribal populations on the coastal plains, the Katkari have not participated actively in the mainstream political life of non-tribal villages. The survey data shows that only 91 out of 312 Katkari hamlets in the three talukas have some representation among the five to 10 elected persons that make up the gram panchayat in each nearby non-tribal village. Furthermore, most heads of families (86 per cent) said that they had never attended the gram sabha, the periodic assembly of village members convened by the gram panchayat. Data collected by Tomar and Tribhuwan (2004) for Katkari in Pen taluka shows a similar pattern: none of the Katkari interviewed for that study showed any awareness of the electoral constituency with which they were associated, or had any knowledge of the last gram sabha in their community or any of its development activities.

Poor representation of the Katkari in this important local political and administrative institution belies their weight as a proportion of the general population. In Sudhagad taluka, the Katkari are the largest tribal group, and make up about 20 per cent of the total population. The other communities in Sudhagad taluka are Kunbi Maratha (58 per cent), Thakur (8 per cent), Dalit (2–3 per cent), Brahmins (2 per cent), Agri (2 per cent), and Goldsmiths, Barbers, Marwadi, Dhangar and Muslims (about 8 per cent). Katkari are also significantly represented in many villages in both Karjat and Khalapur talukas.

Despite their numbers, historically the Katkari have had virtually no profile in electoral politics here or anywhere else in the state (Heredia and Srivastava 1994, 118). Politicians and senior government officials at the state level almost never mention the Katkari during the normal course of governing, and rarely target the Katkari as a voting block during election campaigns. When they do appeal to the Katkari collectively for their votes, it is with crass political gain in mind, and Katkari are inevitably forgotten once elections are over. While this is common in electoral politics, neglect of the political relevance of the Katkari is in contrast to the more routine appeal by politicians for the votes of most other scheduled tribes in the state.

Emerging Youth Leadership

The initial response of the research team to the absence of an established gauki or other form of traditional local organization among the Katkari was to support the development of new organizational forms. These took the form of gaothan action committees. While typically comprising mainly middle-aged and older Katkari men (and occasionally women), young men often assumed critical roles in these groups. As so many Katkari adults were non-literate and unschooled, educated youth were in a better position than the elders to compile and complete the requirements for caste certificates and other documents needed to protect the hamlet and to access information on government services of various kinds. Leadership by male youth in these matters emerged often at the urging of male village elders, although the elders used their influence to convene meetings of the gaothan action committees. This section provides an example of male youth leadership that had a significant impact on the course of the inquiry into the gaothan problem and the ongoing struggle for rights and recognition.

As noted in Chapter 4, groups of young men emerged as strong leaders in efforts to scale up the gaothan initiative to communities beyond the initial study group. In Mil Katkarwadi, the youth of the gaothan action committee were instrumental in acquiring caste certificates and other legal documents needed by the Katkari to access government schemes and make demands regarding gaothan and dalhi land rights. Along with this work on basic documents, the youth group helped 10 different Katkari communities prepare and submit formal applications for a gaothan, without any assistance from members of the research team. They also helped some 200 families in Mil Katkarwadi and surrounding hamlets get ration cards, caste certificates, death certificates, registrations of legal heirs and other documents relevant to the specific needs of individuals and families. Through this process, the youth learned the details of the procedures and became adept at completing applications on their own. Three of the Mil Katkarwadi youth began to spend time in front of the local tehsildar's office; they sold their services to help people prepare affidavits and acquire other documents. They helped each other do this work by taking turns going to the tehsildar's office while the others worked and contributed part of their daily wage to each other. Katkari from as far as 15 km away came to their village seeking their help. This small band of para-legals gradually became a vital resource in the Khalapur area. Their clients were not only Katkari but also other Adivasi who needed assistance and couldn't afford to pay the fees charged by conventional agents. The youth usually charged about Rs 150 for the paperwork associated with a caste certificate, a much lower rate than similar services offered by non-tribal agents (usually Rs 1,000). Interviews with these youth show that over a period of several years, they helped to issue more than 800 caste certificates, plus many other basic documents. In recent years, they have focused on ensuring that school children have caste certificates and therefore remain eligible for various benefits.

Image 6.1: Bansi Ghevde discusses gaothan applications with a group of youth in Mil Katkarwadi. These young paralegals became a vital resource in the Khalapur area

This initiative shows the enormous potential of youth leadership to organize and mobilize members of their own community around Adivasi rights. The various accomplishments of the youth group in Mil Katkarwadi are exceptional, but many other youth leaders emerged during the inquiry and have contributed consistently to their communities. The gaothan action committees, comprising youth in part, have survived over time, and many reconstituted themselves as forest rights committees during the period of application for dalhi lands. Some 15 independent youth groups formed in the 30 or so villages in Khalapur taluka where the inquiry has been active and remain strong on their own. They respond in a meaningful way to various administrative needs of the community and even to broader problems. For example, these groups have helped people working at brick kilns keep accounts and demand proper payment for the bricks they produce. People say that kiln operators cannot systematically exploit and harass families working at the kilns because the youth are available to help in situations of abuse and do so frequently.

The defiance and courage of the male Katkari youth is echoed in the story of Nagya Mahadu, a Katkari youth who participated in the 'jungle satyagraha' inspired by Mahatma Gandhi's salt satyagraha. In 1930, Nagya Mahadu and other Katkari defied British authority by cutting grass in the forest near the village of Chirner in Uran taluka, an act forbidden by law. Police opened fire on the Katkari, killing Nagya and 12 others. The incident was almost forgotten when activists in the area came across a reference to him in a government gazetteer. Their research and activism, mainly in the Pen and Panvel region, eventually led to a yearly *yatra* (pilgrimage) in his honour and official recognition on the martyrs' memorial commemorating the freedom fighters in Chirner village.[1] A programme on Nagya Mahadu continues to be organized on 25 September in many talukas, including the Katkari Forum for Justice in Sudhagad (discussed in a later section of this chapter).

The advantages of youth-based leadership in terms of courage, energy and literacy are both encouraging and fragile. Leaders among the youth groups are increasingly seen by the political parties in the area as ripe material for their own purposes and are being drawn into the machinery of particular parties seeking to increase their support within Katkari communities. As well, compared to the traditional gauki, youth groups are less cohesive and their leadership less rooted in the community. As in most Indian societies, male youth are seen differently from older men by the community at large. They must prove themselves constantly, while male elders are listened to and given immediate respect. Male elders are able to convene the whole village to meetings and have some coercive power with respect to village norms, such as deciding on penalties for failing to contribute to collective work and setting compensation to resolve internal disputes.

---

[1] Vaishali Patil of the Ankur Trust and Madhu Patil of the Yusuf Meherally Centre initiated and facilitated a process of consultation and mobilization of other activists (including Dnyaneshwar Patil) and Katkari (including Nagya Mahadu's grandson) to recognize this unsung hero.

In examining the male youth organizations that emerged during the inquiry, it is unclear what influence, if any, women and female youth have on their activities and priorities. The need remains for an organizational form that can take responsibility for the whole village, and consistently integrate women and female youth into the decision-making process. The overall challenges that seem to be emerging for Katkari communities involve retention of the best youth leadership, sustaining those groups that exist and supporting development of new potential that may include inter-community organizations. Over the course of the inquiry, only in Sudhagad taluka did the latter kind of organization exist, in the form of a longstanding but largely moribund collective organization. As discussed later in this chapter, efforts to revive this organization are today creating conditions for the Katkari to work across communities on issues of common concern, albeit with many limitations.

Revitalizing a Regional Organization

In 1982, a number of Katkari men in various communities scattered throughout Sudhagad taluka created the Katkari Forum for Justice (Katkari Nyaya Nivada Panchayat), a regional association to address disputes. It now represents 82 Katkari hamlets in the taluka. The hamlets are grouped into two clusters: 42 hamlets surround Pali town while another 40 hamlets are around Parali town, about 18 km from Pali. According to the founding leaders, people from these communities came together because the Katkari were routinely treated as criminals by outsiders. They also used to fight a lot among themselves. 'We started the forum to help people break from bad customs. People were very poor and didn't even have shirts or pants.' The Katkari elders desperately wanted to change the image of the community and create a forum for addressing problems facing the community.

For over 20 years, the Katkari Forum for Justice focused on the resolution of conflicts within Katkari communities as well as conflicts between communities and outside groups. Many of these concerned the abandonment of young brides by their new husbands and fights that emerged between families and the hamlets where they lived. Its work was ad hoc and waxed and waned over the years. By early 2000 it had become inactive, meeting only occasionally and failing to maintain full representation from all member hamlets. Conflicts within communities were being managed more and more by the police, leaving the forum with no clear purpose. Members began to question if its existence was justified.

The Katkari Samaj Mandir

In 2009, members of the Katkari Forum for Justice began to discuss an idea they had talked about before and that they felt was critical to the development of the Katkari community as a whole: the need for a Katkari meeting place in Pali town – a Katkari samaj mandir.

While both Parali and Pali have markets, Pali's is much larger. Katkari men, women and children travel in buses or walk long distances to sell their produce in the Pali markets. This includes firewood, but also non-timber forest products and both dried and fresh fish. It is also the headquarters for Sudhagad taluka. While not centrally located in the taluka, people have no option but to visit Pali since various government offices and other key services are located there. The town houses the tehsil office where government schemes are administered, the Revenue Department, the Bank of India where old-age pensions are collected and deposits made and the primary health care centre where basic medical treatments are available. The town also hosts the main taluka police station, the bus stand, colleges, various doctor's offices and clinics and the courthouse.

Katkari who visit Pali town face a lot of difficulties. Travel takes a long time due to poor public transport. Walking along rough trails or on dangerous roadsides is the only option for many villagers. Once people arrive in Pali, there is no place to safely store any produce that remains after the market day ends. Nor do people have a place to keep the things they purchase from the market. There is no place to sit and relax or even to eat food. If they miss the bus home, they have to sleep at the bus stand or somewhere on the road. There is no place to stay overnight for people who have to come back the next day for their work in the government offices or for treatment in the primary health centre. Not a single Katkari person owns property in Pali, so no relatives or friends are able to offer accommodation. Sick people and those trying to access government services face considerable hardship and inconvenience waiting for appointments and treatments. Furthermore, there is no place for the Katkari to organize meetings. Hundreds of Katkari who come to Pali town each day have no place of their own and have no option but to sit on the roadsides. They can be seen everywhere in the town, especially in public spaces such as stairways and the street. By contrast, caste communities like the Maratha, Dalit, Marwadi, Agri and Brahmins have built community centres (samaj mandirs) in Pali town to cater to their need to congregate. The samaj mandirs are used by members of these communities to sit, relax, eat food, keep belongings, hold meetings or even sleep overnight, if the situation so demands.

In the past, some Katkari leaders had met with elected representatives and government officers to request a samaj mandir for the Katkari community. According to the members of the forum, this request had been outstanding for more than 15 years. Politicians from different political parties made promises during these meetings, in return for assurances of votes from the Katkari community. The Katkari even registered an organization under the name of Priyadarshani Sudhagad Taluka Adivasi Kalyankari Sanghatana to fulfil the legal requirements needed to qualify for government aid. For years, the Katkari had been voting for various political leaders who promised to build a samaj mandir in Pali for their community, but none had done anything. The forum had become completely disenchanted with politicians and asked the research team to meet with them to discuss their struggle and new ways to achieve this goal.

In August 2007, some 20 Katkari men, all members of the Katkari Forum for Justice and representing 11 different villages, gathered to discuss the problem. One of the participants was also a sarpanch, while two participants were also members of gram panchayats associated with their hamlets. Together, they comprised a critical mass of male leadership within the larger Katkari community in Sudhagad. Still, the discussion began with some participants blaming others for the sorry state of affairs and failure to establish a Katkari samaj mandir. The research team offered to mediate by supporting a discussion of deeper causes and potential solutions more meaningful than those tried in the past. We used the problem tree method, which many were already familiar with. The core problem ('We have no samaj mandir') was written on a card in bold letters and participants began to discuss the main causes. Each cause was written on a separate card and placed in the row below the core problem. Participants were then asked about the causes of the main causes. Efforts were made to understand the sub-causes of the causes till the third or fourth levels were reached.

Initially, a few participants dominated the discussion, a problem managed by constantly verifying the information with others and encouraging them to add details. The process gradually became very intense as a jumble of participants spoke passionately about various causes and explanations. Making sense of the contributions became a challenge, something we managed by probing deeper to arrive at a clear and distinct cause, and asking participants to sort the same causes into piles. Eventually, first-level causes and associated chains of reasoning emerged, summarized as follows:

1. None of the political parties has helped the forum get a samaj mandir. They only make promises so they can get votes. This happens because Katkari are illiterate, ignorant and divided. Moreover, Katkari people cheat political parties by taking a politician's money and then voting for someone else. Each election a different candidate from a different political party has made promises to build a Katkari samaj mandir, through their political workers in Katkari hamlets. There is no unity among Katkari people because of the various political groupings in communities. Outsiders create these divisions.

2. Government officials do not help either. This, they argued, was linked to a lack of effective leadership among the Katkari for influencing and pressuring the government. This leadership vacuum is also linked to the lack of unity among the Katkari. Adivasi political workers and activists themselves create divisions among people in hamlets for political and monetary gains.

3. There is no suitable government land in Pali town for the construction of a samaj mandir. All plots of land within Pali town are privately owned. Moreover, the current land prices are very high (up to Rs 100,000 per guntha). Land prices were lower in the past but Katkari people were not organized around the issue of the samaj mandir at that time. Katkari were also unable to obtain land from the government in the past (when suitable government land was still available), due to their lack of knowledge about the procedures for doing so. Earlier, when the Katkari had made a formal application to the government for a grant of land, their request was refused because the Katkari panchayats were not registered as a legal entity. When the Katkari did eventually set up a registered society, the government no longer had any land within Pali town. So the Katkari did not bother to approach the government for land again.

4. The forum does not have enough money for the construction of a samaj mandir and cannot raise the money from the community. This problem is connected to a lack of employment, high expenditures on alcohol and a lack of land and other productive assets among its membership.

5. Membership in the Katkari forum has declined and the forum has become weak. Many Katkari families do not enrol as members due to lack of faith in the managing committee members and little

knowledge of the forum's activities or potential. Recent performance of the forum does not demonstrate benefits to the Katkari.

6. The forum lacks knowledge of the legal procedures needed to get financial support from the government. The leadership is afraid to approach government officials. Moreover, government officials are reluctant to give information about sources of support and political leaders actively mislead the Katkari. People blindly follow their instructions and often take the wrong path.

Following a tea break, participants began to explore the effects of the core problem, listing nine main effects and associated chains of reasoning, as follows:

1. Sick people who come to the hospital for medical treatment are unable to rest properly while waiting for services. This aggravates their illness.
2. Katkari who come to the headquarters to do official work cannot stay long enough to get proper advice and guidance on their official problems. As a result, they are unable to access government schemes. There is no improvement in the situation of the Katkari.
3. Katkari who come to the market to buy or sell their produce have no safe place to keep their goods. Quite often, they are forced to sell their goods at very low prices.
4. Katkari do not receive proper attention from the police. This neglect and disregard prompts them to borrow money from others to 'deal with' the police cases. This contributes significantly to indebtedness, especially among the poorer Katkari families.
5. Government officials ignore the Katkari community since they are unorganized and divided. As a result, there are no improvements in the Katkari situation.
6. Katkari do not have a 'rightful place' at the taluka level. Instead they must seek favours from members of other communities and stakeholders; this creates obligations and forces them to go along with what others say.
7. There is no place for the forum to hold meetings or organize services, making it difficult to function effectively or properly. Without a common space, the forum cannot help people address basic problems such as land demands, legal documents, etc. This fosters the perception among people that the forum does not do anything for them. Membership in the forum has not increased and its resources remain limited. As a result, Katkari people do not have a forum to fight for common causes.

The picture of the core problem that emerged from the analysis amazed the participants. They remarked that they had never before thought about the many roots of this single problem and the many negative effects it has on the entire Katkari community in Sudhagad taluka. Everyone present in the room felt that if the problem was so important, why were they not doing anything to resolve it? Participants began making various suggestions to resolve the problem, referring to different parts of the problem tree. Many of the suggestions returned to the notion of seeking help from different political parties. After reminders of prior experience with politicians, however, these were rejected by participants as they struggled to find alternatives. Everyone was convinced that they had to do something by coming together as a community instead of relying on others and creating divisions along political lines.

Eventually, people began to consider ways they could address the problem themselves, without the expectation of political party support. Buying a plot of land in Pali, instead of waiting for government land to become available, became the focus of the discussion. Many participants expressed serious doubts about the willingness and ability of Katkari families to contribute money to purchase land. However, Ghogarkar, the forum chairperson, reminded the group that the forum had collected Rs 19,000 in small fines from Katkari families in just one year. These were related to many small offences committed by individuals and families. He saw a possibility of collecting much more if the amount demanded from each family was very small. Another participant suggested they begin with seeking contributions from the poorest members of their own community. This, he said, would ensure that poorer families had equal rights to the samaj mandir. One by one, the participants endorsed these suggestions and resolved to each visit five or six neighbouring villages to raise awareness about the value of a Katkari samaj mandir and the need for monetary contributions from every Katkari family. These ideas enthused the Katkari participants so much they also struck a small committee to start looking immediately at plots of land that might be for sale in Pali.

Within two months of the problem tree assessment, the forum had raised Rs 50,000 from Katkari families in 40 hamlets, a remarkable accomplishment considering the dire economic situation of most families and the community as a whole. They had stuck to their decision to collect at a level appropriate for the poorest of the poor – Rs 5 per person. Virtually every family in every village contributed this amount.

While the funds were not sufficient, in February 2008 the forum purchased a small parcel of land on the edge of Pali with the assistance of an interest-free loan from members of the research team. The location of the land had a significant historical connection for the Katkari: it was directly on the walking route that people from many Katkari hamlets normally took to get to Pali. Right next to the property was a large tree where people sat to rest after the long walk, and prepared to enter the town proper. Eventually, a building was erected through more fund raising in Katkari communities, an anonymous financial contribution and assistance from one of the research team members who had recently built his own house in the town and was familiar with the permit and construction processes. By early 2010, the building had a solid foundation, brick walls and a tin roof, but no windows, doors, gate or other amenities. Since that time the samaj mandir has become a place of importance to the Katkari. Many now sit there, drink water, rest for some time and then proceed into Pali. The building provides a quiet space for sick people to sleep if they need to. They have a storage space for wood or other products not sold during the day at market and a place they can rest until the following day. They also have a space for meetings, to be equipped in time with a large table, chairs and a filing cabinet. The forum also aspires to hire someone to sit there, much like youth in Khalapur do at the tehsildar's office, and to offer assistance to Katkari in need of government paperwork, information on government schemes, explanations of letters received from the clinic and other programme work or legal work. The Katkari samaj mandir has become a place the Katkari can call their own in Pali town.

Strategic Planning

Building the shell of a samaj mandir marked a significant turning point for the forum. It celebrated in February 2010 with a special inauguration of the building with flowers, incense and the ritual breaking of a coconut. A large cotton mat was donated for the occasion by the research team. The executive of the forum, Dwarkanath Lakhma Ghogharkar, having presided over the long years of its existence, announced during the inauguration his satisfaction with progress, and his decision to step down. He said, 'We have made progress by helping people break from bad customs. We have also built a Katkari samaj mandir. It is important that we continue to look outward, beyond what we have accomplished so far. Now is time for the younger generation to lead.'

The research team was aware of these plans and, in prior consultation with the executive, proposed to facilitate a strategic planning exercise to help the forum make a smooth transition to new leadership. Some 22 members of the forum had gathered, representing most of the associated hamlets and villages. In recognition of the significant accomplishment represented by the construction of the samaj mandir, and the very positive mood of the group, the facilitators launched the planning process with an appreciative question – what things were going well in their communities and where could improvements during the last 10 years be clearly seen? After discussing the question, participants agreed that it was time to build on these strengths when setting the forum's future priorities. They also decided that a time-frame of two years was needed as a planning period, because the challenges were many and the resources of the forum very limited.

Areas of improvement in the lives of the Katkari were elicited from the group and discussed one by one. Sticks were placed on the floor progressively like the spokes of a wheel, and objects selected to represent each topic. These were placed at the outer end of each stick as visual labels for spokes radiating from the centre. The research team used this variation on the Socratic wheel as the method for facilitating the discussion because of its visual and simple wheel presentation.[2]

One person in the group said that various Katkari had established small businesses in recent years and that this was an emerging livelihood option. He and others in the group gave examples, such as very small brick operations, a tree nursery, vegetable growing, shops selling provisions and charcoal contracting. He noted that entrepreneurial Katkari with knowledge of the brick industry and easy access to skilled workers had responded to the emerging demand for bricks near urban areas and the doubling of brick prices. They had set up their own very small units close to Katkari communities and the small towns and villages experiencing a housing boom. Others said that even in more remote locations, Katkari had been able to access government livelihood schemes to purchase a pair of ploughing bullocks, establish a small herd of goats or set up a small shop. A brick was selected by the group to represent the idea of new businesses. Everyone recognized, however, that only a handful of individuals had actually made this livelihood shift successfully.

---

[2] For detailed instructions and adaptations of the Socratic wheel method, see Tools and Software at www.participatoryactionresearch.net.

Image 6.2: Members of the Katkari Forum for Justice do strategic planning using markers and symbols to show accomplishments and set priorities for future action

Most Katkari were still dependent on casual agricultural wage work and bonded employment on large brick operations in various parts of the state. They decided to give a score of 1 out of 10 to show that the current situation was nevertheless a slight improvement on the past. When it came to setting a goal for the topic, many remarked that despite the positive trend there were many limitations as well, especially with respect to the management capabilities of the Katkari. They said that money and assets such as bullocks from government schemes were often poorly spent, used for other purposes, or sold off. They also felt that the forum had little need to play a role in this process and could not be responsible for managing schemes and putting energy into enterprise development. Besides, they noted, successful enterprises are usually individual, not group endeavours. Based on this discussion they set an improvement target of 2 out of 10 over the next two years. While the forum would continue to inform people about government schemes and help young people interested in brick or nursery enterprises to get management training, it would not treat this topic as a high priority for the organization.

Government employment was another area where participants said there had been some improvement in recent years. Paper money was selected as a symbol for this change and participants rated the current level at 1. People said that they have always had access to government jobs, due to employment reservations, but that many didn't stay in such jobs. One of the participants provided an example from his own experience as a government watchman. He and his cousin had been offered jobs as part of a quota programme. The cousin lasted four days only. He didn't show up at the work site at all, for fear of being separated from his family. For a year he received notices from the government about the job. Looking ahead, however, participants recognized the potential value of these jobs to youth and that competition for them was now fierce. Even with employment reservations, bribes are needed to get government jobs such as entry into the police or as a watchman. Other types of private sector employment were also increasing and of great interest to young men who wanted to be tractor drivers or to work in company security. The forum set a goal of reaching 3 out of 10 for livelihood improvement over two years. To achieve this, they said they would encourage and assist applications for government jobs and organize career guidance for educated youth. Some even suggested that senior members would coach and accompany candidates to interviews to ensure that they received proper attention.

Cleanliness as an expression of pride and a minimum standard of living was also identified by the group as an area where improvement from the past could be seen. Using a traditional white cap to symbolize the topic, the group gave it a current rating of 2 out of 10. They said that earlier people did not take baths for a month or more, houses were very dirty, utensils were not cleaned properly and areas surrounding houses and the hamlet were littered. One participant told of how he set an example by having a clean house, ensuring his children went to school, taking a bath daily, wearing washed clothes, reducing litter around the house and providing clean food in the house. He also felt that illnesses had declined as a result. The group agreed that there was a strong need for improved cleanliness within the community as a whole. They set a goal of reaching a level of 5 over the coming two years, through a campaign that the forum would lead for disposing of plastic bags in a proper manner. Such bags, they felt, symbolized the litter in their community because they never rot and are highly visible. By eliminating plastic bag litter, the general message of cleanliness would be conveyed.

Harassment by police, symbolized by a stick used to beat people, was an area where participants felt significant improvements had occurred over the previous years, already reaching 7 on the scale. This improvement, they said, was mainly due to the work of the forum to reduce conflict and sort out problems within the village. Katkari were better organized around conflict management as well, so the incidence of police abuse had reduced considerably, they felt. Now, police don't pick up Katkari randomly for any crime; there must be evidence that the person was involved in some way. The group decided that the forum needed to remain vigilant about police harassment and to continue its past work on legal aid and conflict resolution, with a view to achieving a level of 8 over the coming two years.

Alcoholism, symbolized by a discarded plastic water bottle often used to hold alcohol, was an area where participants felt great dissatisfaction and concern. They rated the current level of improvement at less than 1. Participants also recognized that this was a difficult problem to resolve. When husbands drink, women also drink, even when pregnant. Then there are fights, leading to the abuse of women. Various participants expressed concern about the future impact of this practice on youth in the community, influenced as well by increasing levels of alcohol consumption among non-tribal youth in the area. They noted that past efforts to control the problem by banning the making of alcohol, including requests for help from the police in enforcement of the ban, had come to naught, or simply shifted production from Katkari communities to other Adivasi communities. Katkari families had lost livelihoods as a result of the ban, but they had not stopped drinking. Reduced availability also simply drove people to the town of Pali to drink, where the addiction was even more expensive. While local spiritual leaders had inspired some Katkari to stop drinking, they had little broad influence. For all these reasons, reflecting what participants considered to be a very persistent and difficult problem, they felt that as a forum and a community they could only aspire to very modest improvements, perhaps reaching a level of 1 over the following two years. Actions by the forum would focus on discouraging families from taking advances on wages to spend on drinking during festivals.

Improvements in the practice of customs related to marriage and other religious ceremonies (*pujas* of various kinds), symbolized by a flower necklace brought for the occasion of inaugurating the meeting, was identified as an area where the forum had overseen significant improvements. The group gave this factor a 5 out of 10 for the current level of improvement. The main focus of this work had been to control the pressures from the wider Indian society to host elaborate and costly marriages. Unlike Hindu families, the Katkari traditionally followed a bride price system rather than dowry, and organized their own marriages. Feelings of inferiority arising from this difference had created continuous pressure to amplify the marriage ceremony, including issuing invitations to large numbers of people, inviting Brahmins to officiate and organizing a puja. In response, the forum had established norms for expenditures to be incurred during marriages and specified the amount of bride price paid to different parties. These norms had been written down and were widely used in the hamlets. During the assessment, members of the forum resolved to continue to promote these norms and to monitor their implementation. The group also reaffirmed earlier decisions to authorize its representatives to impose fines on families that did not respect the norms. As a group, they agreed that over the following two years the forum should pursue a modest overall improvement to the 6 level.

Education was another area where participants felt that some improvements had occurred in recent years. The school drop-out rate seemed to be going down. Children in the critical 6 to 14 years age group tended to be in school and there were more schools being built in Katkari hamlets. Although still few in number, more Katkari children were studying beyond the 10th standard. Using a pen to symbolize this topic, participants set the current level at 2. Still, they noted that many Katkari parents did not take education seriously because they themselves were not literate. Moreover, even educated children could not get jobs without paying bribes. Parents wondered about the relevance of education for the Katkari. They decided as a forum, however, to continue to create awareness about the value of education by meeting with groups of parents. They also resolved to lobby the government to build schools in Katkari communities and set a goal of reaching the 4 level over the next two years through these actions.

Finally, improvements in housing and appliances such as televisions, fridges and bathrooms, symbolized with a flat stone for a foundation and a piece of brick for a wall, were also noted, and rated at the 3 level. While most Katkari families had in the past lived in wattle and daub houses, more were making houses with a stone foundation and brick walls and acquiring household amenities. Rapid progress was now expected by the forum, since many families had started collecting materials on their own rather than waiting for a government scheme.

One person reported that in Kumbhargharwadi hamlet, 25 or so new houses had been built recently, demonstrating that people could act on their own. The forum felt that it could support this trend by sharing stories of how people were building their own homes and reminding people that by building their own homes they were also reducing the threat of eviction by landholders. They set a target level of 5 within a two-year time-frame.

The wheel-like display on the ground of the current situation and the target levels that the participants set for further improvements became the basis for group priority setting and strategic planning that the forum could undertake (Figure 6.1). The participants reviewed each spoke represented by a bamboo stick and a symbolic object representing the current and target levels and decided which ones to focus on over the following two years. Four areas where the gap between current and target levels was greatest were singled out for special attention from the forum: government jobs, education, cleanliness and housing. People agreed that these were important to all communities within the forum and consistent with the forum's mandate and capabilities. The various actions identified during the process were summarized and agreed to by the group as a whole.

Participants also revisited the alcoholism question. While they felt they could not be ambitious in this area, they expressed concern that improvements made in the past were slipping back. Non-tribals were drinking more, and this was influencing the younger people, creating a serious threat to the community. The forum needed to pay attention to this problem, even though the target level was modest. It was consequently added to the forum's strategic plan and commitments were made to discouraging the taking of advances and tightening up the rules around buying alcohol for marriages and festivals. Past successes in controlling norms for marriages were recognized as a strength the Forum could use to impose sanctions and fines against behaviour related to alcohol consumption.

The president of the executive committee concluded the strategic planning exercise by calling on members of the forum to keep the priority topics in mind in the work they were doing in their hamlets and to dedicate their time accordingly. He also expressed surprise at how the process had stimulated so much discussion, both in appreciation of what was improving in their communities, and in recognition of what was still critically wrong.

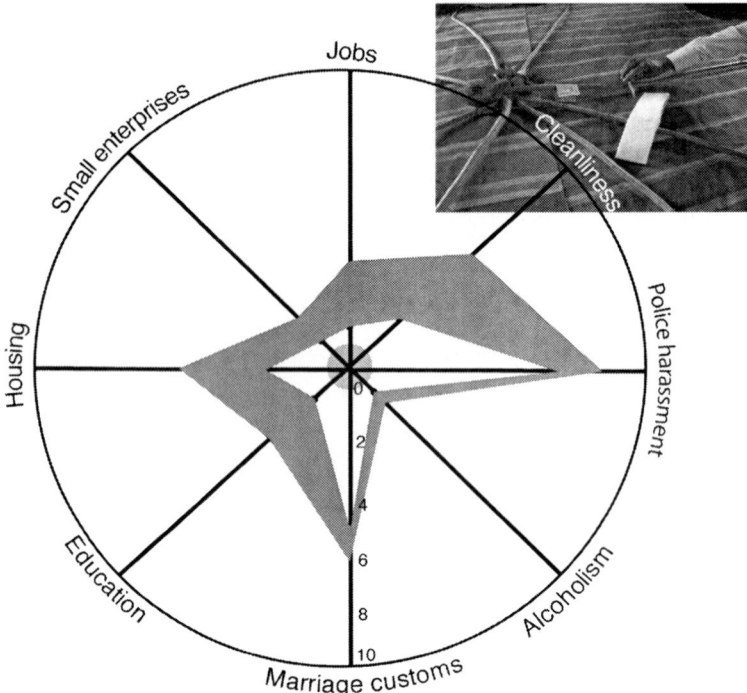

Figure 6.1: Eight areas of interest to the Katkari Forum for Justice and the broader Katkari community

Source: Author's field notes, February 2010, Pali, Maharashtra.

Note: The figure shows the current level for each area (inner shape) and the target level for improvement over the next two years (outer shape). The biggest gaps between current and target levels show areas where the forum intends to give priority attention (housing, education, jobs and cleanliness). The area with the lowest current level of achievement (controlling alcoholism) will also receive attention, not only because it is low, but because the problem is also tending to get worse. The gains expected in controlling alcoholism are nevertheless very modest due to the complexity of the problem and the forum's limited scope to make a difference. Members agreed to treat these five areas as their collective priorities, and to dedicate their time accordingly.

For the research team, the strategic planning exercise showed that the forum had an interest in broadening and deepening the work it did, while maintaining continuity with past actions. The planning process seemed to support a transition in leadership that cut across divides between young men and male elders, and between different hamlets represented by the forum. Like the earlier problem tree assessment, the

Socratic wheel was well adapted to the style of discussion the forum was used to and required little facilitation. It also produced a visual synthesis of the discussion results. As such, it seemed to provide a constructive intervention into the internal functioning of the organization. Questions remained, however. As noted by Kudva (2006), community groups and the non-governmental organizations they work with struggle to sustain organizational gains. To what extent was the method a transferable skill with ongoing utility in the decision-making process of the forum? Will it help the forum move beyond the ad hoc and patchy assistance provided by the research team and other activist organizations working with them? More fundamentally, can the emerging leadership sustain critical processes of knowledge making and deliberative decision making within the forum and between the forum and the broader Katkari community? Baviskar (2008) warns that champions of Adivasi causes, and presumably the methods they use, sometimes suppress the many contradictions that inevitably emerge around leadership, representation and processes of internal democracy. The concluding chapter examines the various changes resulting from the research-in-action and some of the many challenges that remain.

Conclusion

The research process illustrated in this book has tried to change the situation of the Katkari by engaging them in the analysis and interpretation of the constraints they face. Over a period of six years, from March 2005 to August 2011, research-in-action sought to secure a gaothan for 212 Katkari hamlets in three talukas at risk of enclosure and eviction. While the results of this effort seem fragile and uneven from hamlet to hamlet, we believe readers will agree that what emerged was also meaningful and significant.

This chapter highlights some of the observed changes related to the Katkari's vulnerability and the persistent constraints that they continue to face. A separate section contains the research team's recommendations to governments and civil society organizations committed to resolving this longstanding problem. Legal activism is at the forefront of these recommendations and rests on recognition of public responsibility for the failure in the past to secure Katkari village sites. While the Katkari are not just passive victims of this circumstance, politicians and government officials should see the Katkari claims as an urgent demand and ethical obligation that requires a concerted and immediate response.[1]

Observed Change

Overall, Katkari hamlets in the area where the inquiry was active are now moderately more secure than when enclosures and evictions went unnoticed and unchallenged. Landholders are more cautious, due to the

---

[1] For an ongoing discussion of the Katkari claim to a gaothan, and opportunity to contribute to their struggle, see www.rainforestinfo.org.au/ katkari/ index.html (accessed on 14 February 2012) and www.fightingeviction.net.

tangible risk of prosecution under the Prevention of Atrocities Act. Enclosure and full-scale evictions are on hold, at least for the time being. This improvement is a relief from the tidal wave of misery being unleashed on the Katkari by a relentless and well-resourced real-estate boom.

Other signs of real progress can also be seen. The Katkari in three talukas have registered 45 petitions for inclusion in a gaothan. These are waiting in the offices of tehsildars for action to be triggered at the policy level through renewal of a gaothan extension scheme (see later in this chapter). In addition, 52 claims to forest lands were submitted collectively by hamlets under the provisions of the Forest Rights Act. In late 2010, the Forest Department approved individual house plots (ghartan) of 1 guntha each for all registered households in these 52 Katkari hamlets. This gives the affected families secure tenure over the land under their houses – an inalienable base, a home from which to pursue a livelihood and to hope for a better future.

Claims of transformation and human emancipation can also be made. It is encouraging, indeed inspiring, for the research team to know that many Katkari in many hamlets where we worked are now much more aware of their rights than they were, and less fearful of more powerful segments of society. While the threats are far from over, the Katkari's resolve to stay in their hamlets is much stronger than it was at the outset. Importantly, they are active in making demands for gaothan rights. Various Katkari hamlets have physically removed fencing from around their hamlets and made it publicly known that the land is theirs. These visible changes in the level of organization, leadership and self-confidence in the Katkari community are significant accomplishments for a people isolated in silence and hopelessness until a few years earlier.

A recent incident illustrates the depth of the transformation. It does not involve encroachment by a private landholder, but rather the illegal actions of a gram panchayat that was extorting money from Katkari and Thakur households occupying common grazing land on the boundary of the non-tribal village's gaothan. While the lands are formally owned by the Revenue Department, members of the gram panchayat had for several years demanded an annual 'fine' of Rs 2,500 to Rs 5,000 from each family in the tribal hamlet for 'encroaching' on the lands and services of the village. Emboldened by knowledge of gaothan rights and the positive experience of Katkari in some other hamlets, a Katkari woman from the community worked alone to organize other Katkari and Thakur families in the village. She recognized that the lack of organization in the hamlet was an underlying constraint on householders' ability to collectively resist ongoing harassment by local politicians. Eventually, she formed a women-only Gaothan Hakk Kruti Samiti (gaothan rights action committee) and submitted an application to the tehsildar. The group persisted in its demands for over a year, sending several delegations to the tehsildar, resubmitting the application by registered post to the collector and the revenue minister in the state government and raising funds for a private survey of the land. Following an investigation by officials, the application was formally recognized as legitimate and an order issued by the tehsildar to include 41 Adivasi houses on the 7/12 extract (land deed) of the main village. While this is still in the process of being formalized, the affected Katkari and Thakur families no longer have to yield to notices of encroachment from the gram panchayat. This single-handed initiative by a Katkari woman clearly demonstrates that the hearts of the women are not on the ground.[2] It has also pointed the way for actions by other hamlets in the area living on common grazing lands not yet integrated into a gaothan.

The Katkari are also actively participating in broader actions aimed at redressing a range of land rights, including demands for dalhi lands under the Forest Rights Act and tenant rights under various other pieces of land laws. Between 2008 and 2009, more than 1,000 claims to forest lands were developed and submitted by Katkari forest rights committees to the appropriate authorities. They also pressured such authorities to overcome problems in processing the claims. Recently, Adivasi seeking proper implementation of the Forest Rights Act walked for 15 to 20 days from all corners of Maharashtra to Mumbai. This led to a meeting on 15 March 2011 in Mumbai with the chief minister of the state. At this meeting, the chief minister recognized the government's failure and promised to take corrective action. The protest was organized by a number of activist groups, and included six Katkari community-based organizations eagerly participating under their own village banners.

Other direct action by the Katkari has focused on acquiring caste certificates. These documents are critical to affirmation of their identity as an Adivasi people, and to demands for political representation, access to education and jobs and use of special development funds available to scheduled tribes and members of particularly vulnerable tribal groups

---

[2] 'A nation is not conquered until the hearts of its women are on the ground. Then it is done, no matter how brave its warriors or how strong their weapons.' Quote attributed to the Cheyenne tribe of North America.

(PTGs). During the inquiry, the Katkari acquired more than 1,000 caste certificates. That they are demanding these papers in large numbers, and meeting the demand in part through members of their own community who offer para-legal services, is a change that can be attributed fully to the awareness raising and training inherent in the gaothan rights movement. Youth leadership supported the drive for caste certificates and specific livelihood improvements in some communities. The formation of a Katkari labour union in Khopoli and the emergence of small Katkari-run enterprises in Sudhagad are worth celebrating. These are practical gains achieved by male youth tapping into the defiance and courage of Nagya Mahadu, the Katkari youth who died during the independence movement defending rights and livelihoods.

Hope lies in what we believe is a tangible shift among the Katkari in their view of themselves and what is possible. The Katkari involved in gaothan struggles are more aware than ever of the scope for affirming their rights through their own efforts and of the basic organizational practices and administrative procedures such as caste certificates that can help them achieve their goals. They are also keen to encourage and enable their children to attend school, and, as seen by the work of the Katkari Forum on Justice, are aware of the profound impact alcohol abuse has on their community. These shifts in awareness and a rekindling of confidence and self-esteem are to be supported.

Persistent Constraints

Our work with the Katkari suggests that dialogue across boundaries – true and respectful conversations aimed at co-constructing knowledge and searching for solutions – has also changed Katkari and our own understanding of the persistent constraints they face. The primary conclusions from this people-based and evidence-based dialogue are threefold.

First, longstanding neglect of the Katkari by governments and active exclusion by other members of village society remain key impediments to justice for the Katkari. These actions isolated the Katkari from the administrative supports and legal protections available to most members of a scheduled tribe and particularly vulnerable tribal group. They often forced the Katkari into direct confrontations with landholders, battles they usually could not win. New strategies had to be pursued in order to enhance the Katkari's ability to force the government officials responsible to do their jobs. As readers have seen, strategic actions described in this book initially took the form of direct engagement with local gram panchayats, followed later by petitions to government officials at higher levels in both the Revenue Department and the ITDP. These were combined with efforts to engage with many more Katkari communities that faced similar obstacles to improving their living conditions. The engagement process involved exchanges and meetings between two kinds of groups: Katkari individuals and communities that had organized themselves around the gaothan problem, in direct discussions with unorganized individuals and communities that expressed an interest in getting organized. By scaling up the number of communities actively demanding their rights to a village site, the research team presumed that government attention would follow. When these initiatives failed, however, direct legal action was taken by invoking the Prevention of Atrocities Act. The threat of the Katkari taking legal countermeasures by making use of this act had a chilling effect on landholders and put an immediate stop to several cases of eviction in the three talukas where the research was active. It also put the gaothan problem directly on the desks of government officials. It did not, however, address the underlying government neglect at both the political and bureaucratic levels.

Second, weak local organization makes it extremely difficult for the Katkari to build consensus and formulate collective actions, especially those that needed to be sustained over time. The struggle for a gaothan could not be resolved quickly. Persistence was critical to success and could only be provided by strong local organization. Historical forms of Katkari organization at the local level such as the gauki had not survived the shift to new settlements on the plains and the introduction of the panchayat system. The Katkari community, very loosely organized to begin with, had become highly fragmented, both physically and socially. While the gaothan action committees proved to be effective replacements over the short term, sustaining capacities to reflect, plan and organize actions over the longer term remains a significant challenge. This challenge is multi-dimensional, and includes the risk that Katkari demands and Katkari leaders may get drawn temporarily into party politics for partisan reasons and only up until election day.

Third, dependence on migratory livelihoods is felt acutely by the Katkari in every hamlet and is explicitly linked in their minds to the underlying fear of landholders and other more powerful members of village society. Addressing this constraint is both difficult and a long-term affair. It requires that people break the bonds of migration and actively develop alternative sources of income. These actions are critical to reducing the vulnerability of the Katkari to retaliation by landholders and for creating the conditions for resisting exploitation at various levels. This is a daunting challenge, indeed, far beyond the direct control and means of both the research team and the Katkari. We decided, however, to begin the process together, by assessing the livelihood realities of the Katkari more deeply, and exploring ideas for improvements that emerged from the analysis. The Katkari's efforts to acquire livelihood assets such as arable land and to organize themselves for better wages are positive steps. Still, Katkari livelihoods remain extremely vulnerable. Little real progress has been made with respect to the exploitation many suffer at brick kilns. The youngest and the strongest are drawn into bondage, to be discarded, in debt and broken, as soon as their bodies begin to fail.

Reviving the Gaothan Extension Scheme

The ongoing vulnerability of Katkari hamlets, and need for urgent government action, are glaringly apparent. The pressure of the real-estate boom continues and is subject to sudden changes that may prompt landholders to risk enclosing hamlets to sell land occupied by the Katkari. While Sudhagad taluka was originally spared the full brunt of this boom, signs are that this area will be sucked into its maw. The hamlet of Jhapwadi, located next to Wavloliwadi, one of the study villages in Sudhagad taluka, was recently affected by the sale of land next to and including the hamlet. The land has been fenced off, a clear violation under the Prevention of Atrocities Act. Despite this illegality, it remains difficult for the Katkari involved to pressure the police and officials to act in their favour. The new incident shows that gains in security achieved thus far are really only a reprieve and may reverse as property values increase the stakes and as landholders continue to find ways to reduce the risk of prosecution when evicting households.

The gaothan problem, at its root, is not one of rights per se. Various pieces of legislation and related policies at both the central and state government levels affirm, without any doubt, the right of the Katkari to reside where they have lived for decades. As Chapter 4 made abundantly clear, laws also exist to support the extension of existing village gaothans to include Katkari hamlets, both on private lands and on government lands (forest lands and common grazing lands).[3] The law explicitly tasks

---

[3] There are a few cases of Katkari hamlets on temple lands. These can be managed in a way similar to hamlets on private lands.

various levels of government with the legal responsibility to protect one of the most vulnerable and exploited tribal communities in India.

The practical problem lies in the exercise of rights. And it is here that the Katkari need not remain isolated from the mainstream and from the assistance of others. In particular, the Revenue Department for the state of Maharashtra must revive the gaothan extension scheme and ensure that it is properly implemented. Resolving the Katkari gaothan problem can be that simple, if lessons learned from the past and from other schemes and programmes are effectively and efficiently integrated into a revived gaothan extension scheme and related housing schemes focused on the Katkari.

Private land is where the threat of eviction is most acute. By contrast, government forest lands were recently given to the Katkari as housing sites (ghartan) under the Forest Rights Act. These hamlets are now secure. In both cases, however, extension of a gaothan is needed to ensure access to even basic amenities – approach roads, electrification and common meeting spaces. The Bombay Village Panchayats Act, 1958, the Maharashtra Land Revenue Code, 1966, and the Maharashtra Regional Town Planning Act, 1966, all standing pieces of legislation fully supported by Clause (g) of Article 243 of the Constitution of India (Part IX: The Panchayats), give to the state government, and to the Revenue Department in particular, the right to alter the limits of a village. All that is required is a notification by a senior official such as a collector. Directions to extend gaothans have been noted in virtually every five-year plan of the state government since 1951. The most recent example is contained in the Maharashtra State Housing Policy, issued with great fanfare in Mumbai on 23 July 2007 by the then Chief Minister Vilasrao Deshmukh. The policy (Government of Maharashtra 2007, 30) notes that rural housing is to be tackled through gaothan extension and housing schemes (Indira Awas Yojana and Rajiv Gandhi Gramin Niwara Yojana). Section 26 of the policy states: 'All villages face acute shortage of land for house construction. The earlier gaothan extension scheme facilitated land acquisition by Government. This scheme will be revived and the Collectors will be empowered to acquire land through consent.'

This policy, after much effort and money was expended in its development, was not actively implemented, especially in rural areas. The policy also suffered from an unnecessary flaw that should not be repeated in a newly revived scheme. While it empowered collectors to acquire land through consent, the actual mechanism by which this could be accomplished was not specified. Earlier gaothan extension schemes were stronger in this regard, although they vacillated between use of the Land Acquisition Act, 1894, and the Limitation Act, 1963, which allowed for the acquisition of title by 'adverse possession'. In our view, the Land Acquisition Act is the most appropriate means to acquire the private lands where Katkari hamlets are established at present. While property owners dislike both acts, the Land Acquisition Act conserves the principle of just compensation for expropriated lands. One could argue that landholders forfeited their moral rights to the land when, decades ago, they invited Katkari to settle in exchange for labour on their farms. However, expropriation without compensation by virtue of 'adverse possession' allowed under the Limitation Act, 1963, would only sow rancour and resentment against the Katkari for generations to come. As noted in Chapter 4, this was a barrier to implementation of the earlier schemes, and it should not be repeated. Given the small areas affected, and despite high property values, just compensation would be a small price to pay for peace and a good start to Katkari membership in village life.

Justifying the public purpose that would allow the state government to acquire land under the Land Acquisition Act rests on a wide range of policies and acts aimed at supporting the land rights of poor and marginalized populations. These were described in detail earlier.[4] The Bombay Tenancy and Agricultural Lands Act, 1948, recognizes the rights of tenants on both cultivable and homestead land. The Maharashtra Agricultural Land (Ceiling on Holdings) Act, 1961, allocates lands to landless people. The Maharashtra Restoration of Lands to Scheduled Tribes Act, 1974, was formulated to prevent alienation of tribal land. The Scheduled Caste and Scheduled Tribe (Prevention of Atrocities) Act, 1989, has provisions to address or prevent atrocities against Dalit and tribal communities, including land encroachment or eviction. All of these acts augment the basic provisions of the Constitution (Scheduled Tribes) Order, 1950 – which recognizes groupings of historically disadvantaged people – and subsequent provisions designed to 'actively protect' the particularly vulnerable tribal groups.

Another relevant lesson from past and present policy failures is the question of financing for a gaothan extension scheme. An urgent government survey, the best way to expedite the technical work needed

---

[4] There is, of course, much public debate in India at present regarding the validity of these earlier pieces of land legislation, which viewed ownership of property as a lower-level statutory right subject to the exercise of other more fundamental rights (cf. Mahapatra 2009).

to identify hamlets and establish new gaothan boundaries, can be handled directly by the Revenue Department. It would cause only short-term disruptions to what is admittedly an already over-taxed survey service. The cost of acquiring private lands to be included in a gaothan is another matter, however. The number of communities affected in three talukas alone is more than 200. This number may rise once the status of gaothan is better understood among the Katkari living in other talukas. One way to deal with this cost could be for the state government to pay initially and to be reimbursed (after it submits detailed accounts) by the central government under the scheme known as Development of Particularly Vulnerable Tribal Groups. This scheme is managed by the Ministry of Tribal Affairs and implemented at the state level through the Integrated Tribal Development Project. According to this ministry,

> the scheme is extremely flexible because it enables every State to focus on areas that they consider is relevant to their PTGs and their socio-cultural environment. Activities under it may include housing, land distribution, land development . . . or any other innovative activity meant for the comprehensive socio-economic development of PTGs, more particularly for the PTGs who are nomadic in nature. (Ministry of Tribal Affairs 2011, 156)

State government financing at the outset, followed by reimbursement from the central government, was a key feature of gaothan extension schemes in the past,[5] and could be used again now.

Finally, civil society organizations can assume a supporting role in resolving the gaothan problem. Various organizations with a history of service and dedication to the Katkari could contribute to a survey of Katkari hamlets in talukas of the state not covered by this inquiry. This would reduce the risk of leaving out established but often invisible Katkari communities scattered throughout the coastal region. Their involvement would also increase the chances of engaging the Katkari directly in preparing the necessary technical supports, such as proof of residency, history of residency and status as members of a scheduled tribe. By being sensitive and sensible in dealing with the Katkari, and treating them with respect, these organizations could help to achieve some of the deeper goals of a secure gaothan – attachment to place, a decent home and

---

[5] See Resolution (GR) (No. LND.3962/107047-V), dated 2 January 1964, detailed in Chapter 4.

access to employment. Such an approach would also help to create the organizational capacities needed to follow up on appropriate housing and minimal infrastructure once the village site is secure.

Several decades of work by members of the research team on housing programmes among the Thakur, Mahadev Koli and Katkari in Maharashtra underscore the importance of participation and agreement when building houses.[6] The earlier Indira Awas Yojana (IAY) scheme for building houses did not engage families in decisions regarding the size or design of the house, construction materials or the timing of construction. Nor did it involve family members in making bricks or in building the house. These tasks were typically completed by outside contractors. This lack of participation often led to substandard construction and undermined the sense of accomplishment and ownership that can come with building a home. The current IAY no longer engages contractors, and is more flexible with regard to the size and design of the houses it supports, but financing house construction remains a problem for the extremely marginalized groups it is supposed to serve. Thus, the Katkari must compete in the gram panchayat with Thakur and Mahadev Koli families for support from the IAY. This encourages corrupt practices and imposes terms Katkari cannot meet if they are working outside their communities during the main construction season (the dry season, when many are at brick kilns). To overcome these constraints, housing programmes for the Katkari should mostly make use of resources available from the Integrated Tribal Development Project (ITDP), as these can be administered more flexibly.

Rudolf Heredia, an anthropologist who knows the Katkari well, framed the basic principles in support of government intervention as they apply to housing in his 1993 article 'Legislation and Housing'. He uses and extends the 1985 decision of the Supreme Court regarding pavement dwellers in Mumbai to reinforce the link between the right to life and the right to housing. He argues that

> pavement dwellers are forced to subsist on the pavements in order to be close to their place of work. They are too destitute to survive otherwise. Hence eviction from their dwellings would force a separation of the place

---

[6] Housing programmes were undertaken under the auspices of the Academy of Development Science (ADS), often with the financial support of Habitat for Humanity.

of residence from their place of work, which in their dire straits of poverty
would amount to a separation from their livelihood. This surely would
abridge their right to life to the point of negating it. (Heredia 1993, 98)

The failure in the past to address the problem of Katkari shelter and
protect them from eviction is a similar denial of the fundamental right
to life.[7]

While these legal arguments are compelling, in our view political action
should not lose site of the ethical dimension – social justice, solidarity
and appreciation of the public good (Kneen 2009; Farhad Mazhar,
personal communication, May 1, 2011). Government responsibility to
resolve the Katkari gaothan problem does not rest only in the legal realm.
Legal activism and related procedures should not become an excuse to
delay or mire concrete steps in a court of law. Simple direction from
political leaders to collectors to revive the scheme for the Katkari, and
use the Land Acquisitions Act to acquire the requisite land, is the key
message. No new laws or complex legal arguments are needed to establish
this justifiable public purpose.[8] This pragmatic approach has the advantage
of avoiding the confusion, loopholes and failures to implement that have
plagued the development of other pieces of legislation. Mobilizing
sympathetic government officials and members of civil society to call for
political action based on an ethical understanding of the situation is likely
to be more effective than a long legal battle. As noted earlier, government
failure to implement its own policies in the past is an ethical breakdown
demanding immediate and concerted action.

A successful gaothan extension scheme and house and village
development, while certainly not a panacea for all of the difficulties facing
the Katkari, are clearly the minimum steps towards meeting public
responsibilities, both legal and ethical, to one of the most underprivileged
groups in Indian society. Such steps would also provide, if properly
implemented, a positive environment and inspiring story around which
the Katkari can plan to achieve other unfolding and important goals.

---

[7] Rudolf Heredia, personal communication, 18 April 2011.

[8] This position refers strictly to the Katkari gaothan extension scheme proposed in
this chapter. Broader debates regarding a national housing law are also needed.
Such a debate seems over the horizon for now compared to legislation on the
right to education, the right to food and the right to work (Rudolf Heredia, personal
communication, 18 April 2011).

Observations on the Inquiry Process

Maxcy (2003, 85) suggests that in a pragmatic social science 'only results count!' From this perspective, the value of the gaothan inquiry with the Katkari can be judged by the results achieved – modest improvements in the security of Katkari hamlets and significant improvements in the Katkari resolve to stand firm. It is also fair to say that the insecurity and resolve of the Katkari would have been considerably worse without the inquiry. With land prices skyrocketing, pressure was mounting on all insecure hamlets. But for the purposeful, methodical and direct engagement of the research team with Katkari, who then organized gaothan action committees, people in hamlets without secure tenure would have remained uninformed of their rights, shocked by enclosure and eviction threats, uncertain about what to do and fragmented in their response. Many more would have ended up homeless, on top of the many other difficulties and sources of suffering they face. While only a few villages secured tenure, the accomplishment is significant considering the obstacles faced.

The inquiry process has made a difference for the Katkari. It also illustrates a wholesale shift in thinking about how researchers can inquire into real life problems and mobilize, or create, knowledge to address them.

Innovation in the many ways that knowledge is created, shared and used is not something scholars do particularly well. Research methods have changed little in the last 50 years or more. They involve these mainstays: the survey, the interview, participant observation and the focus group. Changes to old practices are, however, vital during a time when people and social groups face great challenges. To solve problems on a world scale, we must create synergies among the living knowledge of people from all parts of the world. This includes the almost one billion poor or marginalized people wrongly branded as 'have-nots' and 'know-nothings' – human beings deemed to have little to contribute to human history.

Engagement with marginalized populations cannot be reduced, however, to participation without informed and thoughtful agreement. The stakes are too high and time too dear for the Katkari or other communities to be drawn into simplistic decision-making processes that ignore not only their own understanding of reality but also the knowledge available to them in the worlds of government offices, legal practices and the interpretive frames of the social sciences. Participatory action research inspired by PRA alone has a tendency to fall into superficiality and quick fixes, or worse yet, forced consensus where none truly exists. Similarly, an extractive and scholarly enterprise bent on generating universal claims or value-free knowledge has little to offer the Katkari. It also has little to offer science. Engagement across boundaries, if it is to advance and realize its transformative potential, must recognize and pursue both careful precision and a sense of caring attention to the people involved. Only then can the pursuit of knowledge combine hope with understanding, to create what (Freire 1994, 8) called an active force against 'hopelessness as a concrete entity'.

This book has attempted to contribute to a rethinking of science itself by combining evidence-based and people-centred thinking and action, thereby bridging gaps between science and democracy. This is in keeping with Kurt Lewin's commitment to 'action research' and the Habermasian tradition of discourse ethics. It uses a theory of civic engagement that recognizes multiple interests and grounds for dissent and offers ways to address them through the exercise of communicative reason and the incorporation of scientific information and evidence-based reasoning in the deliberative process (Chevalier and Buckles, 2012).

While not always successful, the gaothan inquiry rested on the 'skilful means' the research team had to develop and apply to situations that were inescapably messy and unpredictable.[9] To begin with, the gaothan inquiry attempted to *ground* learning in real settings and ongoing processes that provided a sense of meaning and social purpose – the struggle against enclosure and eviction that the Katkari faced. The desired ends were defined intersubjectively and experientially through practical thinking by the Katkari and in dialogue with the research team. Every meeting by the research team with the Katkari began with a discussion of what need or question had prompted the meeting, and what results people expected. The discussion framed and supported decisions *by the group* about what was important and what was appropriate to assess at that time and with the people present. The research team matched its methods to the felt needs of participants, to emerging questions and to salient purposes, as best we could and within the time available for participants to work together.

---

[9] The term 'skilful means' is an adaptation of the Buddhist concept of *upaya-kaushalya*. Also known as the craft of compassion, it refers to the art of helping others realize the potential within a situation and create a shift in understanding and action. Means will be more, or less, skilful depending on how well they embed the ends in the means. For a full discussion of the philosophical grounding of the concept, see Chevalier and Buckles (2008; 2012).

The gaothan inquiry was grounded in action, and the actions that emerged were grounded in research, presented throughout this book as detailed information, analyses and interpretations of important moments in the change process. The inquiry also sought to *mediate* different views and knowledge systems, by engaging people and knowledge from different perspectives and facilitating dialogue across social boundaries, cultural settings and modes of learning. The research team focused initially on mediating people and perspectives within a few Katkari communities, working in small groups where a safe environment for learning could be created. This is a key principle in adult education to help groups find their voice (cf. Vella 2002). Few inquiry events were held with Katkari and government officials present at the same time and none involved the landholders themselves. This was important to building confidence and sharpening thinking; Katkari perspectives on the gaothan problem were vague initially and their positions vulnerable to intimidation and manipulation. As time went on, and interests, values and positions became clearer to the Katkari themselves, local and traditional ways of engaging with others became more prominent in the overall inquiry process, including exchanges between communities, petitions, visits to government offices, direct action (removal of fencing) and even marches as in the case of access to forest lands. Throughout, basic concepts and categories for analysis, including questions of power, meaningful differences and similarities, and factors driving or causing a particular situation, were usually elicited from the Katkari rather than supplied by the research team. While this took time and meant that each assessment began with as few pre-defined concepts as possible, the inquiry sought to mediate between Katkari and researcher knowledge systems and ensure that the thinking process and lines of action were wholly understandable and even enjoyable to those involved, as Fals Borda and Rahman (1991) recommend. The strong advantage of this attention to local terms and concepts was that people could then link immediate needs and concerns to larger systemic issues. The co-construction and interpretation of factors and their causal links helped to raise awareness of how social systems (legal protections, for example) support and resist change. The methods also relied on eliciting local concepts and mobilizing local forms of expression to communicate complex ideas.

An example of mediating modes of communication is an assessment conducted with Katkari and Thakur youth regarding the impact of patron–client relationships on their livelihoods and control over village sites. Two Katkari youth involved in the assessment created a visual representation of a complex concept they wanted to share with the group, that is, the fact that the landholder required that they plant his fields before they could plant their own. As agricultural success is very sensitive to time of planting, this obligation had a serious impact on their ability to engage in agriculture and make the most of their modest land resources. The concept, and its implications, emerged from them in a way that was completely comfortable for them: by using sticks to create an image on the floor of a large field (the landholder's) surrounded by three small fields (their own), with leaves placed only in the large field to show it was planted when theirs were not. This and other symbols for ideas created by the Katkari and Thakur supported a lively discussion of differences and similarities in their experience with non-tribal communities and employers. During a break, a short game of kabaddi launched a new discussion of tactics used by different parties to separate and isolate their opponents.

As noted in the introduction, the task of mediating multiple stakeholders and sources of information did not directly address women's issues. This remains an important limitation of the inquiry, only partly managed by involving women in most of the village-level meetings. While one could reasonably think that a narrow definition of the inquiry purpose – a focus on securing a village site – has no overriding gender dimension, what is done to develop village sites once they are secured certainly does. Broader questions of social, economic and political development within the Katkari community are gendered issues, through and through. Importantly, Katkari women are not typically part of community-level decision-making bodies such as the panchayat and they continue to do most of the domestic work such as cooking and fetching water, all with their children in tow. These are matters that remain largely unmediated in this book, and their significance unknown.

The power of the research team to influence actions and results emerging from the inquiry was also a mediation challenge, reflecting fundamental inequalities built into the relationship. The Katkari understood that the research team was deeply concerned about the gaothan problem and accepted our explanation that it was our obligation to provide them with information and advice about options available to them. The Katkari readily accepted the assistance offered by the research team due to the many years of persistent, respectful and sympathetic support provided to them. Unlike an ethnography, the inquiry was action-oriented from the start and we were fully mindful of our role as stakeholders in the situation. Whenever appropriate, the research team explicitly recognized itself as distinct among the other actors in terms of power, interests and legitimacy (as in the stakeholder analysis assessments). No pretence of neutrality prevented the research team from bringing to the table specific knowledge and values as well. As a result, we cannot be certain that our understanding of a particular situation, relationship or factor did not sometimes dominate conclusions and the decision-making process. However, the research team always sought to listen first and to avoid being excessively directive.

To succeed, a well-crafted inquiry must be people-based and caring; it must respect difference and the multiplicity of ways of knowing. It must also integrate evidence-based thinking, the kind that is achieved through skilful navigation and scaling. *Navigation* means knowing how to select and combine the forms of inquiry, planning and participation that help people deal with complexity (the uncertain, the unknown) in a timely fashion. It means doing the right thing with the right people, at the right time and in the right way, to create a shift in understanding and action. Throughout the book, we have tried to explain why particular assessments were called for and what prompted the selection of specific analytical tools. *Scaling* involves choosing the right level of detail and complexity. It is the art of adjusting inquiry methods and actions to fit the levels of evidence, planning and engagement that are needed to obtain meaningful results.

The gaothan inquiry started with a narrow focus on gaining title to village sites, sparked by enclosure and eviction threats. Initial actions were planned against the backdrop of well-established land and housing rights that should have been enough to solve the problem directly, but did not. Over time, the inquiry shifted to persistent problems that emerged from the initial analysis and arising events such as the landholder confrontation that saw an approved document ripped to shreds after a gram sabha meeting. This shift involved navigating towards a desired outcome through troubled waters and constantly adjusting the focus and time dedicated to each waypoint or set of coordinates along the way. Table 7.1 is a timeline of these waypoints. The distinctive features of the inquiry, like the stone pillar (*ves*) marking the entrance to Siddheshwarwadi, show the dynamics at play during the journey. It was like a voyage at sea: the energy and enthusiasm of gaothan action committees buoyed spirits, obstacles to navigation arose during various gram sabhas, a new aid to navigation appeared as previous government responses were collected through the Right to Information Act (RTI), and a bright beacon flashed, with a warning light as well as welcome insight, through use of the Prevention of Atrocities Act. As with any real-life voyage, the definitive set of waypoints can only be placed on a chart once the ship is safely in port. Knowing that the route would be chaotic rather than orderly, a realization that came early on in the process, was invaluable as it forced the inquiry into a continuous planning mode based on working hypotheses. We pursued these rigorously and with care, while maintaining a steadfast sense of purpose.

Table 7.1: Timeline of key moments or 'waypoints' in the research process

Before 2005: Fifteen years of work by ADS and SOBTI with Katkari communities on land issues (Karjat taluka) and economic development concerns (Sudhagad taluka). Limited interaction with Katkari in Khalapur taluka.

March 2005: Approached by women in Malegavwadi who were concerned about the fencing in of their community by a religious trust. Planning for an inquiry begins.

May to December 2005: A survey of Katkari hamlets in three talukas, to determine the scope of insecure tenure. Diagnostic work in 10 villages, linking the gaothan to issues of immediate concern. The Katkari begin to organize.

January to April 2006: Emergence of gaothan action committees, orientation of the committees on the provisions of the panchayats and development of applications for gaothans using required documents and proofs. Land prices escalate dramatically in Karjat and Khalapur.

April to May 2006: Opposition from a landholder in one village blocks gram sabha resolutions in all but three villages. Public actions are suspended and a new inquiry is launched into the persistent constraints faced by the Katkari community.

June to September 2006: Information released to the research team through the Right to Information Act clarifies the history of earlier gaothan extension schemes and reveals the option of direct applications to higher government officials. Work also begins on livelihood issues to reduce dependence on landholders.

October to December 2006: The unexpected discovery of land titles issued decades earlier in one of the inquiry villages revitalizes interest among other villages and prompts the gaothan action committees to submit applications directly to the tehsildars and collectors.

January to July 2007: Gaothan action committees lobby government officials. After long delays, officials report that the gaothan extension schemes have been discontinued and that they will not do anything until instructed to do so at the political level.

August 2007 to April 2008: Broader monitoring of eviction threats greatly expands the number of communities involved in the inquiry. Awareness of new enclosures

Contd.

Contd.

heightens the anxiety and insecurity of the Katkari. Suddenly people see eviction as imminent. New organizational forms emerge in Khalapur taluka (youth groups). Efforts to revitalize a regional Katkari forum in Sudhagad taluka begin.

May 2008 to January 2009: Youth groups intensify and broaden the collection of documents, including proofs of residence and caste certificates. Youth begin to offer para-legal services. Over a number of months, dozens more gaothan applications are submitted to tehsildars.

June 2008 to January 2009: The Forest Rights Act has been passed in 2007 and actions are launched in 2008 to develop individual applications for dalhi forest lands. The government discourages work on collective rights, but applications are submitted anyway for villages on forest lands.

January 2009 to September 2010: Encroachments on individual and village lands prompt use of the Prevention of Atrocities Act. Enclosures and evictions stop in the areas where the inquiry has been active, but continue in areas closer to Mumbai.

February 2010 to May 2010: Attention shifts to engaging with the ITDP and the development of a focused petition for a special gaothan extension scheme for the Katkari. Officials of the ITDP express different priorities and a preoccupation with only tribal populations living in designated areas.

June 2010 to December 2010: 52 communities get forest land and the rights to ghartan (individual land plots).

January 2011 to March 2011: A Katkari woman in Mohachiwadi, Karjat taluka, files an application for gaothan for the tribal hamlet located on common grazing land. Wavloliwadi in Sudhagad taluka is enclosed after the landholder dies and Katkari residents are threatened with eviction.

Source: Author's field notes, 2005–2011

The integration of science and democracy that guided the gaothan inquiry, while combining methods and information of different types, was not simply an exercise in mixed methods. What mattered most when navigating was the fit between process and purpose and the art of judging the right strategy to apply in a given context (Chevalier and Buckles, 2012). In the Katkari inquiry, different methods were selected to fit each purpose, including simple rating exercises to identify livelihood priorities and more advanced analytical tools such as Domain Analysis to deepen understanding of livelihood strategies. Importantly, the results of one line of inquiry, whether it was the assessment of the conditions affecting a petition to the gram sabha or statistics on the number of insecure villages, were fed into subsequent assessments and actions. The outputs or results of one step were used as inputs to the next. The sequencing of activities

was never fixed, however. Engaging with the Katkari in the struggle for
a village site inevitably came up against emerging issues, sudden changes
in circumstances, and broader constraints on transformation embedded
in the situation: class and caste exploitation, exclusion from the levers of
administrative power, and the lack of any effective form of Katkari
political organization. The working hypotheses underlying these concerns
guided the inquiry in important ways. To paraphrase Lewin, a good theory
of the persistent constraints Katkari faced when trying to exercise their
rights was most useful. It helped the research team navigate in the midst
of complexity, uncertainty and unpredictability.

Of all the 'skilful means' the research team applied, mobilized in others,
and supported, making sense of complexity was what made the inquiry
meaningful and powerful. In *sensemaking* lies the ability to construct
meaning by integrating information, analysis and insights into stories and
explanations that inspire and persuade. For example, the relationship
between knowing and doing was elicited through group discussions with
the Katkari about the causes and effects of an insecure gaothan and the
means and ends to change the situation. These discussions transformed
their understanding of how the gaothan linked to other matters of concern
to them, and showed what was possible if this constraint were to change.
More generally, short cycles of data collection, analysis, interpretation
and decision making were built into every assessment with the Katkari
to make sure that sensemaking was part and parcel of each meeting.
The concluding stories were co-constructed, immediately shared, validated
by the group and applied to the formulation of new lines of action or
research questions. This stands in sharp contrast to the protracted, long
cycles of conventional research that produce volumes of text that have
no impact and are not shared. Because every group assessment was
complete and immediately shared in important ways, the writing and
documentation of results and decisions was incidental to the emergence
of understanding and the ongoing work that the Katkari were involved
in.

The five 'skilful means' of research-in-action – grounding, mediation,
navigation, scaling and sensemaking – represent a wholesale shift in
thinking about how researchers inquire into real-life problems and
mobilize, or create, knowledge to address them. This written account of
the experience, reconstructed as thoroughly as we could and supported
by detailed field notes and records of key words and signposts of Katkari
meaning, is not in any sense a translation of the Katkari voice. Writing
this book was not a collaborative exercise with the Katkari, who are

neither authors nor reviewers of the final product. To share authorship with the Katkari would be a pretence that either naively gives them undeserved credit or deceptively appropriates a distinct voice. The literary production of the gaothan story, and the theory of knowledge making behind the approach, is a construction in and of itself, to be judged by how well it engages another group of stakeholders – practitioners and theorists of participatory action research that want to work with integrity by integrating the idea and practice of democracy in the realm of knowledge creation.

The telling of the gaothan story continues to unfold along two parallel tracks, one embedded in the day-to-day life and land struggles of the Katkari themselves and the other in the writing and future uses of this text, by the research team and by readers. One need not be confused with the other. The Katkari are direct authors of their own history of action research into the gaothan problem and they are responsible for the sensemaking that took place in the real world over the years and through crucial decisions and ongoing actions. Those scenes of rich, meaningful and powerful interpretation are populated by real Katkari voices, and convey the meaning Katkari give to the complex information, relationships and interpretations that emerged through the inquiry. The book is not and need not be some memory of those scenes. Like music in the air, the actual events are gone forever. New history will be made and recorded, however, so long as researchers and development practitioners cultivate and enhance the skilful means they need to see and hear what people have to say.

Bibliography

ASER Centre. 2007. 'Annual Status of Education Report 2007'.
http://www.asercentre.org/ngo-education-india.php?p=Download+ASER+reports

Baviskar, Amita (1995). *In the Belly of the River: Tribal Conflicts over Development in the Narmada Valley*, New Delhi: Oxford University Press.

_____ (2008). 'Pedagogy, Public Sociology and Politics in India: What Is to Be Done?' *Current Sociology*, 56(3): 425–33.

Bebbington, A. (2004). 'Theorising Participation and Institutional Change: Ethnography and Political Economy'. In Samuel Hickey and Giles Mohan (eds), *Participation – From Tyranny to Transformation? Exploring New Approaches to Participation in Development*, London: Zed Books, pp. 278–83.

Béteille, Andre (1992). *The Backward Classes in Contemporary India*, New Delhi: Oxford University Press.

_____ (2008). 'The Concept of Tribe with Special Reference to India'. In S. K. Chaudhury and S. M. Patnaik (eds), *Indian Tribes and the Mainstream*, New Delhi: Rawat Publications, pp. 21–44.

Bokil, M. (2002). 'De-notified and Nomadic Tribes: A Perspective', *Economic and Political Weekly*, 12 January 2002, pp. 148–54.

_____ (2006). *Katkari – Vikas Ki Visthapan?* [*Katkari – Development or Displacement?*] Mumbai: Mauj Prakashan Gruh.

Bose, Nirmal Kumar (1967). *Problems of National Integration*, Simla: Indian Institute of Advanced Study.

Brara, Rita (2006). *Shifting Landscapes: The Making and Remaking of Village Commons in India*, New Delhi: Oxford University Press.

Breman, Jan (1996). *Footloose Labour: Working in India's Informal Economy*, Cambridge: Cambridge University Press.

_____ (2010). *Outcast Labour in Asia: Circulation and Informalisation of the Workforce at the Bottom of the Economy*, New Delhi: Oxford University Press.

Brown, D. (2004). 'Participation in Poverty Reduction Strategies: Democracy Strengthened or Democracy Undermined?' In Samuel Hickey and Giles Mohan (eds), *Participation – From Tyranny to Transformation? Exploring New Approaches to Participation in Development*, London: Zed Books, pp. 278–83.

Chalam, K. S. (2007). *Caste-Based Reservations and Human Development in India*, New Delhi: Sage Publications.

Chambers, Robert (1993). *Challenging the Professions: Frontiers for Rural Development*, London: Intermediate Technology Development Group.

————— (2008). 'PRA, PLA and Pluralism: Practice and Theory'. In P. Reason and H. Bradbury (eds), *The Sage Handbook of Action Research*, London: Sage Publications, pp. 297-318.

Chaudhury, S. K. and S. M. Patnaik (2008). *Indian Tribes and the Mainstream*, New Delhi: Rawat Publications.

Chevalier, Jacques and Daniel Buckles (2008). *SAS2: A Guide to Collaborative Inquiry and Social Engagement*, New Delhi: Sage Publications.

————— (2012). *Participatory Action Research: Theory and Methods for Engaged Inquiry*, London: Routledge.

Coady, Moses (1939). *Masters of Their Own Destiny: The Story of the Antigonish Movement of Adult Education through Economic Cooperation*, New York: Harper.

Cooke, Bill and Uma Kothari (eds) (2001). *Participation: The New Tyranny?* London: Zed Books.

Cornwall, A. (2004). 'Spaces for Transformation? Reflections on Issues of Power and Difference in Participation in Development'. In Samuel Hickey and Giles Mohan (eds), *Participation – From Tyranny to Transformation? Exploring New Approaches to Participation in Development*, London: Zed Books, pp. 75–91.

Council for Social Development (2010). *India Social Development Report 2010: The Land Question and the Marginalised*, New Delhi: Oxford University Press.

Dalvi, Surekha and M. Bokil (2000). 'In Search of Justice: Tribal Communities and Land Rights in Coastal Maharashtra', *Economic and Political Weekly*, 35(32): 2843–50.

Das, Veena (ed.) (2003). *The Oxford India Companion to Sociology and Social Anthropology*, New Delhi: Oxford University Press.

Dash Sharma, P. (2006). *Anthropology of Primitive Tribes in India*, New Delhi: Serials Publications.

De Silva, G. V. S, Niranjan Mehta, Poona Wignaraja and Md Anisur Rahman (1979). 'Bhoomi Sena: A Struggle for People's Power', *Development Dialogue*, 2: 3–70.

Devalle, Susan B. C. (1992). *Discourse of Ethnicity: Culture and Protest in Jharkhand*, New Delhi: Sage Publications.

D'Souza, Dilip (2001). *Branded by Law: Looking at India's Denotified Tribes*, New Delhi: Penguin.

Fals Borda, Orlando (1979). 'Investigating Reality in Order to Transform It: The Colombian Experience', *Dialectical Anthropology*, 4 (1): 33–55.

Fals Borda, Orlando and M. A. Rahman (1991). *Action and Knowledge: Breaking the Monopoly with Participatory Action Research*, New York: Intermediate Technology Publications/Apex Press.

Freire, Paulo (1970). *Pedagogy of the Oppressed*, New York: Continuum.

—————. (2004). *Pedagogy of Hope: Reliving Pedagogy of the Oppressed.* New York: Continuum International Publishing Group.

Fuchs, Martin and Antje Linkenbach (2003). 'Social Movements'. In Veena Das (ed.)., *The Oxford India Companion to Sociology and Social Anthropology*, New Delhi: Oxford University Press, pp. 1524-63.

Gadgil, M. and Ramachandra Guha (1992). *This Fissured Land: An Ecological History*, Berkeley and Los Angeles: University of California Press.

Gaikwad, Nancy (1995). 'Katkaris: A Tribe Seeking an Identity'. In Navinchandra Jain and Robin D. Tribhuwan (eds), *An Overview of Tribal Research Studies*, Pune: Tribal Research and Training Institute, pp. 26-38.

Gangopadhyay, P. and S. Gangopadhyay (2006). 'A Study on Nutritional Status of Kolam of Maharashtra'. In P. D. Sharma (ed.), *Anthropology of Primitive Tribes in India*, New Delhi: Serials Publications.

Ghatage, Babasaheb (2008). 'Welfare of Nomadic Tribes: A Case Study of Maharashtra'. In Jagan Karade (ed.), *Development of Scheduled Castes and Scheduled Tribes in India*, Newcastle: Cambridge Scholars Publishing, pp. 19-31.

Ghosh, Kaushik (2006). 'Between Global Flows and Local Dams: Indigenousness, Locality, and the Transnational Sphere in Jharkhand, India', *Cultural Anthropology*, 21(4): 501–34.

Government of India (2012a). 'A- 11 State Primary Census Abstract for Individual Scheduled Tribe – 2001' Census of India, accessed March 1, 2012 http://censusindia.gov.in/Tables_Published/SCST/scst_main.html

———— (2012b). 'Maharashtra Housing Profile' Census of India, accessed March 1, 2012. http://www.censusindia.gov.in/Census_Data_2001/States_at_glance/state_profile.aspx

Government of Maharashtra (2007). *Maharashtra State Housing Policy*, Mumbai: Housing Department.

Guha, Ramachandra (1994). 'Fighting for the Forest: State Forestry and Social Change in Tribal India'. In Upendra Baxi and Oliver Mendelsohn (eds), *Rights of Subordinated People*, Oxford: Oxford India Paperback.

Gupte, A. K. (2006a). The Bombay Village Panchayats Act, 1958 (with latest amendments, short notes and case laws). Pune: Hind Law House.

———— (2006b). The Maharashtra Land Revenue Code, 1966 (with latest amendments, short notes and case laws). Pune: Hind Law House.

Habermas, Jürgen (1984). *The Theory of Communicative Action*, Volume 1: *Reason and the Rationalization of Society*, trans. Thomas McCarthy, Boston: Beacon.

Heredia, Rudolf C. (1993). 'Legislation and Housing', *Economic and Political Weekly*, 16–23 January, pp. 97–100.

Heredia, Rudolf C. and Rahul Srivastava (1994). *Tribal Identity and Minority Status: The Kathkari Nomads in Transition*, New Delhi: Concept Publications.

Hickey, Samuel and Giles Mohan (eds) (2006). *Participation – From Tyranny to Transformation? Exploring New Approaches to Participation in Development*, London: Zed Books.

Human Rights Features (2003). Prevention of Atrocities Act: Unused Ammunition. http://www.hrdc.net/sahrdc/hrfeatures/HRF83.htm (accessed on 21 July 2011).

Jain, Navinchandra S., G. P. Ramteke, S. R. Shevkari and Robin D. Tribhuwan (1995). 'Demographic Profile of Tribals in India, with reference to Maharashtra'. In Navinchandra Jain and Robin D. Tribhuwan (eds), *An Overview of Tribal Research Studies*, Pune: Tribal Research and Training Institute, pp. 1–19.

Jayakumar, E. C. (2006). 'Incidence of Atrocities on Scheduled Castes on the Rise', *Man in India*, 86 (1–2): 143–53.

Kamat, S. (2001). 'Anthropology and Global Capital: Rediscovering the Noble Savage', *Cultural Dynamics*, 13(1): 29–51.

Kannabiran, Kalpana (ed.) (2007). *The Rule(s) of Law: Critical Essays on Criminology in India*, New Delhi: Sage Publications.

Kapoor, Dip (2007). 'Gendered-Caste Discrimination, Human Rights Education, and the Enforcement of the Prevention of Atrocities Act in India', *Alberta Journal of Educational Research*, 53(3): 273–86.

Karade, J. (ed.) (2008). *Development of Scheduled Castes and Scheduled Tribes in India*, Newcastle: Cambridge Scholars Publishing.

Kela, Shashank (2006). 'Adivasi and Peasant: Reflections on Indian Social History', *Journal of Peasant Studies*, 33(3): 502–25.

Kennedy, M. (1908). *The Criminal Classes of Bombay Presidency*, Bombay: Government Central Press.

Khedkar, Rajeev, A. Kumar, B. K. Bangare, B. Mate and B. G. Pardhi (2002). 'The Role of Uncultivated Foods in the Food Security of Tribal Communities of Raigad District', Unpublished Report, South Asia Network for Food, Ecology and Culture, Hyderabad.

Kijima, Y. (2006). 'Caste and Tribe Inequality: Evidence from India, 1983–1999', *Economic Development and Cultural Change*, 54(2): 369–404.

Kneen, Brewster (2009). *The Tyranny of Rights*, Ottawa: The Ram's Horn.

Koli, Manohar (2008). 'A Study of Social and Legal Dimensions of Atrocities against Scheduled Castes and Scheduled Tribes'. In Jagan Karade (ed.), *Development of Scheduled Castes and Scheduled Tribes in India*, Newcastle: Cambridge Scholars Publishing, pp. 32–52.

Kothari, A., N. Singh and S. Suri (1996). *People and Protected Areas: Towards Participatory Conservation in India*, New Delhi: Sage Publications.

Kudva, Neema, 2006. 'Shaping Democracy through Organizational Practice: The NGOs of the Tribal Joint Action Committee in Karnataka, India' *International Journal of Rural Management*, 2(2): 228–43

Kumar, Vijay (2006). *Tribal Welfare and Development in India*, New Delhi: Anmol Publications.

Lewin, Kurt (1948). *Resolving Social Conflicts: Selected Papers on Group Dynamics*, New York: Harper and Row.

Mahapatra, Dhananjay (2009). 'Should Right to Property Return?' *Times of India*, 28 February. http://timesofindia.indiatimes.com/India/Should-right-to-property-return/articleshow/4202212.cms (accessed on 2 August 2011).

Maharatna, Arup (2005). *Demographic Perspectives on India's Tribes*, New Delhi: Oxford University Press.

Maxcy, S.J. (2003). 'Pragmatic threads in mixed methods practice in the social sciences: The search for multiple modes of inquiry and the end of the philosophy of formalism', in A. Tashakkori and C. Teddlie (eds), *Handbook of Mixed Methods in social and behavioral research*. Thousand Oaks, CA: Sage, pp. 91-110.

May, P. A., J. P. Gossage, A. Marais, L. S. Hendricks, C. L. Snell, B. G. Tabachnick, C. Stellavato, D. G. Buckley, L. E. Brooke and D. L. Viljoen (2008). 'Maternal Risk Factors for Fetal Alcohol Syndrome and Partial Fetal Alcohol Syndrome in South Africa: A Third Study', *Alcoholism, Clinical and Experimental Research*, 32(5): 738–53.

Mies, Maria (1999). *The Subsistence Perspective: Beyond the Globalized Economy*, London: Zed Books.

Mines, Diane P. and Nicolas Yazgi (eds) (2010). *Village Matters: Relocating Villages in the Contemporary Anthropology of India*, New Delhi: Oxford University Press.

Ministry of Tribal Affairs (2001–11). *Annual Report*, 2000–11, New Delhi: Government of India.

Municipal Corporation of Greater Mumbai (2009). *Mumbai Human Development Report 2009*, New Delhi: Oxford University Press.

Naval, T. R. (2004). *Legally Combating Atrocities on Schedule Castes and Scheduled Tribes*, New Delhi: Concept Publishing Company.

Nijman, Jan (2008). 'Against the Odds: Slum Rehabilitation in Neoliberal Mumbai', *Cities*, 25(2): 73–85.

Oommen, T. K. (ed.) (2010). *Social Movements I: Issues of Identity*, New Delhi: Oxford University Press.

Pretty, J., I. Guijt, J. Thompson and I. Scones (1995). *Participatory Learning and Action: A Trainers Guide*, London: International Institute for Education and Environment.

———— (2008). *Dishonoured by History: 'Criminal Tribes' and British Colonial Policy*, New Delhi: Orient Longman (Revised Edition).

———— (2009). 'Starvation among Primitive Tribal Groups', *Economic and Political Weekly*, May 2009, xliv (18): 13–16.

Radhakrishnan, P. (2003). 'Backward Castes/Classes as Legal and Political Entities'. In Veena Das (ed.), *The Oxford India Companion to Sociology and Social Anthropology*, New Delhi: Oxford University Press.

Rahman, Md Anisur (1993). *People's Self-Development: Perspectives in Participatory Action Research – A Journey through Experience*, London: Zed Books and Dhaka: University Press Limited.

Reason, Peter and Hilary Bradbury (eds) (2008). *The Sage Handbook of Action Research: Participative Inquiry and Practice*, London: Sage Publications.

Roy Burman, B. K. (1983). 'Transformation of Tribes and Analogous Social Formations', *Economic and Political Weekly*, 18(27): 1172–74.

Sanyal, S. (2006). 'Primitive Tribal Groups in India: An Appraisal'. In P. D. Sharma (ed.), *Anthropology of Primitive Tribes in India*, New Delhi: Serials Publications, pp. 5-14.

Sarkar, A and S. Dasgupta. 2000. *Ethno-ecology of Indian Tribes: Diversity in Cultural Adaptation*. Jaipur: Rawat Publications.

Sathe, M. D. 1988. 'Katkari Labour in Charcoal Making', *Economic and Political Weekly*, July 30 1988, 1565–68.--

Satheesh, P. V. (2009). *Why PRA?* Pastapur Village: Deccan Development Society.

Sax, William (2010). 'Village Agency'. In Diane P. Mines and Nicolas Yazgi (eds), *Village Matters: Relocating Villages in the Contemporary Anthropology of India*, New Delhi: Oxford University Press, pp. 89–106.

Shah, Alpa (2010). *In the Shadows of the State: Indigenous Politics, Environmentalism, and Insurgency in Jharkhand, India*, New Delhi: Oxford University Press.

Sinha, Surajit (2010). 'Tribal Solidarity Movements'. In T. K. Oommen (ed.), *Social Movements I: Issues of Identity*, New Delhi: Oxford University Press.

Spivak, Gayatri Chakravorty (1988). 'Can the Subaltern Speak?' In Cary Nelson and Lawrence Grossberg (eds), *Marxism and the Interpretation of Cultures*, London: Macmillan, pp. 66-111.

Srinivas, M. N. (1987). *The Dominant Caste in Rampura and Other Essays*, New Delhi: Oxford University Press.

Swagata and Nirupama (2008). 'Government Endeavours: The Failure of Social Justice Theory in Practice'. In Jagan Karade (ed.), *Development of Scheduled Castes and Scheduled Tribes in India*, Newcastle: Cambridge Scholars Publishing, pp. 167–78.

Tayal, B. B. and A. Jacob (2005). *Indian History, World Developments and Civics*, District Sirmour, Himachal Pradesh: Avichal Publishing Company.

Tomar, Y. P. S. and Robin D. Tribhuwan (2004). *Development of Primitive Tribes in Maharashtra: Status, Continuity and Change*, Pune: Tribal Research and Training Institute.

Uma Devi, K. and Neera Bharihoke (2006). *Tribal Rights in India*, New Delhi: Serials Publications.

Vaid, N. K. (1992). *Tribal Development*, New Delhi: Ashtam Prakashan.

Vella, Jane (2002). *Learning to Listen, Learning to Teach: The Power of Dialogue in Educating Adults*, San Francisco: Jossey-Bass.

Von Fürer-Haimendorf, Christoph (1982). *Tribes of India: The Struggle for Survival*, Berkeley: University of California Press.

Weling, A. N. (1934). *The Katkaris: A Sociological Study of an Aboriginal Tribe of the Bombay Presidency*, Bombay: The Bombay Book Publishers.

Whitehead, Judy (2007). 'Sunken Voices: Adivasis, Neo-Gandhian Environmentalism and State-Civil Society Relations in the Narmada Valley 1998–2001', *Anthropologica*, 49(2): 231–43.

Xaxa, Virginius (2003). 'Tribes in India'. In Veena Das (ed.), *The Oxford India Companion to Sociology and Social Anthropology*, New Delhi: Oxford University Press.

Index